Kicking Against The Pricks:
An Armchair Guide
to Nick Cave

By Amy Hanson

First edition published in 2005 by
Helter Skelter Publishing
South Bank House, Black Prince Road,
London SE1 7SJ

Copyright 2005 © Amy Hanson

All rights reserved
Cover design by Chris Wilson
Typesetting by Caroline Walker
Printed in Great Britain by CPI, Bath

All lyrics quoted in this book are for the purposes of review, study or criticism.

A CIP record for this book is available from the British Library

ISBN 1-900924-96-X

Kicking Against The Pricks: An Armchair Guide to Nick Cave

By Amy Hanson

Helter Skelter
publishing

ACKNOWLEDGEMENTS

There are very few musicians in any generation who come along and create a viable, corporeal and diffuse canon. Nick Cave is one of those rare gems. So, then, biggest thanks go to Cave and all members of the Boys Next Door, The Birthday Party and The Bad Seeds, without whom this book would have never been schemed.

Many thanks, also, must go to Sean Body and Helter Skelter who helped me bring this book to life!

For my own attempts to collect Nick Cave's songs and story together within the framework of the book, there are so many people who allowed me to pick their brains. Firstly, thanks to Nick Cave, who always has interesting things to say. Especial thanks must go to Robert Forster and Robert Vickers, who so generously shared their memories, not only of Nick Cave and The Birthday Party, but of the Indie scene in Australia and England. Many thanks, too, to Dale Griffin for his own memories of encounters with the group. And a big round of applause to everyone who agreed to talk to me off the record, and to Dave Thompson who generously shared his own archive material and interviews with Nick Cave, Mick Harvey, Marc Almond and Chris Bailey.

Finally, thanks to…Ella & Sprocket, Samantha Sheckler (and Mom, Dad and baby Jake Sheckler), Dad & Jane, Marcia, The Possum, Bob & Karin (who entertain with gusto!), Jo-Anne Greene (who has the world's biggest Einstürzende Neubauten collection), Kate Blair, the ladies of COS, and especially Anne Smith, who is always available for tears, hi-jinks and bottles of good wine!

The publishers would like to give special thanks to Bleddyn Butcher.

AUTHOR'S NOTE

KICKING AGAINST THE PRICKS: AN ARMCHAIR GUIDE TO NICK CAVE represents a discography that focuses not just on when a song was released, and where it can be found (there are plenty of excellent online discography sites which do that) but rather on when a song was recorded or released for the first time.

This book, then, is the first of its kind to be published around the life and times of Nick Cave, the Boys Next Door, The Birthday Party and the Bad Seeds, with other, notable, collaborations appearing within the framework of these three bands to provide an accurate historical and musical background to Cave's catalogue of singles, albums, remixes, films, compilations and more.

Although a discography provides the framework for the book, it is not complete – comprehensive, but not complete. There are purposeful omissions; this is not an attempt to document every single time Cave set the recorders rolling and turned on a microphone, but rather to present the most important bulk of Nick Cave's entire career, mapped out in chronological order, no matter the partnership, collaboration or band.

Based upon years of avid collecting, listening and exploration, *Kicking Against The Pricks: An Armchair Guide To Nick Cave* draws material from interviews conducted with many of the book's key players from 1995 through 2004, as well as including first-hand material that dates back to the 1970s. Other sources, including quotes and excerpts from other press sources, are acknowledged in the text and in the bibliography.

While the complex history of Nick Cave's musical career and personal life is important, for our purposes what becomes most important are the songs; some twenty-five years' worth of material. Assumptions are made that the reader has more than a passing familiarity with the work of Nick Cave, and has already absorbed at least some of the myriad biographical information available online, in print and as detailed in Ian Johnston's *Bad Seed: The Biography Of Nick Cave* and Robert Brokenmouth's *Nick Cave: The Birthday Party And Other Epic Adventures*. This book, then, is an attempt to add a sonic story.

HOW TO USE THIS BOOK

For hopefully obvious reasons, *KICKING AGAINST THE PRICKS: AN ARMCHAIR GUIDE TO NICK CAVE* is laid out chronologically by year, with all entries then following, again, in chronological order. The emphasis is on material considered to have been released officially, although a small number of bootlegs and semi-official releases are noted in the text when relevant. In terms of line-ups, these are set out for each album and detail the core of musicians in each band – the highly varied guests of Nick Cave on record will be found mentioned in the comments. Also, each member is given a credit for their *main* instrument and it shouldn't be forgotten that the Bad Seeds are a resourceful bunch (Mick Harvey is capable of playing an entire album himself) and it would probably take another book to fully document the range of instruments that they have played on each album. Within these parameters, the following headings should be similarly self-explanatory. But, just in case....

SINGLE/EP: includes 45rpm, 10-inch, 12-inch, EP and CD single releases, including collaborations with other artists. In general, only basic UK catalogue numbers are given – any given single might well appear in a dozen different permutations, with some tracks exclusive to one pressing, but others common to all of them. Rather than double the size of the book with repetitive lists and largely similar numbers, all versions of each single are rounded up into one entry, identified by the most simple of the many catalogue numbers.

ALBUM: includes LP, cassette and CD full-length releases, and Various Artist/Original Soundtrack compilations featuring newly recorded material.

LIVE: Officially released concert recordings are listed by date of original show, where known.

SESSION: Unreleased studio material, or recordings subsequently released on compilations and anthologies (detailed in Appendix One), listed by date of original recording where known. Undated material is listed either following the main chronological sequence, or where it would seem to fit in regard to the band's repertoire of the time. When in doubt, performances are dated to the year in which the song was first recorded. Material by associated spin-offs is not included.

RADIO/TV: Specially recorded material cut for radio/TV broadcast.

VIDEO Material released on VHS or DVD.

FILM: Movie work initially unavailable in any other format.

For ease of reference/cross-reference, every song is individually numbered according to the year in which it was recorded (the first two digits – 77, 78, 79 etc) and by the release's position within the above sequence. Unreleased songs known to have been recorded at listed events are noted UNR (UNRELEASED). Subsequent (live, radio or re-recorded) appearances of the same song receive a new number. However, alternate mixes from the original session, or commercial remixes of a previously released recording, when issued under the original title, retain the original number, suffixed a, b, c etc.

Releases by associated groups are unnumbered.

Further material is included in appendices (I) Compilations and Anthologies; (II) Videos and Visuals.

And finally... to many of those that are fans of Cave, his work will always be inextricably linked with the Bible: at times in his career it seems to be his only source of inspiration – it is certainly the most consistent by far. In deference to this, the career has been clearly divided: the Boys Next Door and Birthday Party eras where he seems periodically consumed with a messianic rage that was his hallmark is dubbed The Old Testament. The gentler, more reflective personality that began to emerge from *From Her To Eternity* onwards (and which reached it apotheosis with *The Boatman's Call*) is contained within the New Testament. And, naturally, all side-projects by the Bad Seeds are christened the Acts of the Apostles.

INTRODUCTION

By the mid-1970s, rock 'n' roll, in all its guises, was indisputably cast as an Anglo-American phenomenon. You could count on two hands the number of bands who had truly impacted on those scenes from elsewhere, and though it was snobbery, it was also inevitable. The industry focussed upon the industry centres. Beyond them, in those unmapped regions where A&R men feared to tread, and even the hardiest touring bands trembled to venture, the best you could say was that – well, at least the bands tried.

In Australia, bands *tried* to sound American. The biggest groups would always be the ones that came from overseas, and the domestic market's own attempts to retaliate offered little more than a Xerox of what had gone before: Air Supply, the Little River Band and Sherbet were all ersatz-American AOR bands whose sense of national identity ended when they put away their passport.

Painfully shy of its own cultural heritage, Rolf Harris was the closest thing Australia had to a successful musical export, and his impact spread across the board: a blending of traditional folk and mildly twisted comedy. It not only spawned a handful of international hits, it also provoked a massively influential rock'n'roll cover – Alice Cooper's juju-laden mangling of the bearded didgeridoo-king's 'Sun Arise' in 1971.

Away from the commercial mainstream, however, the isolation was not all bad. Exclude peer pressure from any musical equation, and even the most formulaic genre is going to get skewed. When bands cannot follow their leaders, they interpret them instead. In Melbourne, Jo Jo Zep & the Falcons and the Sports were nominally pub rockers, but musically they spun off in their own direction several bar chords earlier.

In Sydney, the Filth took their musical lead from the MC5, and their visual impetus from the Stooges' *Metallic KO*: 'they were incredibly terrifying,' remembers one mid-70s observer, Nicholas Edward Cave, 'a self-mutilating, violent kind of group. They were just a bunch of psychos, but they were interesting.'

And, in Brisbane, the capital of Australia's most conservative state, there was The Saints, a massively influential band that was and would remain the touchstone for nearly every band of their ilk to come. Released at approximately the same time as the first Ramones LP hit the streets in the States, and six full weeks before either the Sex Pistols' 'Anarchy In The UK' or the Damned's 'New Rose' even reared their heads, The Saints' debut 45, 'I'm Stranded', was a shocker. Not only did the band sound more like the Ramones than that august band themselves, but The Saints arrived at the same conclusions in total isolation, not only from 'da bruddahs', but also from the music scene that spawned it all to begin with.

'The Saints were a massive influence in their attitude towards things,' Cave recalls. 'They would come down to Melbourne and play these concerts which were the most alarming things you've ever seen, just such anti-rock kind of shows, where the singer [Chris Bailey] wouldn't come on stage, and when he did, he was this fat alcoholic. It was so misanthropic it was unbelievable, and the whole band were like that. They were so loud!'

By this time, Cave and his own contemporaries had realised that something equally violent and unshackled, was occurring in London and New York: 'For me, and the people who really knew what was going on in that area, we were already aware of how cool it was to go on stage and be obnoxious.'

Punk permeated Australia by word-of-mouth. In 1975, Cave's first band was still toying with a suitable name, even as they worked up a live set that comprised what Cave remembers as '75% Alex Harvey songs.' Phill Calvert elaborates: 'There was a different name every week. We played school dances etc.' Within a year, the band members had discovered Iggy Pop, 'and that titillated our schoolboy sensibilities no end'; six months after that, imported Punk records turned their musical tastes right around once again.

Cave explains: 'The Ramones I thought were a great band who I listened to a lot, and the Sex Pistols. But we were able to look at it with discretion; we had things to compare it to.' According to his school friend Mick Harvey, 'it was an advantage to be in Australia, and so far away from what was happening [elsewhere], because it was all a piece of knowledge. There was nothing tainted about it, you could take it seriously or not.' The absence of peer pressure comes into play once again.

'We weren't swept along by the whole Punk thing, thinking "oh Punk rock, everything's great, let's get everything, let's listen to everything",' recalls Cave. 'We did listen to everything, but we were able to differentiate. The Pistols we thought were a great band, and the Ramones we thought were a great band, but the Damned were shit. And we didn't reject everything else wholesale when Punk came along, so we were still listening to the Stooges, Alex Harvey, a lot of Country music, Blues music, other stuff. So there was all that kind of mixed in together.'

Like its American counterpart (and unlike its British), Oz Punk developed along social, rather than political, lines. Cave explains, 'In Melbourne where we grew up, there's a river [the Yarra] that divides the city, and the side of the river that I was on, St Kilda, was where the junkies and the prostitutes and all that sort of stuff hung out. The other side [Carlton] was where the universities were, and we loathed each other.

'There would be parties on that side of the river, which we would go to and get our heads kicked in, and parties on our side where the same sort of thing would happen. My side of the river was just about taking drugs, and making nasty music, and their side of the river was about making a point and changing the world and so on.'

The musical divide was indeed pronounced. In August, 1977, Cave's band had renamed themselves The Boys Next Door, and Phill Calvert recalls, 'It wasn't until we trimmed down to a four-piece and changed the name to The Boys Next Door that we started to play in pubs and at university gigs etc. That was probably the real starting point for the band. It started out with a lot of covers and a few originals and then slowly we worked all of the covers out...usually only retaining one or two...which would be our take on that song.' That month the band slammed through their first ever show as a Punk group, and swiftly established themselves as the best band in St Kilda. Six months later, Ian 'Ollie' Olsen's Young Charlatans grabbed a similar hold on Carlton. The rivalry between the two was already hot when Charlatans guitarist Rowland S Howard, decamped across the river to join the Boys Next Door in late 1978.

Olsen's band, says Cave, 'were from the other side of the river, the experimental side. They got into electronic music, and were less rock 'n' roll inspired.' It was a process which culminated in the fondly remembered, but ever-so-precious Whirlywirld, harbingers of the proto-electronic sound which would dominate the early 80s. Olsen himself, Howard adds, 'was the first person I ever met who assumed that he was naturally superior to everybody else. [He] had the ability to make you think he was a complete genius.' Cave and co, on the other hand, went out of their way to make you think they were complete psychos.

Although it was some time before Nick Cave reaped the benefits sowed by the burgeoning scene, he was never oblivious to music. Even as a young child, the lad was active in his local church choir, 'going to church three times a week'. Those earliest hymns were all absorbed into his subconscious and, although his own rock 'n' roll persona would be startlingly different, it was obvious much later on that all that youthful exuberance and theological education had sunk in. Indeed, the young Cave actually made his recorded debut at this time, as the Wangaratta choir recorded a Christmas single, coupling 'Silent Night' and 'O Little Town Of Bethlehem'. This seems to have been released to churchgoers and family members only – one wonders whether Cave himself has kept a copy... and why it isn't on the *B-sides & Rarities* box set?

It was after the church choir, and before the formation of the Boys Next Door, however, that Cave became steeped in the power of popular music. All he needed was a band of brothers to complete the picture. He found precisely that in the gaggle of school friends with whom he would first beat out a tune.

Coming of age in the Seventies, it was only natural that Cave would latch on to the superstars of the day, and it was the Sensational Alex Harvey Band and Alice Cooper who were his greatest heroes. But Cave himself was no slave to the one-and-ten-hit wonders of his peers, as he dipped also into much broader waters, there to digest the songs of people like Johnny Cash, Hank Williams and Tom Jones as well.

But, Alex Harvey remained the coolest of all, and Cave still asserts that the iconoclastic Scotsman remains one of his greatest ever influences. The

Sensational Alex Harvey Band formed in the very early 1970s, after Alex ditched a meandering solo career for a full time line-up that comprised Zal Cleminson, Chris Glen and Hugh and Ted McKenna. A slow start found the band struggling for a foothold but, once they had found one, their fearless blending of vaudeville theatre and Hollywood schlock knew no limits. The 1972 classic 'There's No Lights On The Christmas Tree Mother, They're Burning Big Louie Tonight' was an early peak, a grisly rock and roll carol that cloaked in holly and mistletoe the execution by electrocution of a notorious gangster: an image that remained with Cave when he staged a far more sinister take on the same theme with 'The Mercy Seat,' some twenty years later.

It's easy to see what it was in Alex Harvey that appealed to the young Cave. The Scotsman's persona was intense, built upon an energy that translated effortlessly from the studio to the stage, where he'd cavort with wild eyes and crazy hair, playing to the camera and audience in a striped French t-shirt. But, even beyond those visual trappings, Alex plied a rock 'n' roll stripped straight from a comic book devil, to make an impression on just about everyone who saw him. For Cave, the entire package was a supernova of utter excess transformed to pure excitement.

Besides, it was far more entertaining for Cave to ape someone like Alex Harvey, than to follow the staid rockers that continued to inform the Australian music scene. And it was through Alex, and through the Sex Pistols and The Saints and even Saint Iggy Pop himself, that Cave formulated his own earliest attempts at a stage presence.

At that time, it was Alex Harvey covers that set the stage for nearly all the free-formed jams and embryonic band rehearsals that Cave himself was involved in. He remembers that 'from when we were fifteen or so, I was playing with Mick Harvey and Tracy Pew. We had a couple of our own songs, but basically it was just Alex Harvey's stuff, and a bit of Alice Cooper...'

Obviously, this tack served Cave and his friends well, preparing them for the musical revolution which was just on the horizon. In 1974, spurred on by the rising (if visible only with hindsight) flames of the proto-Punk explosion, Nick Cave put together Concrete Vulture within the confines of his Caulfield Grammar School band. Alongside Mick Harvey, drummer Phill Calvert, guitarist John Cochivera, sax playing Chris Coyne and bassist Brett Purcell, Concrete Vulture was a rag-tag assortment of boys – and they were boys – gigging at school, at parties and at church youth group meets arranged by Mick Harvey's minister father. The musicians' influences were disparate, even then. Phill Calvert, for example, 'learnt marching drumming from age eight to eleven. After that I was self taught. So I had the basics. I listened to a bit of Jazz, both cool (Miles and Coltrane) and free freak-out stuff like Ornette Coleman. I was also big into soul and R&B drummers from the 60s...James Brown etc. You can probably hear some of that mix of stuff.'

Indeed Harvey, very early on, proved to be adept at organising the band, their contacts and their gigs. It was a role that he slipped into and never really let go of, a source of satisfaction as well as frustration as the years passed. It has been said that without Harvey's business acumen, Cave's early ventures would have been penniless many times over. He was also in tune with Cave's musical ambition and they soon found themselves, as a live act, operating in the same kind of atmosphere and with the same kind of attitude as a lot of bands of the day. 'We'd played concerts before the Punk thing happened, and we could play reasonably well,' Cave said. 'But we were playing kind of raucous noisy gigs anyway. And it didn't take that much to change our sound in order that we became a Punk rock group.'

Although Cave's first band was never meant to be an ongoing concern, but rather a way to fill hours in an otherwise bland existence, by the time the boys drifted out of grammar school in 1976 they'd kept it all going, with Tracy Pew replacing Purcell. This new band, still nameless, continued to rehearse and gig occasionally throughout 1976-77, and began defining themselves as a small presence within the local music scene.

The Boys Next Door's first Punk show, at Ashburton church hall, was disrupted by skinheads, and shut down by the police; their second, at Swinburne Tech, was punctuated by maniacal Ramones covers. Immediately, Mick Harvey acknowledged, 'we fit in with what people's idea of a Punk group was like,' with Cave the consummation of what a Punk front man should sound like. With his hair cut Sid Vicious style, a raging, spitting, screaming monster, he looked, as journalist Richard Guillart wrote, 'just dangerous enough for everyone to stay out of his way.'

Competition for the Boys Next Door's throne was limited. Of the other bands on the Punk circuit, Cave remembers, 'some were better than others; there were some good bands, and there were really some very strange bands that were never recorded.

'Filth... the Baybeez (Melbourne's answer to the Ramones, apparently)... the Primitive Calculators were a great group; there was the early Moodists playing around, and a band called The Reels.'

Punk's grasp on Australian inner-city life became a stranglehold as news filtered back of various exported successes in Britain and America. Recruited to EMI, The Saints' 'This Perfect Day' made the UK Top 30 in August, 1977; Radio Birdman signed to Sire... by early 1978, the Aussie major Mushroom had formed a Punk-specific subsidiary, Suicide, and was picking up anything that moved.

So, with their boots and bright faces pointed firmly toward the future, the Boys Next Door continued their regime of jamming and gigging. At shows that ran the gamut from Melbourne's London Tavern and Swinburne College, to the Preston Institute Of Technology and the Royal Oak Hotel's Tiger Lounge, they were making a transition: leaving behind a straight covers repertoire and peppering audiences with their own rough'n'ready interpretations of Punk, with songs such as 'Dive Position', 'Friends Of My World' and 'Shivers'.

However, the band didn't have enough in the bag to go out completely on their own and these early shows still included several notable cover songs: among them David Bowie's 'Andy Warhol', Iggy Pop's 'China Girl', and

Screamin' Jay Hawkins' 'I Put A Spell On You', which Cave remembered, 'I first heard in a bar somewhere when I was very young, and I never heard anything like it.' That classic was augmented by what was one of the Boys Next Door's signature set pieces, Nancy Sinatra's 'These Boots Are Made For Walking'.

The Go-Betweens' Robert Vickers remembers them at this time. 'I never played on a bill with [them], but saw them a number of times going back to 1978 when they were the Boys Next Door and were a much more sedate but still very good, art rockband.'

Vickers' observation is an important piece of early history. Whereas most fledgling bands of the era were content to beat their way through three chords of insta-Punk, Nick Cave and his buddies were egotistical, and smart enough to want more. From very early on, they strove to add their own stamp to the Punk scene. At the very most, it was an intelligent choice, a brilliant stroke of forward thinking aspiration. Or, perhaps, it was just dumb luck from a bunch of kids who didn't know what the hell they were really doing – on stage and in life.

By the end of the year, the Boys Next Door had become a quintet, welcoming guitarist Rowland S Howard into the band as he fled the dissolution of the Young Charlatans. In Howard, as in Harvey, Cave would find a double, a worthy sparring partner, and a masterful collaborator. Howard's addition would completely change the direction of the band, adding that clever spark, so bright yet impenetrable, that would come to make The Birthday Party's sound instantly recognisable.

THE OLD TESTAMENT

THE BOYS NEXT DOOR &
THE BIRTHDAY PARTY

1978

(SINGLE) These Boots Are Made For Walking
7801 These Boots Are Made For Walking
7802 Boy Hero
ORIGINAL RELEASE: Suicide 103140, March 1978

COMMENTS: A limited edition (1,000-1,500 copies). Nancy Sinatra may have created kitsch with 'These Boots Are Made For Walking,' but Cave's snotty, off-key version served as a fitting recorded debut for the Boys Next Door. Although Cave has said that the band were not readily influenced by Punk, preferring instead to draw from a vast pool of Country, Blues, Glam and classic rock, there is no denying the snarl of Punk in this cover.

Written by Lee Hazlewood for Sinatra's 1966 *Boots* LP, the blonde singer's version rocketed to the top of the US charts. The Boys Next Door, however, had less of an impact on the scene. Both on vinyl and on a version captured on bootleg at the band's August 1977 Swinburne college gig, the sparse instrumentation conveys menace – ragged and ramshackle and completely at odds with the pop singles that dominated the charts of the time.

The Suicide label itself was dreamed up when the Mushroom major decided to highlight the burgeoning local Punk scene. Just in case the experiment was a dismal failure – and to avoid any direct linkage with the parent label's traditional *milieu* – a new, suitably nihilistically named subsidiary was called for. While Suicide may have had a Punk-sounding name, its staff remained dyed-in-the-wool suits, and the Boys Next Door quickly found that they weren't just able to get up and play. Power shifted from the hands of babes, to a record company that put the band at their beck and call.

'Boots' was present in the band's live set, and Cave averred that 'we used to play that song, and I think they considered it to be a favourite for us to record.' In an interview in 1983, Rowland S Howard recounted how neither he nor the band were particularly enthused by the song's selection. 'That was sort of a record company idea more than anyone else's.'

The Boys Next Door were still a vague entity, even to themselves and calculating releases were pretty much beyond them. Though they were capable of moments of sheer brilliance, they were few and far between and it was a stroke of luck that they were helped along by the higher ups at the record label, who had a more evolved commercial sense and gave them a profile early on.

And, although the song passed quickly out of the band's own repertoire, to be relegated to the bootleg circuit, it would be revisited at least once more, when the Bad Seeds' Barry Adamson recorded a version for his 1991 *Delusion* soundtrack.

The flip, written by Cave and Mick Harvey, was one of the first Boys Next Door originals to make a live appearance, back in August 1977.

(ALBUM) compilation: *Lethal Weapons*

7801 These Boots Are Made For Walking
7803 Masturbation Generation
7802 Boy Hero
ORIGINAL RELEASE: Suicide VXL 2407, May 1978

COMMENTS: The *Lethal Weapons* compilation was intended to showcase the late-1970s crop of Australian Punk bands. The Boys Next Door contributed three tracks to the comp – both sides of their debut single, plus 'Masturbation Generation', a song that according to Cave, was titled by Gary Gray, vocalist with The Reels. 'He gave that title to me for a song I'd written called "I'm So Ugly", or something like that.'

The Boys Next Door's three songs were recorded by Greg Macainsh, singer and bassist for local Glam-pop band Skyhooks (and also ex-Reuben Tice and Frame). Alongside bands like Teenage Radio Stars (who themselves would metamorphose into the Models) and JAB, the Boys Next Door proved to be a handful of head hairs above their peers, becoming one of the few to actually go on to bigger things. Neither was the experience as pointless as some subsequent historians like to make out, as *Lethal Weapons* handed the band a bigger boost than playing gigs ever could. It gave them an arena and, for the first time, nation-wide exposure to an army of Aussie Punk curiosity seekers.

Despite this exposure, Phill Calvert insists that the band's demos for the compilation were actually stronger than the finished recordings. 'We cut them on our own with the engineer (could have been Mike Shipley...not sure). I wish we still had those tapes...I remember them as rougher and tougher than what ended up on the record. It was at a studio called Media Sound...which became Platinum Studios in the 80s and is now called Sing Sing South.'

The original Suicide release of this album was available on both black and white vinyl. Mushroom itself reissued the set in 1983. (Mushroom Records L27112)

(RADIO) 3RRR Christmas Party, 12 December 1978
UNR Boy Hero
UNR Conversations
UNR Shivers
UNR Mouth To Mouth
UNR A.K.A.
UNR Dive Position
UNR The Nightwatchman
UNR Caroline Says
UNR Something About Our
UNR I Mistake Myself
UNR Personality Crisis
UNR Grand Illusion
UNR Somebody's Watching
UNR China Girl

ORIGINAL RELEASE: Unreleased. Broadcast live to air 12 December 1978

COMMENTS: This early set was put out through the airwaves just in time for the 1978 holiday season. Triple R Radio in Melbourne was an early champion of local independent music. Beginning as an outlet for purely educational broadcasting, by 1978 they'd switched formats, giving fans of the underground scene an outlet. No matter how radically early Punk was changing the musical landscape, it was still taboo as far as the mainstream was concerned. Radio stations like 3RRR were to have an enormous impact on getting alternative music out to a greater number of people than those who relied on club hopping to find the era's tastemakers.

1979

This year found the band continuing to groom themselves musically and expanding their gig circuit, playing some of their first ever 'big' shows. However, it wasn't roses all the way for the Boys Next Door. Joining a multi-band tour that included fellow Suicide acts Cold Chisel, The Angels and Flowers, the band were not exactly showered with accolades – they were even booed right off the stage at Melbourne's Festival Hall in March. They were a support band, and treated as such by the audience. In truth, The Boys Next Door created a horrible racket at times, while the band themselves were often worse for the wearing. They were paying their dues – the hard way.

But even those disappointments were counterbalanced by the adrenaline rush that came from being on stage. They were rising stars on the club circuit, even if that was as far as they would go. Appended to the Mushroom label, they were included on several notable compilation albums, giving them a taste of what was on the horizon. And, while the label's support would ultimately prove tepid, simply being on a label gave them the boost they needed to push further. Mushroom's ambivalence, however, would come at a cost.

(ALBUM) compilation *From The Archives*
7901 Scatterbrain
7902 Enemy Of State
ORIGINAL RELEASE: Missing Link, 1979

COMMENTS: A nice compilation of local bands featuring one group of impresarios billed as two distinct acts. 'Scatterbrain' was recorded on a primeval 4-track recorder in Phill Calvert's bedroom and appears under the Boys Next Doors name. However, the second song, a cover of Ollie Olsen's 'Enemy Of State', was a product of the mysterious Torn Ox Bodeys.

(SINGLE) Shivers
7903 Shivers
7904 Dive Position

ORIGINAL RELEASE: Mushroom K7492, May 1979

COMMENTS: 'Shivers', written by Rowland S Howard, had previously made a mark on the music scene when he wrote and recorded the number with his first band, The Young Charlatans. And it was 'Shivers' that fitted so naturally, almost preternaturally, into the Boys Next Door's canon. Both Cave and Howard would revisit this song from time to time over the years, with one of Cave's most notable resurrections coming when he laid down backing vocals on a 1996 cover by the Israeli band the Witches, for their *Undercover* LP.
The Boys Next Door second single was released with two different sleeves.

(ALBUM) *Door Door*
Line-up: Nick Cave (vocals); Mick Harvey (guitar); Tracy Pew (bass); Phil Calvert (drums).
7905 The Nightwatchman
7906 Brave Exhibitions
7907 Friends Of My World
7908 The Voice
7909 Roman Roman
7910 Somebody's Watching
7911 After A Fashion
7904 Dive Position
7912 I Mistake Myself
7903 Shivers

ORIGINAL RELEASE: Mushroom D 19227, May 1979

COMMENTS: Although this album was partially produced by the Boys Next Door themselves, it remained the record they loved to hate – all the more so after they grew into The Birthday Party and discarded any suggestion of a pop background. Cave, for one is particularly vehement regarding the set, describing anyone who actually admitted liking the album as 'unfortunate people.'

At this early stage in his career, the Cave voice was barely formed. Basically, sometimes he was singing, sometimes he wasn't. In fact, he later told *The Offence* 'I think my singing style at that particular period was totally repulsive. It was really disgusting.' And in truth, there were many people at that time that would have agreed with that assessment.

Even the presence of engineer Tony Cohen couldn't save the band from what Howard remembers as 'just a really ridiculous situation.' Cohen would soon be called a guru – recording some of the hottest, hippest bands around. His style counted for something, his skill behind the boards soon became the stuff of legend. At the time, though, working at Richmond Recorders, Cohen produced more restrained acts during the day, switching to the shadowed studios at night to cut tracks with bands few others would touch – the Boys Next Door included.

What happened to the Boys Next Door on this album was that they were swayed by, and accountable to, the label heads – and the tinkering of *Door Door* was done with maximum exposure, using an MOR sensibility that would shift stock, but not necessarily capture how the band themselves viewed their material.

The resulting album presented two different faces of the Boys Next Door. The first six tracks were produced by Les Karsky (a former member of the British pub-funk band Supercharge) at Alan Eaton Studio in June 1978. The overall feel is very late 1970s new wave, with the band's sound most reminiscent of Rikki And The Last Days Of Earth, those now-forgotten English future-Punks whose one album remains a heavily guarded secret among the proto-Ultravox crowd.

Slick, smooth and twisted in skeins of New Wave ethos, the songs on this album are derivative of many bands of the era. And, while Cave has so often disparaged this earliest output, the fact remained that the band were doing exactly what they were told to do – as he recalled two decades later. Cave said: 'We were given a producer who was this fucking idiot, who didn't have a fucking clue about anything, we had a record company who had absolutely no idea about anything, and we had a manager who took us into the office one day, handed us these diagrams of clothes he wanted us to wear, and said "listen boys, I've been on the phone to London. Punk's out, Power-pop's in."'

And the Boys Next Door were still so inexperienced that they blithely went along with whatever they were told. With aural hindsight, however, it's easy to see why, even if they had been completely thrilled with what they were doing, they didn't continue to crank out new wave power pop by the bucketful.

By the late 1970s, the world was glutted with bands just like this – some better, some worse than the Boys Next Door. In order to make a mark – a recorded mark anyway – it's important to remember that live, the band sounded nothing like this; and if they wanted to advance they had to blast out in their own way, splatter their sound. They needed to re-create themselves and The Birthday Party would become the vehicle for their reinvention.

The album was reissued on CD in 1993 – Mute Door CD 1 and Mushroom 1993 MUSH 32033.2.

(SINGLE) Scatterbrain
7901 Scatterbrain
ORIGINAL RELEASE: Crystal Ballroom CBR-1, November 1979

COMMENTS: What better way to bolster your fan base than to DIY your own give-away single? Culled from the *Archives* compilation, 'Scatterbrain', was passed as a freebie to gig-goers at the band's November 1979 Crystal Ballroom shows.

The flip was The Models' 'Early Morning Brain'.

(EP) *Hee-Haw*

7913 A Catholic Skin
7914 The Red Clock
7915 Faint Heart
7916 Death By Drowning
7917 The Hair Shirt
7918 The Plague

ORIGINAL RELEASE: Missing Link MLEP-3, December 1979; except 7918 out-take included on *The Birthday Party: A Collection* (Missing Link LINK 22)

COMMENTS: *Hee-Haw* was recorded during July/August 1979 at Richmond Recorders. Engineered by Tony Cohen, the songs were produced by the Boys Next Door and Keith Glass – their manager.

One notices a complete turn around for the band from the *Door Door* fiasco. Still reeling from the disappointment of their debut outing, the group had learned several life lessons about the business of business and the process of recording. Coming into the studio, they had it in mind to just let it all go, and turn their sound into something quite startling, something which, according to Howard, would be: 'Adventurous…after what we considered to be the humiliation of *Door, Door*, which is like the tamest thing possible, we just reacted very violently against that record in the most extreme direction away from that.'

In that, they certainly succeeded. The motley collection of songs on the EP had moments of wild free-form, snippets of psychedelic mania, and even a little twang thrown in for good measure. Sweetly naïve – certainly. A very good start? Most definitely.

After a somewhat grating opening across 'Catholic Skin,' with its Punky bass sound, the band experiments mightily on 'Death By Drowning' with a squeak of sax that anticipates some of Bauhaus' early honkings. Cave rebelled against some of *Door Door*'s smoother pop-inflected vocals – his hoots and yowls punctuating Howard's guitar slash. Finally, we can see something happening. That the band were experimenting with their sound, based on what they'd heard in their own back yards and coming across the ocean from Britain and America, is obvious. How could they not? They were very young, after all, and still getting the hang of it all. Disparate elements of definable music styles emerge momentarily, before being swept away into the freewheeling maul of the band's own design.

By the time we get to 'The Hair Shirt', which is enthusiastically gritty and spare, it's obvious that, even when the band seems to be hanging by the seat of their pants – and just barely – they must have had some kind of plan. Brash and exuberant, there is an intensity to the delivery that jostles with its careful organization. It must have caused some confusion for those who only found the song for the first time when they picked up the 1983 reissue, now credited to The Birthday Party.

As a whole, *Hee-Haw* was a brilliant swansong for the Boys Next Door.

These songs were subsequently reissued by Missing Link in 1983 (ING 008). By the time the set got a fresh airing from 4AD in 1989, it had metamorphosed into a thirteen track compilation re-titled *The Boys Next Door/The Birthday Party,* (CAD 307 CD). That set would again see the light of day in 1997 as Henry Rollins championed the band's set on his own 2.13.61 imprint. In tandem with the US indie Thirsty Ear, Rollins would also spearhead a massive re-issue program that gave many new fans access to these early recordings for the very first time.

1980

Eager to expand their horizons beyond the Melbourne and provincial Australian Punk scene, the group decamped to London, England, as The Birthday Party, where, they hoped, they would finally catch a break – something that had eluded them so far in Australia. The new name, usually believed to be taken from Harold Pinter's groundbreaking and disturbing play but actually inspired by a scene in Dostoevsky's *Crime and Punishment,* was something of a statement. Cave had inherited a love of literature from his father: Cave has often spoken of being read passages of great works from Joyce, Dostoevsky and other literary giants (as well as the Bible) and it was to be an important influence for the rest of his career. The conscious literary reference in their name signalled their ambition and determination to provide something that was non-mainstream in a different way from most Punk music.

Although the rich stew cooking in England remained somewhat elusive to those below the equator during the 1970s, by the turn of the decade, Punk had not only arrived, it was leaving as well. If every other Punker and his own brother were making the pilgrimage to London, Cave figured that he too would throw in his lot and try his luck in that soggy city.

The Boys Next Door played their last ever gig under that name at the Seaview Ballroom in Melbourne on 28 February. By the beginning of March, they'd touched down in London, having flown across oceans and continents.

It must have been some kind of culture shock; or at least weather shock. Flipping the equator and landing upside down in a country they'd only ever dreamed about didn't pan into the nirvana the band had hoped. Even changing their name couldn't make the magic happen, at first.

Although The Birthday Party would make a dent in London's still violent, viable scene, the band and Cave, in particular, discovered, that not only did they dislike the capital, they really, really hated it! 'We abhorred everything about London, found it to be one of the greatest disappointments of our lives. After living in Australia and reading constantly about England – what an amazingly exciting place it was – we finally got there and found this horrible, very constipated society.'

However, Phill Calvert offers a more positive spin on the adventure. 'London was great. It was just that we were very broke and trying to get our band going. Of the first year there, I remember on about the first weekend there we saw The Cure at The Marquee club. They could really play...sounded just like their first record except live...we thought that if all of the bands in London could play like that we were in for serious competition. A few weeks later I saw Siouxsie and the Banshees and then later The Teardrop Explodes, Simple Minds and a few other bands, and realised that not many bands in London at that time were up to matching their records with their live performances.'

Indeed, the miasma that dogged The Birthday Party came very close to breaking them. The band, Cave said, 'became this terrible, monstrous kind of group, simply in reaction to what we saw there.'

But that reaction, and people's reaction to The Birthday Party, was also influenced by the band themselves and the company they kept, along with the dull vistas of London. The group, Rowland S Howard recalled for *Alternative Press*, 'had an innate belief that we were so much better than everybody. That's an important thing, it's important that a band should be "you against the world."'

The Birthday Party discovered the truth of that when they dropped by the Rough Trade offices, shortly after they arrived in London. Howard continued, 'they listened to things like "The Friend Catcher" and "Mr Clarinet" and all that, and Geoff Travis said to me, "I think you're a very good group, but you're too much like the Talking Heads, and you're too unemotional". And so I said "OK, OK" and we went away.'

Neither were the Talking Heads the only point of comparison. Joy Division and The Pop Group, too, were frequently aligned with The Birthday Party. It was, shuddered Howard, 'a continuous process.' As they railed against the mainstream clutching at straws at times to find their own voice, it was Punk against the world, Cave against the world, The Birthday Party against the world.

Which is to say that they still made an impact – most certainly they did. From their Birthday Party debut on 29 June, 1980 at London's Rock Garden, to their last gigs in London in October, the band scored a couple of successes. Not only did they nail down their first ever session for DJ John Peel – on 10 September – they were picked up on by the important 4AD indie label. Ivo Watts, the label's mephisto, happened upon the band in what was only their second Birthday Party show, at the Moonlight Club on 7 July. He liked what he saw, and went back for more the following month. By the time the band returned to Australia, they'd inked a deal with 4AD.

Good/bad, light/dark – a black and white dichotomy awaited The Birthday Party as they compared their homeland with their most recent home. But the grey areas between the two states were filled with an infinite number of shades. London had been a time to learn – to absorb, to bask in the globs of gob spat by audiences across the city, and soak up the mores of their better known peers.

That experience drove them back home after just seven months, and only a handful of gigs. Once back down below the equatorial line, however, The Birthday Party would strengthen. Cave, Harvey, Howard, Pew and Calvert would reinforce their resolve to continue on a path that they decided was completely of their own forging.

By November the band were in Melbourne, awaiting the release of the *Boys Next Door/Birthday Party* compilation and picking up their gig schedule as if they'd not been away. Notable shows of the season included a few gigs with the Go-

Betweens in December. Go-Betweens' Robert Forster remembers these shows fondly. 'Always a good combination I thought...The Birthday Party going gangbusters, very exciting and full. [And then], the Go-Betweens a sort of opposite. [I remember] raising the curtain for them, and then finishing the night in style.'

These shows were followed by an end of year extravaganza at the Crystal Ballroom where a Phill Calvert-less Birthday Party ripped through a set that comprised nothing but Stooges covers.

By the end of the year, they'd re-entered Richmond Recorders for another stab at their post-Punk legacy – commencing recording material for *Prayers On Fire*.

(SINGLE) Happy Birthday
8001 Happy Birthday
8002 Riddle House

ORIGINAL RELEASE: Missing Link MLS-16, February 1980

COMMENTS: Released before the band had yet to breathe an ounce of English air, this single was initially given away as a freebie at their gig at the Crystal Ballroom on 16 February, 1980.

Both songs were recorded at Richmond Recorders, during August and September 1979 and January and February 1980. Released, of course as a Boys Next Door single, the original pressing predates the band's name change; was limited to just 750 copies; and exists both with and without a picture sleeve.

With its beetle-bash riffing and Cave's shambolic homage to newfound transition, one wonders just how happy a birthday it would have been. The backing vocals leave something to be desired, but hearing Cave woof makes up for any other flagging enthusiasm. This band was rarely afraid to experiment – and this song, in particular is an apt study of what directions The Birthday Party would take. 'Riddle House', meanwhile, wraps itself around Pew's fat bass and owes much to the burgeoning dark wave oeuvre that was becoming a force in the UK. While it can't be well argued that the earliest incarnations of The Birthday Party were influenced by, and wielded their own take on, what would be so horrifically pigoeonholed into the Goth tag, it's also equally impossible to keep the band in that box.

(SESSION) Richmond Recorders, January-February 1980
8003 Hats On Wrong
8004 Guilt Parade
ORIGINAL RELEASE: *The Birthday Party/The Boys Next Door* compilation, November 1980

COMMENTS: Sessions at Richmond Recorders would produce much of the band's output for the remainder of the year. These two tracks, however, remained unreleased until being compiled onto the year's-end compilation.

THE BIRTHDAY PARTY

(SINGLE) Mr Clarinet
8005 Mr Clarinet
8001 Happy Birthday
ORIGINAL RELEASE: Missing Link MLS 18, July 1980/4AD AD114, October 1980

COMMENTS: A stunning debut, 'Mr Clarinet' is completely derivative of the sonics that ebbed and flowed as the band cast off the clothes of one incarnation, to don those of another. Although it was originally issued only in Australia, copies winged their way northward, imported into England following The Birthday Party's own relocation to London where it proved to be an utterly uncompromising introduction.

At the very beginning, when word was just starting to percolate through the clubs, the *NME* simply cast the band aside as 'an avant-garde Australian group', completely overlooking the fact that what the band did across 'Mr Clarinet' – the utter barrage of intensity and purpose that penetrated the muck – was nearly exactly what so many home-grown and *NME*-championed outfits were themselves churning out. Could it have been The Birthday Party were doing it better?

Although the high treble and guitar punch of the single certainly echoes the clatter and band of their contemporaries, the song extends far beyond most bands' formulae, showcasing Cave's ragged delivery. Indeed, it's his heartfelt rage that becomes the only instrument to drive the drums down. If there's any incongruity to be found here, it lies solely within Pew's very mushy bass line, which he recorded alone. The bassist was not around for the take, so his band mates recorded their parts, leaving him to continue alone, and then smooth away the roughness into the final mix. In commercial terms, the single proved to be fruitless – not an even halfway successful exercise.

(RADIO) John Peel Show, 10 September 1980
8006 Cry
8007 Yard
8008 Figure Of Fun
8009 King Ink
ORIGINAL RELEASE: *The John Peel Sessions* Strange Fruit SFRSCD 098, 2001

COMMENTS: The Birthday Party's first John Peel session, recorded and broadcast long before most of the country had even heard of the band, hit listeners like a series of savage pokes in the eye. One minute you were listening to the traditional period-Peel fodder of discordant midlands art rock, with a raucous singer and an angular sax solo – and then all hell broke loose, across four songs that possibly remain *the* acid test for all those fans post-'Wild Roses' who say they have been fans since the early days.

Screaming, screeching, clattering and crunching, all the usual terms can be applied to this recording, but with one major difference. Most of the people who used such terms knew what to expect, from either reputation or past experience. But there weren't many of them around, that evening in September 1980.

(SINGLE) The Friend Catcher
8010 The Friend Catcher
8011 Waving My Arms
8012 Catman
ORIGINAL RELEASE: 4AD AD12, October 1980

COMMENTS: Although now running as The Birthday Party, the band were still honing songs that had long been part of the Boys Next Door live set, including a fiery cover of Gene Vincent's 'Catman' and 'The Friend Catcher'.

The song was an especial favourite of John Peel, who provided its only UK radio airings; indeed, Rowland S Howard remembered, 'he was always saying very kind things about the group on the radio' and, given the shoddy treatment the band were receiving from the music press, they needed all the accolades they could get.

'The Friend Catcher' is joyfully noisy, Howard's blaze of brilliant feedback completely undermining whatever structure the band had in mind for this song. Indeed, he was so caught up in attempting to tame the cacophony that, according to legend, he actually prolonged it, cracking his feet on the effects pedals in a desperate attempt to silence the screech. Although he would subsequently claim that he knew what he was doing all along, explaining that he was 'using the studio technology...to make it all much bigger.'

(ALBUM) *Fast Forward*
8008 Figure Of Fun
8007 Yard
ORIGINAL RELEASE: Fast Forward 002, December 1980

COMMENTS: This Australian monthly cassette magazine debuted in November 1980, promising to showcase the best in Australian indie and Punk acts, a market whose own expansion could be deduced from the growth of *Fast Forward*: from six or seven tracks in the early issues, to 20 a time later in life. Alongside an interview with Rowland S Howard and Nick Cave, the sophomore issue of *Fast Forward* featured two tracks from the band's recent Peel session, while The Birthday Party shared this issue with Vital Cortex, Graeme Pitt, Stuart Coupe and Clinton Walker.

1981

Once again, the band reconvened at Richmond Recorders for sessions that encompassed both the *Prayers On Fire* album and the 'Nick The Stripper' 12-inch. And, again Tony Cohen was at the helm. Once wrapped, the band filmed their performance at Melbourne's Crystal Ballroom at the end of February. That clip, shot by Evan English and Paul Goldman, better known as The Rich Kids, and edited by John Hillcoat, was used for the band's promo video.

The Go-Betweens' Robert Vickers caught up with The Birthday Party again. By this time he'd relocated to New York City, where he was ensconced in that city's thriving Punk scene, but he did catch a gig or two during a trip home to Sydney. 'I was very impressed and went backstage to meet them. They were the hippest thing going on the Australian Punk scene at that time, but I guess living in New York made me interesting enough to talk to.'

Not too daunted by their wobbly moment in London the previous year, the band was back in that city by the beginning of March and hit the club scene with a vengeance, gigging across town. Around this time, two key personnel in the Nick Cave story appear: Magazine bassist Barry Adamson and *NME* photographer Bleddyn Butcher catching The Birthday Party for the first time, when they supported Colin Newman of Wire on 19 March.

Adamson, of course, would join the Bad Seeds when they emerged from the wreckage of The Birthday Party in 1984. Prior to that, the bassist carved a peerless reputation for himself alongside Howard Devoto and Magazine, one of the most innovatively exciting bands of the late 1970s. Australian expatriate Butcher, meanwhile, became one of The Birthday Party's most stalwart supporters in the music press and beyond, and developed a close friendship with Cave. It is Butcher's stunning pictures that grace the cover of the live Birthday Party album released years later, and it was he who drew many people's attention to the group in the first place, as well as providing guidance and a familiar accent to give them encouragement.

The Birthday Party were able to hold their own against myriad bands, in whose company Cave's long, lean and mean antics seemed completely incongruous and there were memorable gigs with the likes of Theatre Of Hate and Modern English. By the end of June, the group hit the sticks, leaving the confines of London for a snappy eight-date tour of the UK, opening (alongside Subway Sect) for 4AD label mates Bauhaus.

Bauhaus were promoting their 'The Passion Of Lovers' single and The Birthday Party were thought to be a neat fit for the tour. Pete Murphy wore the graceful mantle of Goth King, with his cohorts as court beside him. If we accept that dubious imagery, the aggressive and egregious Cave, was the perfect hard court jester – leaping and screaming with the cacophony of The Birthday Party bearing as much of the brunt of his rant, as the audience in front of him.

When Bauhaus took the stage, one knew what to expect from Pete Murphy and his crew. When Cave and The Birthday Party stepped out into the lights, the ensuing set could go in any number of directions. And that was what set The

Birthday Party apart. They may not have been better than their peers, and certainly often they were not, but they were always interesting, grimly compelling.

Although The Birthday Party often sought to escape the earliest tendrils of Gothic rock, visually, stylistically and even in their attempts to draw their music into new dimensions, they remained very much in accord with the nuances of the day. It was only within their own refusal to kowtow to the labelling that the band can be said to have resisted such pigeonholing and, of course, their own manoeuvres were so fiendishly subtle that most people missed the joke. The ghoulishly tongue-in-jugular 'Release The Bats' was The Birthday Party's attempt to ruthlessly parody the imagery with which they had been saddled.

The whirlwind was wrapped up at the Cambridge Corn Exchange on 27 June, and all concerned celebrated the finale with hi-jinks. These included Bauhaus lobbing shaving-cream-slathered plastic plates at The Birthday Party during their set, and The Birthday Party reciprocating by pinning Pete Murphy to the stage and decorating his bare stomach with a huge, black markered penis.

What a shock then, for The Birthday Party to commence their first ever journey outside of England (and Australia, of course) with a ten-day tour of the US. Although that country had laid claim to the Punk revolution not long after Britain unleashed its own version, it seemed perhaps, that America wasn't quite ready for The Birthday Party. Their shows in New York, Philadelphia, Boston and Chicago were underwhelmingly attended.

Several shows were shut down due to the band's 'bad behaviour'; another, at New York's Chase Park Lounge, was cancelled entirely with only one lone woman in attendance. In Boston, a little over a week later, Bill Reiflen, then drummer for the Punk outfit the Blackouts, remembered that The Birthday Party 'were just horrible. Rowland was doing this weird little dance, and they sounded just terrible.'

However, Robert Vickers again had another inside take on the band and predicted what they would become to the movement. 'When I got back to New York, I was hanging out at CBGBs late one night with a friend from the Bush Tetras, when Lydia Lunch came literally running up to me and said "do you really know The Birthday Party?" like a teenage Beatles fan from *Hard Days Night*. I knew enough about Lydia to know that she took herself pretty seriously, so a reaction like that meant that The Birthday Party weren't just going to be an important Australian underground band, they were going to be influential all over the world.'

Lunch herself caught them at another Chase Park Lounge gig in the beginning of October. And by the end of November, she was in England herself, joining the band on stage during their London Venue show on 26 November, and then again the following night in Manchester at Rafters.

After a brief stint on the continent, The Birthday Party returned to play what was widely touted as their 'farewell show' at London Polytechnic on 11 December. After that, the band jumped ship back home to Melbourne.

They needed the break. The Birthday Party was disintegrating at a rather alarming rate. The latter half of the year had seen the band's bad boy antics escalate to the point that at some shows, it felt like there were as many punches thrown as songs sung. That behaviour had become part of the band's psyche as well as something that was expected of them. This was a dangerous development that was bound to take its toll on all the band members.

Tracy Pew, in the grip of various addictions, had suffered several overdoses during their 1981 London relocation. But, the band didn't stop to take much of a break. Instead they entered Armstrong's Audio Visual Studios with Tony Cohen, not only to mix the rough live tape for the forthcoming *Drunk On The Pope's Blood* EP (to be split with Lydia Lunch) but also to lay down the bones of the next year's *Junkyard*.

(SINGLE) Nick The Stripper
8101 Nick The Stripper
8102 Blundertown
8103 Kathy's Kisses
ORIGINAL RELEASE: Missing Link MSD 479, June 1981

COMMENTS: Recorded at AAV Studios in Melbourne in January 1981, this song grew from a set of self-deprecating lyrics Nick Cave wrote while in the throes of crippling writer's block, during the band's London sojourn the previous year. 'Nick The Stripper' begins with a blues rumble in the vocal, subsequently destroyed by Howard's apocalyptic guitar, a prime example of the band's powerful disparate elements at play, combining in unprecedented force, while Tracy Pew's bass line is even bigger and rowdier than we've yet heard from him. During this particular spate of recording, sundry musicians wandered through the studios, including Phillip Jackson, Stephen Ewart and Mick Hunter from Melbourne's avant-garde Equal Local. The three added their brass chops to the mix.

Keith Glass wanted the band to have a promo clip to back this newest song, and so The Rich Kids (Paul Goldman and Evan English) were recruited to wield the camera, joined by young film student John Hillcoat, who edited the raw footage – an extravagant drug and booze-laden farewell party for the band, who were soon to return to London.

'Blundertown', meanwhile, finds Cave 'singing' for one of the first times since the *Door Door* sessions and, we find that he *is* beginning to discover the range of his voice. This overlooked gem indicates how diverse The Birthday Party were, a marvellous indication of how Howard's presence within the band changed their sound; a precursor to the direction he would take – first as part of Crime And The City Solution and then with his own These Immortal Souls, and future solo projects.

More akin to the dark wave Australian sound that dominated the early part of that country's decade, the song is wholly melodic, driven by clipped drum staccato and a surfish guitar that softens the bite of such lyrics as, 'it's only 12,000 miles to heaven, but the car is broken...'. Even Cave tempers his frothings here, evoking instead weary passion. Rich and textured, 'Blundertown' may have been a signpost for the future.

And 'Kathy's Kisses', well... the band had done better, although Mick Harvey's heavy handed and slightly discordant piano, coupled with Cave's growl reminiscent of Tom Waits, lends it a weird energy. It also could be seen to foreshadow 'From Her To Eternity' as Kathy's kisses metamorphose into that song's protagonist's tearful upstairs neighbour.

The 7-inch single was released with just the A side and 'Blundertown'. The first 1,000 copies of the 12-inch were released with a pink and blue cover. Subsequent pressings appeared with a grey and black cover. 'Blundertown' was carried over and included on the *No Worries* compilation.

(ALBUM) *Prayers On Fire*
Line-up: Nick Cave (vocals); Mick Harvey (guitar & drums); Rowland S Howard (guitar); Tracy Pew (bass); Phill Calvert (drums).
8104 Zoo-Music Girl
8105 Cry
8106 Capers
8101 Nick The Stripper
8107 Ho-Ho
8108 Figure Of Fun
8109 King Ink
8110 A Dead Song
8111 Yard
8112 Dull Day
8113 Just You And Me
LP BONUS TRACKS
Japan/Greece
8118 Release The Bats
811 Blast Off
AUSTRALIAN/UK CD BONUS TRACKS 1988
8102 Blundertown
8103 Kathy's Kisses
OUT-TAKE
8107a Ho-Ho
ORIGINAL RELEASE: 4AD CAD 104, April 1981; 8107a on *The Birthday Party: A Collection* (Missing Link LINK 22), 1985

COMMENTS: With the band's UK label racking the album two months before Mushroom, *Prayers On Fire* was The Birthday Party's official debut LP.

The sessions for *Prayers* fell between December 1980 and January 1981 when the band spent nearly all their time, including the Christmas holiday, bunkered into AAV Studios in Melbourne. All tracks were recorded here, except 'Dull Day' and 'Just You And Me' which placed the band back at their old haunt, Richmond Recorders. Again, the songs were self-produced, with Tony Cohen engineering. The first 1,000 copies of the Australian Missing Link pressing (LINK 14) were on red vinyl.

A masterpiece of whacked-out time signatures and some otherworldly key changes, the set knocked the British fans and press back like a ton of bricks. No one, no one at all, seemed to know quite what to do with The Birthday Party

– or exactly what to make of them.

Although the band were now regularly garnering good reviews, they were still having a difficult time scoring larger pieces in the London music press, and continued to suffer the racial backlash of their Australian origins. This was especially frustrating because the band were well aware that their material, though savage and uncompromising, far outshone anything else their immediate peers were pumping out.

With so many of their live shows during this era based on tormenting and assaulting the front rows of the audience, it's easy to look back and see why The Birthday Party weren't perhaps as beloved as they felt they had a right to be. Cave could intimidate, and the days of spitting by or at bands was passing as cleaner, more fastidious post-Punk bands suited up and strutted onstage in London's clubs.

Very different to *Hee-Haw*, *Prayers On Fire* was littered with odd effects. 'Capers', one of two Rowland S Howard contributions, in particular, is a glorious mish-mash that finds Cave's odd vocal echo plodding along behind quite a chipper cacophony. And, while that song became a phenomenal study in what could only be called post-post-Punk, Howard's other song, 'Ho-Ho' didn't follow the same blissful path.

With similar intent, Cave's ever so slightly out of tune, and time, vocals were probably intended to come off as they do. However the result is sloppy enough to make one wonder if the take was recorded before or after the band had drunk fellow studio mates Split Enz's twelve bottles of Christmas champagne. Both tracks are notable, too, in that they featured a co-write with Genevieve McGurkin, founder of Honeymoon In Red and These Immortal Souls and one of Howard's longest standing collaborators. (An alternate version of 'Ho-Ho', featuring lead vocals from Cave, was recorded but shelved; Missing Link later employed it as a highlight of the *A Collection* compilation.)

On the opposite side, however, was 'King Ink,' one of the album's set pieces and one of a handful of songs that Cave had written during the band's 1980 London residence. Like 'Nick The Stripper,' with which it can be well paired, 'King Ink' is not only stuffed with wry self-deprecation and self-loathing, but also with a braggadocio that lies oddly, but comfortably in the same space. The latter finds Cave feeling like a bug, hating his 'rotten shell', while in the former, he's become 'a fat little insect, a fucked little insect'. Of the two 'King Ink' is a darker, deeper, more grievous portrayal of a rotten soul. And, with muddy, wet guitar the song becomes poetic music *à la* French writer Jean Genet.

In 'A Dead Song' lies one of the first fruitful collaborations between Cave and his then girlfriend Anita Lane. Funny, somehow sweet and completely ragged, it is underpinned by Pew's remarkable bass lines, highlighting why he remains one of the era's most underrated bassists.

(RADIO) *John Peel Session* 28 April, 1981
8114 Release The Bats

8115 Rowland Around In That Stuff
8116 Pleasureheads Must Burn
8117 Loose
ORIGINAL RELEASE: Strange Fruit SFPS 20, 1987

COMMENTS: Although one could argue that, in studio and on vinyl, the band strutted their stuff to great effect, it's when they were live at the BBC that The Birthday Party were able to actually pin down some of the rancorous passion that a lot of their recorded output would never match. This session is no exception to that rule. 'Release The Bats', of course is the lynch-pin that holds the whole performance together, and was the live favourite that firmly planted the band in Goth's front pocket. This version, anyhow, clips along just as it should and sounds more subdued than it did on the subsequent single. ('Release The Bats' was included on the *Mixed Peel* mail-order cassette presented free with *NME* – Strange Fruit/NME 033).

'Loose', which sounds more like the Stooges original than did the Boys Next Door's in-concert assault on 'Funhouse', was a nice diversion, marking one of the rare times that the band actually set a cover version to tape. Retaining the Stooges' own surfabilly mentality, at the beginning at least, the resulting mash is very reminiscent of The Cramps. Another stage staple, 'Loose' would make an encore appearance in another live incarnation on The Birthday Party/Lydia Lunch *Drunk On The Pope's Blood* EP.

'Pleasureheads Must Burn' was also known as '(Sometimes) Pleasureheads Must Burn' and was a pounding drum driven thrash that inexplicably dove into a crazed free-form – dare we say – Jazz interlude. This song has only ever been made available as a live version, splayed out across the Peel Session, the film footage from the *Pleasure Heads Must Burn* video, *Drunk On The Pope's Blood, Live 1981-1982* and on the *It's Still Living* compilation – it has never seen a studio version.

As for 'Roland Around In That Stuff', which was re-titled thus when Howard was out of the room, and is a vitriolic deadpan, well…you get the picture.

(SINGLE) Release The Bats
8118 Release The Bats
8119 Blast Off

ORIGINAL RELEASE: 4AD AD 111, August 1981

COMMENTS: 'Release The Bats' was produced by The Birthday Party and Nick Launay in London in 1981. Launay, of course, was the extraordinary Townhouse producer whose association with PiL, most notably on their *Flowers Of Romance* LP, was a highlight in a career that had already taken in the Slits and Killing Joke.

Launay's method of working, he's said, is to 'go in prepared, give it everything you've got...but don't take it too seriously.' And that methodology proved to be a perfect fit when it came time to begin 'Release The Bats'. Now, nearly 25 years on, Launay still recalls Cave's vocals on the single as one of his favourite ever moments in the studio.

The song, a tongue-in-cheek jab at the droves of black-clad, white-faced, lanky haired Goths that were beginning to take notice of The Birthday Party, has become for many, the quintessential Birthday Party track, and detrimentally so, since they were capable of much better. But it was a stylish and hard-hitting dose of bad temper laced with sardonic humour.

The title itself is a masterstroke; indeed, the band needn't have recorded a single down stroke or drumbeat – no one would have noticed. Although the song remains one of the simpler numbers in the band's canon, its undeniable glee sets it aside as proof that The Birthday Party weren't even close to morose. Conceived, Mick Harvey says, 'as a comedic interlude, recorded "because it happened almost by accident"' 'Release The Bats' certainly contains some wry caricature going on amid the deep rolling bass-led cacophony, leaving Cave to yelp his way from rockabilly ghoul to Gothic Rock demi-God, while stomping firmly on everything in between.

No matter how the song was intended, however, ultimately the joke was on the band. Sure enough, 'Release The Bats' became a mantra for Goths everywhere. Later, Cave would protest furiously against the Gothic Rock tag that enshrouded their reputation. But, with a song title like this, what else could they have expected?

A live staple during much of this period, the song had already enjoyed a successful outing on John Peel's show before finally being cut to single in June. By August, it reached #3 on the UK indie charts. That would be the band's highest peak ever. Of course, those who missed out the first time round were rewarded for their patience when the song was included as a bonus track on the 1988 CD reissue of *Junkyard*.

'Blast Off', meanwhile, was completely lost in the backlash of gothic grandeur from the single's A-side. The utter antithesis of Goth, 'Blast Off' allies itself more closely to seminal bands like The Saints and the ever-present Stooges than it does to either of The Birthday Party's latest skewered peers – Bauhaus or Joy Division.

It's rough, and remarkably abrupt, with Cave's vocals reduced to bitter bites that are nearly lost in the high trebled guitar, heavy drums and rolling bass that always hover near the front. But even all that cannot quash the sax and organ that seemingly have no place in such a vehement song, but work to such beautiful effect. When Cave draws out the torturously long 'Blast Off', one can't help but imagine the lanky figure of Iggy Pop lurking in the shadows, as the baby-fresh faces of Sonic Youth's Thurston Moore and Big Black's Steve Albini take copious notes from the sidelines.

The single's sleeve is comprised of a still from the recent 'Nick The Stripper' video. Missing Link would repackage the songs as a 12-inch singles in April 1983 (MISS 37.12)

(SINGLE) Mr. Clarinet
8005 Mr. Clarinet
8001 Happy Birthday
ORIGINAL RELEASE: 4AD AD114, October 1981

COMMENTS: Belatedly for the Brits, a domestic issue of the early Missing Link single

(LIVE) The Venue, London 26 November 1981
8120 Junkyard
8121 A Dead Song
8122 The Dim Locator
8123 Zoo-Music Girl
8124 Nick The Stripper
8125 Blast Off
8126 Release The Bats
8127 Bully Bones
8128 King Ink
8129 Pleasureheads Must Burn
8130 Loose
ORIGINAL RELEASE: *The Birthday Party: Live 81-82* 4AD CAD 9005 CD 1999, except 8130 on *Drunk On The Pope's Blood*

COMMENTS: The band's first official live album, almost two decades after the fact, pulled from three 1981/1982 era shows. The first, from the London Venue, had previously been excerpted for the *Drunk On The Pope's Blood* EP.

The sound quality is rather good, and the band is well into its stride. 'Junkyard' is particularly claustrophobic and was a magnificent outing for this as-yet-unreleased song – Cave in particular sounds as if he's fighting for breath and words under the slowly churning violence of Howard's guitar. One can see how this fright-show would perhaps have been hard for the uninitiated to be near.

It's still surprising to discover just how incredibly heavy and meaty this band were live. They made a much bigger sound than any other quintet had a right to and again demonstrated an ethic that held them apart from their peers. That they were using the formulae that made Goth so huge is without question, but they were vomiting it back with such a bite that what could have been called just plain old art rock became so much more than even that. Listening to The Birthday Party in concert one can't help but feel that there's something at stake – for the band, for their audience, for the very fabric of post-Punk music.

An apt illustration of this is the monumental version of 'King Ink', one that enshrines the awesome power of the band: Cave's vocals explode and writhe underneath the bludgeoning, primeval rhythm section, and Howard lays on top a devastating interchange of thudding, volcanic riffs from his top strings and hysteric squalls from the rest of the fretboard.

'A Dead Song', while lost somewhat within the strength of the set's other staples, bashes along all beetle-bound as usual with the briefest of spoken introductions from Cave, who sounds at death's door at the beginning of the second song in the set. 'The Dim Locator' still sounds, somehow, typically 'Australian' – a giveaway of the band's musical roots. One of the chief wonders of this album – aside from the extraordinary music – is to listen to the audience reaction. No doubt there were Birthday Party fans present but there must have also been a crowd of people who had never witnessed anything like it in their lives before (there always was at a Birthday Party show) and the air of bemusement, at best, and terror, at worst, really does seem detectable amidst the ragged cheers.

(RADIO) *John Peel Show* 10 December 1981
8131 Big Jesus Trash Can
8132 She's Hit
8133 Bully Bones
8134 Six-Inch Gold Blade
ORIGINAL RELEASE: *The Peel Sessions: The Birthday Party II* Strange Fruit SFPS 058, 1988

COMMENTS: The Birthday Party's third John Peel Session arguably caught the group at its visceral peak – at least so far as their London sojourn was concerned. Honed by so much recent live activity, and finally granted the media exposure they felt they deserved, the group had a confidence that shines through every minute of this scintillating performance. 'Big Jesus Trash Can', in particular, impressed as an example of the new material that was already flowing. The other three songs previewing the gestating *Junkyard* were less immediate, but it made the forthcoming album a mouth-watering prospect.

1982

1982 was a turbulent year for The Birthday Party. It was the year that bassist Tracy Pew was sentenced to serve time for drunk driving and unpaid fines in January. 'I am the Ripper!' responded Tracy. The band's upcoming US dates were cancelled, and they replaced Pew for the duration with a rotating roster of bassists that included Magazine's Barry Adamson, and Harry Howard, Rowland's brother.

The year also kicked off with the continuation of the *Junkyard* sessions in Melbourne. Alongside these, the band were also putting the finishing touches to their half of the forthcoming *Drunk On The Pope's Blood* EP.

The band also made it to Greece to headline, alongside New Order, the first and third nights of a three-day festival in Athens. Sandwiched in between The Birthday Party was another off-kilter band – The Fall. There was a sharp contrast to these bands: one a ramshackle outfit driven by a chaotic camaraderie; one overseen by a shrewd svengali figure. But both bands had achieved respect and recognition when they were something like outcasts from the music scene, so a connection was made on this tour.

The Birthday Party were joined on this outing by Jim Thirlwell, otherwise known as Foetus, who added saxophone to a tumultuous version of the Stooges' 'Fun House'. 'At the end of the gig,' Thirlwell recalled, 'I remember Mark E Smith saying that he liked my saxophone because it was so minimal.' Smith was enamoured, and spread his good news to *Masterbag*'s Helen Fitzgerald, crowing that The Birthday Party were 'one band I really like and I would say we have similar vibes. What they played in Athens was real bluesy stuff which I really liked. When I saw them at the Venue [in August 1982], I went home and wrote a couple of songs the same night ... mostly about the audience though, not the band!'

Smith's affection for The Birthday Party was reciprocated. Following the group's relocation to Berlin (immediately after that Venue gig), guitarist Rowland S Howard admitted, 'for the first time since we left Australia, we felt part of some sort of "scene." There was nothing like that in England. The Fall were the only group we felt any affinity to.'

The two bands came close to an even firmer link after Fall manager Kay Carroll and Birthday Party publicist Chris Carr began discussing trying to attract major label interest in their charges with a so-called Gods of Indy package deal; the Go-Betweens and the Moodists were among other bands considered for inclusion. Nothing came of the notion, however, and slowly the parties drifted away. The Birthday Party gravitated towards Mute, the Go-Betweens to Sire. And The Fall remained with Kamera, at least for the time being.

In August, The Birthday Party relocated to Berlin – to live, to work, and to steep themselves in another culture. This time, there was one less ticket for the journey.

Just a few short weeks after the release of *Junkyard*, the best, and most successful (it reached #73 in Britain) Birthday Party material to date, Phill Calvert quit the band. Quit, or was fired (He would go on to become the drummer for the Psychedelic Furs through 1983, recording just one album, *Forever Now,* with the group).

With Harvey filling in on drums, The Birthday Party launched into another major tour in support of *Junkyard*. On the road, however, Cave and the band noticed a distinct lack of enthusiasm for the music. By 1982, the market was oversaturated with Birthday Party sound-alikes and, although they had a strong fan base, competition for new supporters was stiff. A disappointing tour was to be yet another blow for the band.

(LIVE) Astor Theatre 15 January 1982
8201 King Ink
8202 Zoo-Music Girl
8203 The Dim Locator
8204 She's Hit
8205 A Dead Song
8206 Pleasureheads Must Burn
8207 Junkyard

8208 Blast Off
8209 Release The Bats
8210 Nick The Stripper
8211 Big Jesus Trash Can
8212 Dead Joe
ORIGINAL RELEASE: *It's Still Living* Missing Link ING 009, May 1985

COMMENTS: Recorded and mixed by Tony Cohen, this album was released in 1985, long after the band's own dissolution and even longer still since they'd severed ties with the label. Issued without the band's consent, this album appeared as Nick Cave was gaining some momentum with the Bad Seeds. The show itself was a corker. The band focussed on their recently released songs, with a healthy handful of *Junkyard*'s upcoming gems thrown in for good practice.

(SINGLE) Dead Joe
8213 Dead Joe
ORIGINAL RELEASE: Tactic Music, *Masterbag* BAG 005, February 1982

COMMENTS: This take, from the same Matrix Studio sessions that produced Junkyard's 'Kiss Me Black' and 'Kewpie Doll' features Barry Adamson on bass, and is completely different from the version which appeared on *Junkyard* itself. Brighter and more bitter, Cave's vocals muddy themselves in the middle of an absolute storm of guitar; indeed they careen in a shattered approximation of metal on tar on flesh, and it's only Adamson's bass that keeps the song pinned to earth. This particular cut, originally released as a magazine freebie, would finally appear as a bonus track on the 1988 *Junkyard* reissue.

'Dead Joe' is a bloody froth of dumb emotion and bile, a caterwauling catastrophe of a song. Rowland S Howard, in particular, despaired of it, telling *AP* magazine that it was 'an incredibly dumb song, but it doesn't matter because rock music can encompass so many things and contradict itself, because it's supposed to affect you on a gut level.'

(ALBUM) *Drunk On The Pope's Blood* A-side only
8129 Pleasureheads Must Burn
8128 King Ink
8123 Zoo-Music Girl
8130 Loose
CD BONUS TRACKS
8107a Ho-Ho
7918 The Plague
7901 Scatterbrain
8214 The Friend Catcher
8213 Dead Joe
8215 After The Fire-works (Tuff Monks)
8216 After, After The Fire-works (Tuff Monks)

ORIGINAL RELEASE: 4AD JAD 202, February 1982

COMMENTS: The long awaited split 12-inch with Lydia Lunch. The Birthday Party took the A-side, Lunch's *The Agony Is The Ecstasy* took the flip. Four live cuts from the Venue show the previous November were mixed at AAV Studio 2 in Melbourne in January 1982.

Loud, and nearly incomprehensible at times, The Birthday Party's part in this particular release was nearly universally hammered by the press. But at least they were given credit for coming up with a show that was so anti-establishment that they actually captured what people in Britain felt was something akin to a true Punk ethic – a point borne out when the remainder of the show was released in 1999. Lunch, however, fared even worse from contemporary critics, her 'unpleasant squawking' convincing some critics that even The Birthday Party now sounded listenable.

The original EP has long been a collectors' item, as an artefact if not a Desert Island Disc. The CD reissue, however, is more-or-less essential, as it rounds up material dating back to the Boys Next Door/Birthday Party transition, including 'Scatterbrain' and the unreleased *Hee-Haw* out-take 'The Plague', previously available only on the Missing Link *A Collection* compilation (that set also served up alternate versions of 'Ho-Ho' and 'The Friend Catcher'). The *Masterbag* take of 'Dead Joe' and the fruits of the band's Tuff Monks collaboration (see below) rounded out a crash-course in Birthday Party rarities.

(SINGLE) Tuff Monks: After The Fireworks
8215 After The Fireworks
8216 After After The Fireworks
ORIGINAL RELEASE: 8215 on Au-Go-Go Records ANDA 22, 1982

COMMENTS: In early 1982 The Birthday Party left London, and their gruelling tour year behind to return temporarily to Australia in order to record their next album. The band was beginning to unravel, and they hoped that a change in locale might hold things together. However, while they did indeed get on with the business of recording new Birthday Party material, perhaps the most interesting thing to come from this sojourn was the brief banding and disbanding of the one-off group the Tuff Monks.

Recorded at AAV studios in February 1982, the Tuff Monks were Nick Cave, Mick Harvey and Rowland S Howard from The Birthday Party, and Grant McLennan, Lindy Morrison and Robert Forster from the Go-Betweens. The two bands had, of course, crossed paths before and with both bands in the same studio at the same time, it was inevitable that something would come of it. This McLennan/Forster penned song would end up not only committed to vinyl, but would also become one of both bands' most notable side projects.

Robert Forster explained that The Birthday Party's 'engineer Tony Cohen was, I think, trying to mix a live Birthday Party album and a single of ours that we had just done ['Hammer The Hammer'] in one night. Various members of The Birthday Party and the three people of The Go-Betweens were there. Nick Cave suggested we do something else. It was done in one night. Nick said he would go and get some instruments. He left in a taxi. Grant and I wrote the music while he was gone.'

So, with music and song newly formed, and Cave returning with an assortment of instruments, 'After The Fireworks' was recorded and mixed in April at Richmond Recorders for release as a single. An extension of the session 'After After The Fireworks' would later be included on the *Drunk On The Pope's Blood* CD re-issue (see above).

The song is ragged, and sounds exactly like it was – a quickly laid down ramble, with rolling drums, piano and Cave caterwauling through the music with improvised lyrics. It's a nice study in art rock, and a fascinating piece of both bands' early days – an important document for fans of either band.

'After The Fireworks' would eventually be revitalized on the *No Worries* compilation and again via the Go-Betweens' own re-issue of *Send Me A Lullaby* (Circus/Jetset TWA46) in 2002.

(LIVE) *Seaview Ballroom*, 19 February 1982
8217 Junkyard
ORIGINAL RELEASE: *Composite Signals* VHS, 1984

COMMENTS: The Birthday Party had three tracks on this remarkable compilation, the first of its kind to be released in Australia and filmed by the Single Shot Video Collective. 'Junkyard', was recorded at the band's 19 February 1982 Seaview Ballroom show where they shared the bill with another local band, Safehouse, and borrowed fellow VHS-mates the Moodists' bassist Chris Walsh to replace the absent Tracy Pew. The band would play with the Moodists and the Marionettes the following evening, when those bands were also captured on film.

The Birthday Party's remaining tracks on the video, 'Deep In The Woods' and 'Six Strings That Drew Blood', are taken from another Seaview Ballroom gig, on 9 June, 1983, this time with Tracy Pew back behind his bass. This performance is especially notable – the last The Birthday Party ever played.

The eventual release of the *Composite Signals* package would feature live performances from thirteen Australian indie groups filmed between 1981 and 1983. Other acts included Wild Dog Rodeo, Hunters And Collectors, Essendon Airport, Plays With Marionettes, Beach House, Manhattan Suicide/Wednesday, Equal Local, Government Drums, Equal Local, The Scientists, Sacred Cowboys, Go Circus, and Machinations.

(TV) *Riverside* BBC2 15, March 1982
UNR Dead Joe
UNR Big Jesus Trash Can
ORIGINAL RELEASE: Unreleased

COMMENTS: The Birthday Party's primetime UK television debut on the BBC's fondly remembered, if a little artsy, *Riverside*.

(SESSION) with Anita Lane
8218 The Fullness Of His Coming
ORIGINAL RELEASE: Anita Lane: *Dirty Pearl* LP Mute STUMM 81, 1993

COMMENTS: Post-Phill Calvert, the remainder of The Birthday Party, joined for this session by Anita Lane, resurrected this old number in May 1982. Another co-write between Cave and Lane, the song gave Lane a harder edge than her fans were used to.

Archived for the next decade-plus, this early collaboration with Lane is actually (and aptly) one of The Birthday Party's most fulfilling performances, a stygian fuzz over which Lane slowly intones the lyric (and Cave adds an atmospheric recitation of the title). The overall effect is not too dissimilar to some of Rowland S Howard's work with Lydia Lunch, but remains an oft-overlooked gem in The Birthday Party canon.

(ALBUM) Lydia Lunch *Honeymoon In Red*
8219 Done Dun
8220 Still Burning
8221 Fields Of Fire
8222 Dead In The Head
8223 Comefall
8224 So Your Heart
8225 Dead River
8226 Three Kings
CD BONUS TRACK
8227 Some Velvet Morning
ORIGINAL RELEASE: Widowspeak WSP 12, April 1988

COMMENTS: Honeymoon In Red was a loose collective between Lydia Lunch, Tracy Pew, Rowland S Howard, Nick Cave, Mick Harvey, and Genevieve McGuckin. The sessions for this were conducted in Berlin in June 1982, with the sheer number of members persuading the participants to view the project as an entire new band rather than Lydia Lunch with.....or The Birthday Party with....

Much controversy surrounds these sessions and the final tapes that eventually made their way out on Lunch's Widowspeak label. Initially recorded for the indie, Rip Off, that label never collected enough cash to actually release the album. It was shelved, and nearly forgotten. However, some five years later, Lunch and the album's original producer Clint Ruin – aka Foetus, aka Jim Thirlwell, returned to the tapes, remixing and tweaking the tracks in May 1987.

Along for the ride at that time was Martin Bisi. This vocalist and guitarist and producer was, and remains a little known pioneer in the experimental rock arena, working with bands most closely allied with Bill Laswell's collective; Afrika Bambaataa, Bootsy Collins et al; he did step out of that arena, most notably to produce Sonic Youth, later on.

Bisi also brought Sonic Youth's Thurston Moore along to overdub several of the original guitar parts for this posthumous remix.

According to Lunch, no member of The Birthday Party was pleased with the album's projected public release. Cave, who'd sung on just two tracks, 'Done Dun' and 'Dead In The Head', didn't want his name used on the album. And neither did Mick Harvey.

The rupture between the members of The Birthday Party and Lydia Lunch was only infused with even more real or imagined vehemence as *Honeymoon In Red* was prepped for packaging. Lunch recalls 'I was perturbed because I didn't know what had happened to cause such a massive split.' Both Cave and Harvey completely denied any rumours of rancour. Where they took offence was, rightly, that the album, under the fingers of Thirwell, Lunch and others, had been completely re-worked, thus rendering The Birthday Party's initial contributions something else entirely. It's precious, yes, but valid as Harvey explained in Ian Johnston's biography of Nick Cave.

'We were quite happy about them releasing the album, just as long as it didn't have our names on it. They'd gone back in and re-worked the songs. We'd worked on ten or eleven songs and the only reason five remained untouched was because they couldn't find the multitracks. The six tracks they got their hands on were completely mutilated and changed from anything vaguely resembling what we'd started doing. I didn't see any justification for putting our names on it, we had nothing to do with what had happened to the recording.' The inference for many was that the Lunch camp merely wanted to market with a sticker that read 'Recorded with The Birthday Party in 1982' and the album duly made its debut in 1988. Cave and Lunch's 'Done Dun', co-written with Murray Mitchell, was also released as the B-side to Lunch's 'The Crumb' 12-inch single in 1988. Widowspeak WSP 13.

'Dead In The Head, meanwhile,' was a Birthday Party set staple during the summer of 1982, when Lunch toured with the band.

(LIVE) Bremen, Germany 1 July 1982
8228 Big Jesus Trash Can
8229 Dead Joe
8230 The Friend Catcher
8231 Six-Inch Gold Blade
8232 Hamlet Pow, Pow, Pow
8233 She's Hit
ORIGINAL RELEASE: 4AD CAD 9005 CD, 1999

COMMENTS: A radio Bremen broadcast that eventually appeared on the *Live 1981-1982* album; these tracks – six through sixteen on the LP – were recorded during the band's show in Bremen on 1 July 1982; one stop on the short tour The Birthday Party undertook with Lydia Lunch and Die Haut. This excerpt omits a rousing version of 'Release The Bats' and a savage 'Funhouse' featuring a guesting Lunch.

Although this is a generally ragged performance, with 'Dead Joe' sounding particularly sloppy, the band do turn in a stunning version of 'Six-Inch Gold Blade'. A big, bass-led song in which Cave spins an absolutely horrendous tale with a delivery that belies the brutality – something that he already did well, and honed to stunning effect in later years. 'She's Hit', meanwhile, has an opening which is reminiscent of Bauhaus, but, at seven minutes long, it has time to turn into a Birthday Party staple.

One song from this show, 'Hamlet (Pow, Pow, Pow)' was released in 1995 on the Henry Rollin's fired *213 CD* sampler.

(LIVE) Köln, Germany 2 July 1982
8234 Hamlet Pow, Pow, Pow
8235 Funhouse
ORIGINAL RELEASE: Compilation *Kino Aus Der Kassette, 1982*

COMMENTS: This German language cassette zine features two Birthday Party tracks from their Köln Germany show on 2 July. 'Funhouse' features Lydia Lunch lending her pipes.

(SINGLE) Die Haut Der Karibische Western
8236 Die Faulen Hunde Von Tijuana
ORIGINAL RELEASE: Zensor CM2, 1982

COMMENTS: Christoph Dreher, Remo Park, Martin Peter and Thomas Wydler – Die Haut – relocated to Berlin in the early 1980s to carve a name for themselves in the city's booming musical underground. Activists, politicos, Marxists, musicians, Die Haut formed as Die Mieter (The Tenants) in 1981, in homage to the American experimentalists, The Residents, and turned in their own kind of warped rock 'n' roll.

By June 1982, they'd already soaked up much that Berlin had to offer, and now found themselves paired on tour with The Birthday Party, who were by now ensconced in the city and the two bands formed a significant bond.

This single was recorded the following month at South London Cold Storage, an old meat packing warehouse, as Cave and Lydia Lunch joined Die Haut in the studio. Cave whistles on 'Die Faulen Hunde Von Tijuana', the B-side of the single. The session was engineered by guitarist Charles Bullen of This Heat, a band of supreme experimentalists during the early 1980s.

The single was reissued in 1990 on CD (WSFASF 99).

(ALBUM) *Junkyard*
Line-up: Nick Cave (vocals); Mick Harvey (guitar & drums); Rowland S Howard (guitar); Tracy Pew (bass); Phill Calvert (drums).
8237 She's Hit
8238 Dead Joe
8239 The Dim Locator
8240 Hamlet (Pow, Pow, Pow)

8241 Several Sins
8242 Big Jesus Trash Can
8243 Kiss Me Black
8244 Six-Inch Gold Blade
8245 Kewpie Doll
8246 Junkyard
CD BONUS TRACKS
8213 Dead Joe
8118 Release The Bats
8119 Blast Off

ORIGINAL RELEASE: 4AD CAD 207, July 1982

COMMENTS: This album marked a transition for the band, as Mick Harvey eventually took over Phill Calvert's drum stool and Barry Adamson made a guest appearance playing bass on 'Kiss Me Black' and 'Kewpie Doll'. Those two tracks were recorded in London at the Matrix Studio with Richard Mazda engineering, while the rest of the LP comes from the AAV studio sessions with Tony Cohen over December 1981/January 1982.

The original pressing, on Missing Link, was delayed, waiting for artist Ed 'Big Daddy' Roth to finish his cover. Roth had come to fame as the builder of horrific hot-rod Frankenstein cars constructed from scrap yard junk in California in the 1950s – cars that were never meant to be driven, but simply to be admired; deconstruction and resurrection as sculpture. A regular on the Hot Rod circuit, Roth began airbrushing and selling t-shirts at shows to finance his art. Before long, he'd created a veritable zoo of utterly depraved characters, the most notable, of course, being Rat Fink, the craziest rat on the block. He'd also entered the recording world, cutting several albums as Mr. Gasser (featuring Ed Roth), and the Weirdos.

By the 1970s, he'd become the darling of the Punk rock underground and designed countless record sleeves for a host of bands, including The Cramps and Voodoo Glow Skulls. It was extremely fitting, then, for Roth to add his brush stroke to *Junkyard*.

Although 'Big Jesus Trash Can', has gone down in history as one of this album's seminal songs, it's still a hard listen, whether live or from the studio. However rocky and riddled with disintegrating, and grating, noise it may be, 'Big Jesus Trash Can' still bears *some* kind of relation to rock 'n' roll – an in-your-face response to anyone who cried that the band couldn't possibly become any more ragged and raging than they'd already proved they could be.

Cave tries on his depraved Preacher Man alter ego and finds that he likes the fit just fine. Holy Rollers had better run for cover as Cave predicts heads will roll in Texas. But still, it feels like judgement day is coming – albeit one that is filled more than expected with a rich undercurrent of humour and unabashed mirth even. It demonstrates how Cave's lyrics were developing in ways that made it clear that Cave was going to break beyond the confines of Punk and Goth pretty soon. Not for the first time, he found a skill in bringing experiences to life – those that the musician himself has never experienced – the mark would set him and all his line-ups from here on in apart. And here, 'Big Jesus Trash Can' runs riot, proving the point.

'Dead Joe', remains one of the best examples of the tack the group were now taking as they completely cut ties with their past, and focussed instead on a terrifying hybrid of hard rocking, no-wave noise. Beginning at quite a clip and ending somewhere short of warp speed, the song was a hectic helter-skelter run, a purposeful race to the finish, lyrics pouring pell mell, while the musicians thrashed with abandon. And that was live. On vinyl, however, the song was manipulated under a far more controlled approach, allowing Cave's vocals to come further to the front, some menace to keep the instruments from riot.

The song was also stained with some of the bad blood washing across the band. Calvert was barely hanging onto his drum kit when the album sessions commenced, and his relationship with his colleagues continued to slide downhill from there. It was grim. When the rest of the band felt that he couldn't nail down the timing for this song to their satisfaction, he was un-stooled and replaced by Mick Harvey.

(**LIVE**) Manchester Hacienda, 22 July 1982
8247 Dead Joe
8248 A Dead Song
8249 Junkyard
8250 Release The Bats
8251 Pleasureheads Must Burn
8252 Big Jesus Trash Can
ORIGINAL RELEASE: *Pleasure Heads Must Burn* VHS IKON 7, 1988

COMMENTS: Originally released on VHS in 1988, and reissued on DVD by Cherry Red in 2003, *Pleasure Heads Must Burn* comprised 14 tracks and captured two Birthday Party gigs at Manchester's legendary Hacienda club. The minimal two side-of-stage cameras that are familiar from a string of other releases from the same source document a reasonable show in grainy profile – the sound quality is acceptable, and watching the performance all these years later can leave a nostalgic lump in the back of the throat as one wonders, would the Nick of stripper fame have *ever* countenanced releasing *The Boatman's Call*? Though it doesn't carry much sense of *the band* in performance, it clearly conveys the magnetism and menace of Nick Cave the frontman.

(**TV**) *Gotterdammerung VPRO,* 21 July 1982
8253 Junkyard
ORIGINAL RELEASE: *Pleasure Heads Must Burn* DVD, Cherry Red CRDVD 20, 2003

COMMENTS: Against a striking backdrop, red and edgy, Tracy Pew broods in freakish cowboy drag. No matter that Cave was the frontman, and the band were all bad-ass, there's something about Pew's static presence that draws the eye regardless. A magnificent performance of the new album's title track, and a veritable highlight of the DVD.

(LIVE) Athens Greece 17 September 1982
8254 Funhouse
ORIGINAL RELEASE: *Live 1981-1982* 4AD CAD 9005 CD, 1999

COMMENTS: With Jim Thirlwell on sax, an unlistenable caterwaul offers up a completely deconstructed version of the Stooges' seminal chest-beater.

(RADIO) John Peel Show 22 November 1982
8255 Pleasure Avalanche
8256 Deep In The Woods
8257 Sonny's Burning
8258 Marry Me (Lie! Lie!)
ORIGINAL RELEASE: *The John Peel Sessions* Strange Fruit SFRSCD 098, 2001

COMMENTS: The fourth and final Birthday Party Peel Session. Clean and full of swing, the sonics of this session prove that the band were very well-honed – when they wanted to be. While history so often remembers the sloppy and sometimes haphazard appearance of their live performance, The Birthday Party were often dedicated to providing the best sound that the circumstances themselves warranted, and that on this occasion was exemplary.

The session's producer, ex-Mott The Hoople drummer, Dale Griffin remembers that 'they seemed quite edgy amongst themselves, a lot of the time, but still were able to re-configure themselves into apple pie order for recording. One of my favourite moments though, was when Mick refused to play drums any longer and he went "on strike". Weird. He was a first rate drummer. I seem to recall he wanted to play guitar. It was a bizarre half hour or so before normal service was resumed!'

Written by Rowland S Howard, 'Marry Me (Lie! Lie!)' is a swing-laden mope – well executed by Cave, but heard better when Howard re-recorded it for his These Immortal Souls' *Get Lost (Don't Lie)* album in 1987. A particular favourite of Howard's, the song was often played live in its Birthday Party incarnation, while he would also revisit 'Deep In The Woods', in 1994 during his solo tour.

The session's highlight, however, has to be the gloriously manic version of the new song, 'Sonny's Burning'. It opens with a burst of staccato drumming from Harvey before Cave and Howard tussle for control of the song, which seems to be spinning out of control all the time, and building up in horror too, even when Cave comically yells, 'Don't interrupt.' One of the best and most extreme of The Birthday Party songs.

(LIVE) Brixton Ace, 25 November 1982
8259 Fears Of Gun
8260 Hamlet (Pow, Pow, Pow)
ORIGINAL RELEASE: *Pleasure Heads Must Burn* DVD, Cherry Red CRDVD 20, 2003

COMMENTS: Filmed for broadcast by the BBC, these two performances are better known for their inclusion on the *Pleasure Heads* DVD – although neither is exactly stunning quality, as a darkened stage serves to hide most of the band's best attributes. The DVD, incidentally, also appends a very brief interview snippet from another UK TV show, the extraordinarily short-lived *Whatever You Didn't Get*.

1983

1983 was a year of comings and going that would see the band making great music and gaining acclaim but ultimately breaking up.

The Birthday Party had, by this time, a plethora of admirers. Go-Betweens' Robert Vickers recalls, 'Later on...when I joined the Go-Betweens and moved to London I got to know them better, especially the wonderful Tracy Pew who often stayed with us.

'The Birthday Party were the leaders among the group of Australian bands who moved to London in the early 1980s...the Go-Betweens, The Triffids, The Moodists and a host of others. They were the most charismatic and the most self-destructive; the most successful but the worst organised. They never had places to live and moved around like a travelling circus with a wild collection of fascinating girlfriends who had come over from Australia with them.'

Severed from 4AD and now signed to the prestigious indie Mute, the band were a creative house-on-fire, holed up in Berlin during April to record their label debut – the *Mutiny!* EP, with even the addition of Einstürzende Neubauten's Blixa Bargeld unable to resuscitate the now seriously ailing band. Both Cave and Bargeld were charter members in their own dual appreciation society at home in Berlin. In *King Ink* Cave speaks wonderingly of the first time that he saw Blixa Bargeld and Einstürzende Neubauten – each of them saw a kindred spirit at once and their lives and careers soon became inextricably linked.

Berlin proved to be a continual spark for the band, disillusioned as they were with the backbiting of London, but unwilling to call it a day and go home. They found Berlin to be a city of multitudinous fascinations, although Marc Almond later pinpointed an attribute that The Birthday Party would do well to battle against. 'Berlin...lacks passion. It is about penetration, intercourse, fellatio.

Never about making love.'

But for The Birthday Party, the city afforded them a place to indulge whatever fancy they took and to play alongside a veritable treasure trove of experimental musicians. No more were they constrained by the tight Gothic collar that choked and cloaked them in London. Here, they were encouraged in a way that was much closer to what they had envisioned the band to be in the first place.

Bargeld explained Berlin to *Mojo* Magazine, saying 'The Punk revolution had its own flavour in West Berlin, because you didn't have to serve in the army. Since the war, Berlin has been a demilitarised zone, and so anybody who wanted to avoid the draft moved to West Berlin, which gave the city a unique chemistry.'

The Birthday Party had long since sung Neubauten's praises, with Cave showering accolades on Bargeld's head, naming him 'a man on the threshold of greatness...a Christ akimbo on Calvary.' Pretty heady stuff to live up to, but Bargeld was more than just a charismatic frontman (like Cave) and restless musical innovator. His untutored and, by his own admission, antagonistic attitude to the guitar as an instrument made his appointment as 'guitarist' a very astute and potentially very exciting addition to The Birthday Party and their calculated mayhem.

But, smooth sailing proved to be elusive, despite the creative fire the band were forging – indeed, they were recording some of their best music ever during this 1983 interlude. However, even as one door opened, another was about to shut as Mick Harvey announced he was quitting the band on the eve of their latest American tour. Although a replacement was found – Marching Girls' Des Hefner joined the band at the last minute – there was to be yet another bombshell.

In July Rowland S Howard, too, quit the band – the last straw. There was no point in going on. The Party was over. There was no point in delaying what was now so obviously inevitable.

(LIVE) Hacienda, Manchester 24 February 1983
8301 Hamlet
8302 Pleasure Avalanche
8303 Six-Inch Gold Blade
8304 Wild World
8305 Six Strings
8306 Sonny's Burning
8307 She's Hit
ORIGINAL RELEASE: *Pleasure Heads Must Burn* IKON VHS FCL, 198

COMMENTS: Coupled with that earlier Hacienda performance on 22 July 1982, these seven tracks completed the *Pleasure Heads* live document and are notable for the addition of a third, even more blurred camera at the back of the hall.

(EP) *The Bad Seed*
8308 Sonny's Burning
8309 Wild World
8310 Fears Of Gun
8311 Deep In The Woods
ORIGINAL RELEASE: 4AD BAD 301, February 1983

COMMENTS: Recorded at Hansa Studios in Berlin during October 1982, *The Bad Seed* EP found The Birthday Party continuing to re-work their sound in the wake of Phill Calvert's departure.

The highlight of this set by far is 'Sonny's Burning', the nihilistic forebear to 'The Mercy Seat'. The band, despite their recent meltdown, sound completely revitalized. As the tale unfolds, it's revealed to be a white hot shot of agony, a bitter torture tale as the mythologized Sonny becomes 'some bright erotic star' swinging precariously from the gallows in the midst of Harvey's off-kilter drum staccato and Rowland S Howard's guitar scars.

Mercifully short, because more really would have been too much, 'Sonny's Burning' may indeed be remaindered with The Birthday Party's own remnants but, in its fits and starts, and especially across Cave's vocals, the song was a prescient, if early, glimmer of the band's Bad Seeds rebirth. A nearly invincible and fully formed powerhouse, 'Sonny's Burning' which here opens with the (arguably tongue-in-cheek) cry 'Hands Up Who Wants To Die', remains one of the few all-band collaborations to be recorded. A version of this song, without the opening tagline, was immortalized on The Birthday Party's final, November 21, 1982, John Peel Session.

'Wild World', meanwhile, is creamy languish in the guise of spoken word and Beat-style poetry – along the lines of what The Fall were doing, but punctuated here by Harvey's drums and Howard's bitter little bites of guitar. This was performance art at its early 80s best, and a potent reminder of just where this band came from.

Distilling the essence of the film *The Ring*, and a premonition of *Murder Ballads*, 'Deep In The Woods' lies in that space that is quintessentially Birthday Party, but comes out with the feel of something that remains unformed, a song that has left its full potential somewhere back along the way. Again, poetry for the dark masses, there's nothing like a little death to get the party started, especially when Howard's guitar propels Cave to manic revolutions some three and a half minutes in. One would have hoped, however, that he had left a little of his now-too-often-prevalent grunting to other songs.

When the EP was finally re-issued in 1988, it was bundled alongside the band's final recording – *Mutiny!*.

(LIVE) Seaview Ballroom 9 June 1983
8312 Deep In The Woods
8313 Six Strings That Drew Blood

ORIGINAL RELEASE: *Composite Signals* VHS, 1984

COMMENTS: The last ever Birthday Party concert was not, as it turned out, a cause for mass gnashing and wringing of hands. It was, however, fortuitously recorded by the Single Shot Video Collective and these two performances joined an earlier Seaview excerpt on this excellent VHS.

(ALBUM) Die Haut *Burnin' The Ice*
8314 Truck Love
8315 Stow-a-way
8316 Dumb Europe
8317 Pleasure Is The Boss
ORIGINAL RELEASE: Illuminated Records SUAMS 30, August 1983

COMMENTS: Cave's contributions to these four songs find him less a part of the process and more an innocent bystander to the tinny mayhem, adding lines and breaks when he can get a word in edgeways. Sounding less like The Birthday Party and eerily akin to the horrific no-wave scene in New York, 'Pleasure Is The Boss' kicks out the vestiges of Bowie's 'Jean Genie' across its opening riffs, leaving the drifting 'Stow-A-Way' the most ethereal of the lot, while 'Truck Love' batters nearly everything else aside.
The album was reissued in 2004 on CD with bonus DVD.

(LIVE) *Immaculate Consumptives Non-Stop Revue*, Danceteria New York City 30 October, 1983
UNR In The Ghetto
UNR A Box For Black Paul
UNR Body Unknown
ORIGINAL RELEASE: Unreleased

COMMENTS: Infamous show – mythic bootleg video. Does it exist? The Immaculate Consumptives Cooperative has become the stuff of legend. That it happened is certain. That it was filmed has remained hazy. Marc Almond swears it was, and that he has a copy. Nick Cave says he hopes it wasn't. But, whatever the truth, it remains one of the era's greatest mysteries.
The project itself had been germinating since the very earliest days of 1983. Spearheaded by Lydia Lunch, the kind of woman, according to Marc Almond 'who both fascinated and terrified me.'
Almond himself first became acquainted with Lunch at the Batcave and explained that 'little did I know it, but Lydia had plans for me. In fact she had the next nine months of my life planned out, whether I liked it or not.'
That plan was, of course, the greatest, most ghoulish contemporary cabaret performance ever to be staged. The Immaculate Consumptives revue was to be so outrageous, so over the top, so sinfully arty that Lunch hoped that it would put anything the Batcave ever tried to do to absolute shame.

So, with Almond already in the scope, temporarily divorced from Dave Ball and Soft Cell and currently reinventing himself via recent collaborations with Andi Sex Gang and Psychic TV, Lunch only needed to rope in a couple more members to launch this greatest of triumphs. Jim Thirlwell, and fresh from the unravelling of The Birthday Party, Nick Cave. The event would mark the first time that he ever performed solo.

It was a match made in heaven, this quartet were no strangers. Lunch and Cave enjoyed several collaborations alongside Foetus, who'd also been a long time friend of Cave, dating back to their early Australian days. Almond and Foetus, already friends from Almond's Marc & The Mambas sideline, meanwhile, had been collaborating on their own over the past year, following a dual appearance on Britain's *The Tube,* performing Suicide's 'Ghostrider'.

The show took shape over summer 1983, with some of the group's more controversial antics, Lunch's original plan to be orally raped by an oil-stained, crowbar wielding Cave among them, discarded in favour of a musical event that would showcase the members' talents, both solo and together as a group.

The show itself revolved around each member's own solo performance, although these were connected via a backing tape that was recorded by Blixa Bargeld, Barry Adamson and Mick Harvey and Annie Hogan from Marc & the Mambas.

But the solo performances were also punctuated by other contributions, as Almond explains. 'Each of us did duets with one another before Nick came on and stole the entire show.' Cave's set comprised just two songs, his brooding signature cover of Elvis Presley's 'In The Ghetto', and his own death-of-the-Birthday Party manifesto, 'A Box For Black Paul'.

In fact, 'Black Paul' received only one full airing, on the final night of the Consumptives' existence. The first night, at Danceteria, Foetus broke the piano, kicking the hapless instrument to death during his set, forcing Cave to abandon 'Black Paul' and play the Presley song only.

The second night, Foetus behaved and the piano survived, only for Cave himself to lose interest halfway through the song, and suddenly inform the audience, 'then it goes on like that for another five minutes.' 'I was really pissed off about it,' Foetus remarked later. 'It really broke the atmosphere. But it was a lot of fun.'

The solo pieces at an end, the show wrapped up with all four musicians on stage, thrashing through a raw version of an Almond/Foetus original, 'Body Unknown'. The authors, respectively, sang and drummed, Cave screamed and Lunch strangled her guitar. It was a devastating performance, but it would never be repeated. The Immaculate Consumptives parted company at the conclusion of the third show.

Cave remembered, 'Lydia always had these grand ideas to do things, and she was always very much into roping other people in to do these things with her. I think the Immaculate Consumptives was one of her better ideas. But I don't know if I could be bothered getting something of that type together again, though. Lydia works in a kind of art-event area, and to put a lot of effort into doing three shows that were never recorded, which is what this was about, I wouldn't want to be doing that.' The actual event was 'better to be left in that mythological state, without anyone actually hearing what it was like.'

Referring to his own bootleg video of the performance, Almond admits he has never watched it. 'I've always liked the memory. If I watched it, I'd probably think "oh God!"' It's an emotion Cave readily agreed with.

Indeed, the legend that has built up around the show, all four participants acknowledge, now far outweighs the event itself in terms of significance and historical resonance alike. Even at the time, though, for anybody who cared for such details, the Immaculate Consumptives proved that, beneath the rapid commercialisation of the 'Gothic' movement, and its attendant slide into archetype rock'n'role-playing, its fringes remained as creatively crazed as ever.

(EP) *Mutiny!*
8318 Jennifer's Veil
8319 Mutiny In Heaven
8320 Swampland
8321 Say A Spell
outtakes
8322 Pleasure Avalanche
8323 The Six Strings That Drew Blood
ORIGINAL RELEASE: Mute 12MUTE29, November 1983; 8322-23 on CD reissue *Mutiny!/Bad Seed* 4AD CAD 301, 1989

COMMENTS: Recorded at Berlin's Hansa Studios in April 1983, with Blixa Bargeld playing alongside The Birthday Party, and re-worked in August at London's Britannia Row. This final Birthday Party production was the complete realisation of everything the band had achieved, most markedly on the unerring 'Jennifer's Veil', which not only captured the spirit of Cave's forthcoming Bad Seeds, but also snaked back to everything The Birthday Party had ever done, albeit in a more restrained vein.

A slow drone of guitar, and muddy drum beats that are slower still, it's Cave's voice that drives the song, unravelling the inevitable tale of violence and death, captured in the delicious triple image that shifts between Jennifer's veil, a ship's flags and rigging sails. This remarkable slab of songwriting represents some of the best of the band's material, the lyrics a pure saga of storytelling, an art otherwise sadly lost amid the band's more catch-phrased songs. 'Jennifer's Veil' would help to bridge the gap between bands, surviving long enough past the disintegration of The Birthday Party to become a set staple during Cave's 1984 Man Or Myth shows.

One of the most interesting conceits of the *Mutiny!* sessions, at least in terms of gestation and reincarnation, is 'The Six Strings That Drew Blood'. Not included on the original vinyl EP, and coming to light only for the CD reissue, this particular song exists only in an unfinished, rough mix.

Recorded while the band were under considerable strain and very nearly at the end of their existence, the performance appears to lack cohesion, as the band simply pound through it, leaving Cave to follow with vocals in a kind of sideways slip. But, although it may not be considered classic Birthday Party, what makes it so important is the fact that it *has* survived only in its working form. It's a window into the band's creative process, at a time when they were slicker in their finished form than ever.

Meanwhile, 'Mutiny In Heaven' still finds this band capable of the most extreme kind of music in its last throes. This song is the complete antithesis to Cave's later works with a religious theme, with possibly the most blasphemous lyric set to music. It is a numbing, grimly fascinating horror story, a cross between the Stooges, Dracula and John Milton on smack.

THE NEW TESTAMENT

NICK CAVE AND THE BAD SEEDS

1984

The Birthday Party was dead, disbanded and gone, an imprint that resided only in the memories of those who'd followed the group with a devotion that often bordered on rabid. However, Nick Cave was not gone, not even close to it. And neither was Tracy Pew or Mick Harvey, who had been serious about leaving The Birthday Party but seemed unwilling to sever his link to Cave. This trio was in action by January, with Barry Adamson and guitarist Hugo Race in tow for a handful of shows in Australia. Billed as Nick Cave – Man Or Myth? this new-look ensemble didn't stray so very far from the ideals that The Birthday Party had espoused. Indeed, their set was populated with a schizophrenic mix of Birthday Party favourites, 'Swampland', 'Jennifer's Veil', and 'Pleasure Avalanche', augmented by a handful of newer songs.

By the time spring had arrived, the band had become the Cavemen, with Blixa Bargeld stepping in and Tracy Pew leaving, this time once and for all. It was with this aggregation that Cave played several shows around England and throughout Western Europe. It wasn't long before the Cavemen were renamed the Bad Seeds, but the line-up was still liquid and in September, Race left the Bad Seeds, returning home to Australia to form The Wreckery with Edward Clayton-Jones.

Touring quite heavily by his standards, Cave remained busy for much of the year, although a respite in Hollywood during July, August and September proved especially fruitful and heralded a future career diversion. Not only did he strike up a friendship with post-Punk denizen Henry Rollins, but he continued to work out song drafts. Cave and the soon-to-depart Race also spent a good deal of time collaborating with Evan English and Paul Goldman on the *Swampland* film script. That endeavour, of course, was recycled by Cave into the beginning of his novel *And The Ass Saw The Angel*.

With the band already striving toward a new album, *From Her To Eternity*, many of the songs that peppered these earliest sets were works in progress. One of the year's live staples was the breathtaking 'I Put A Spell On You', (an equally devastating studio take on the song was ultimately to travel no further than the *NME*'s giveaway *The Department Of Enjoyment* compilation).

Cave's reinvention after The Birthday Party seemed to wrong-foot the music press who were faced with a new group, new sounds and new pathos. Their initial reaction to the band was uncertain at first, but the release of *From Her To Eternity* certainly did his reputation no harm. There was also a new breed of fans, kids who perhaps never knew The Birthday Party but were nevertheless transfixed by the lean figure of Cave alternately howling, grunting and singing his way across the stage in sets more clearly influenced by the blues than ever. Where The Birthday Party's works rarely troubled the charts, *From Her To Eternity* would become Cave's first UK Top 40 hit, while his live performances became creatures of legend within hours.

Cave had developed a new, compelling and polarized live persona. Gone were the days of complete cacophony. The disjointed jangle which Cave maintained was now seen to be balanced with a firm Blues style, and the glamour of Tom

Jones and Elvis which showcased Cave's seedily haunting, poetic lyrics.

By November, Cave and the Bad Seeds had returned to the studio to record what would become their second album, *The Firstborn Is Dead*, another instalment in Cave's continued fascination with Elvis Presley (the title, of course, refers to Presley's stillborn twin brother Jesse). The first single from the album, the brooding 'Tupelo', further illustrates that obsession.

(RADIO) *John Peel Session* UK 9 April 1984
UNR I Put A Spell On You
UNR From Her To Eternity
UNR Saint Huck
ORIGINAL RELEASE: Unreleased

COMMENTS: The first solo Nick Cave Peel Session. While his early 1984 gigs had shown that The Bad Seeds had great promise, the band's first recordings, for Peel, realized that promise fully. There, they premiered two new songs, 'Saint Huck' and 'From Her To Eternity', which they'd been working on during sessions at London's Trident Studios during February and March.

The band's own songs were right on the mark, but the highlight of this session remains their superb rendering of the Screamin' Jay Hawkins classic 'I Put A Spell On You'. Hawkins' original is, of course, an unequalled masterpiece of voodoo. It has been covered by many, many artists over the years, each trying and vying to outdo their predecessors in terms of utterly over-the-top histrionics and psychotic free-wheeling blasphemy. It's a spectacular song to cover, from the Crazy World Of Arthur Brown's psychotic psychedelic savaging, to Bryan Ferry's oddly out of step graveyard crawl. But, there are many that would continue to argue that, of all the covers, it was extremely most suited to Cave himself. Spare, and bayou ugly, and even covered with a little moss, it's the insistent riffing of the guitar that sets this song apart. That, and Cave's brutally heartfelt delivery – each line a bitten statement of fact.

(ALBUM) compilation *The Department Of Enjoyment*
8401 I Put A Spell On You
ORIGINAL RELEASE: NME 011, 12 May 1984

COMMENTS: This *NME* compilation cassette featured a host of the day's up and comers, from the Smiths and Lloyd Cole to Husker Dü and the Waterboys, and was available only by mail order from the magazine. It also featured what the magazine billed as a new recording of Nick Cave and The Cavemen's 'I Put A Spell On You'. The NME described the track as being recorded 'in a small studio' in April 1984 by Nick Cave and Hugo Race alone, specifically for the cassette.

(SINGLE) In The Ghetto
8402 In The Ghetto
8403 The Moon Is In The Gutter

ORIGINAL RELEASE: Mute 7 Mute 032, June 1984

COMMENTS: 'In The Ghetto' and 'The Moon Is In The Gutter' were pulled from the March 1984 *Eternity* sessions for the band's first and only accompanying single, released the same month as the album. The A-side, an astute take on Elvis Presley's original, was credited to Nick Cave, featuring the Bad Seeds, and set the stage for what was to come.

A thumping march, slightly sloppy, the song may appear somewhat snarky across Cave's delivery – laced as it was with just a hint of the King's sideways snarl. But it is with the lush guitar sweeps and earnest aura that 'In The Ghetto' captures a different, more corporeal spirit. It's less a cover song, than a plea – for retribution, for justice, for humanity. And it certainly couldn't have been farther from Cave's in-your-face spit and bite that fans were surely expecting. It was a brilliant choice for a break in sound. 'The Moon Is In The Gutter', meanwhile, finds Cave declaring himself 'the king of the blues' and, brief as it is, this slow ramble defies anyone to declare otherwise. The song itself, however, is a bit of a throwaway.

(ALBUM) *From Her To Eternity*
Line-up: Nick Cave (vocals); Mick Harvey (drums, keyboards); Blixa Bargeld (guitar); Barry Adamson (bass); Hugo Race (guitar).
8404 Avalanche
8405 Cabin Fever!
8406 Well Of Misery
8407 From Her To Eternity
8408 Saint Huck
8409 Wings Off Flies
8410 A Box For Black Paul
CD BONUS TRACKS
8403 The Moon Is In The Gutter
8402 In The Ghetto
8701 From Her To Eternity (1987 version)
ORIGINAL RELEASE: Mute STUMM 17, May 1984

COMMENTS: A bridge between the tatters of The Birthday Party and the uprising of Cave proper, the album was recorded in two distinct sessions, the band's first with engineer Flood. The first during September and October 1983 at Trident studios, caught 'Saint Huck', 'Wings Off Flies', and 'A Box For Black Paul'. During this time, the provisional line-up included Nick Cave, Mick Harvey, Blixa Bargeld, Barry Adamson and James Thirlwell and was originally envisioned as a session for a proposed Nick Cave Man Or Myth? debut. Thirlwell shares a writing credit with Cave on 'Wings Off Flies'.

'Saint Huck' is a foreboding slice of cake – not a cakewalk. Part holy-roller and part deep European clatter, one can't help but feel that old Huck would be at home in either Mississippi or Berlin. Vital and urgent, the song lies not with The Birthday Party, nor with the Bad Seeds but is more akin to that quintessential Berliner music, of Bargeld's and Cave's own recent past.

'A Box For Black Paul' follows along in much the same path. Funereal, obviously, but also setting the stage for Cave's future, and a time when he became sonorous, making music for grownups. The song was still difficult, but a long cry from the fiery fuck-up who careened through the earliest days of Punk and Goth. But for now, here, across 'A Box For Black Paul,' simple and even elegant. The song was a live staple and often played at the show as a backhanded introduction for the band, and was rumoured to be about the demise of The Birthday Party.

The rest of the album was recorded during March 1984, again at Trident, and already the nature of the Bad Seeds' birth is apparent. Across a cover of 'Avalanche,' from Leonard Cohen's seminal 1971 *Songs Of Love And Hate* LP, and the Cave/Bargeld collaboration 'Cabin Fever,' the band debuted a more restrained sonic. Yet, without the frenetic drive of The Birthday Party's greatest output, the music was equally large – utterly huge in scope.

Cohen's 'Avalanche,' in particular, received a far more honest reading than Cave's older covers. Cohen still seems to dance on the fringes of the song and probably would have been prouder still of Cave later on in the decade, when he'd bring that same ethic to pass on *Tender Prey*'s 'Mercy.'

Although the album is comprised of recordings that date to the Bad Seeds' most turbulent times, *From Her To Eternity* manages not only to retain much of the raw power that made The Birthday Party so successful, but also is well placed to stand alone in a new arena. Cave has not honed his vocal delivery fully across this album, but with an ear for space between notes, and an understanding that stillness holds as much power as the one-two punch batter of guitars and drums, his lyrical gift is beginning to shine through. Behind him, the band is stripped down and sparse, providing the push that only emphasizes the power in Cave's vocals.

There was no finer example of this than the title track, a lyrical collaboration between Cave and girlfriend Anita Lane, with music by the whole band. It is by far the album's set piece, became an immediate set staple for Cave and was completely reinvented in 1987 for inclusion on Wim Wender's *Wings Of Desire* soundtrack (this version was later appended as a CD bonus track on the album itself).

All in all, it was an immensely successful debut and, in choosing Flood to engineer both sessions, the band made one of their wisest moves yet. Even though they'd already proven themselves as competent self-producers, the magic spark between the band and Flood allowed them to stretch in ways that may not have been initially obvious. It also allowed a vital piece of continuity to slip into place, as well as offering Cave supreme bragging rights in years to come.

'We were working with Flood before he did any work with Depeche Mode and anyone like that; then U2 got hold of him and said, "Make us sound like the Bad Seeds" We know that we work well with him, that he isn't the kind of dictatorial producer type, he's very reliable, knows how to get a solid sound and listens to what we want.'

(LIVE) Stache's, Columbus Ohio 27 June 1984
8411 Blind Boy Willy

8412 A Box For Black Paul
8413 From Her To Eternity
8414 I Put A Spell On You
8415 Mutiny In Heaven
8416 Avalanche
8417 In The Ghetto
ORIGINAL RELEASE: *Nick Cave And The Bad Seeds Live* mail order video in US, semi-official

COMMENTS: In June, the band embarked on a month-long US tour that saw them travel primarily up and down the East Coast, from New York through Washington DC and Boston, Massachusetts. The band hit the Midwest briefly, before playing a handful of West Coast gigs – in Los Angeles, San Francisco and Pasadena, where they supported the psychobilly band The Cramps. By the end of the month, they were in Columbus Ohio for a gig at Stache's.

This show was filmed, directed and produced by Rick Klaus Theis, the American poet, activist and artist heralded for his endeavours in social justice and human rights. The performance was released, semi-officially as *Nick Cave Live*. Aside from a strong six-song performance, the video also includes the band sound-checking a new song, 'Blind Boy Willy', which was an early work-in-progress version of 'Blind Lemon Jefferson'. The video winds up with an interview.

1985

As 1984 came to a close, Cave was back in Melbourne, writing the music for *Ghosts...Of The Civil Dead*, John Hillcoat's powerful, if scattershot, film about prison revolt. Mick Harvey, meanwhile, continued to pull double duty, both with the Bad Seeds and his own Crime And The City Solution, alongside Simon Bonney.

By April, the Bad Seeds were kicking off a short UK tour – this time without Barry Adamson and Blixa Bargeld, who was back in Berlin with Einstürzende Neubauten, cutting that band's *Halber Mensch* LP. Though in a seemingly perilous state, the Bad Seeds merely delved into an ever-widening circle of collaborators and peers, replacing Adamson first with Die Haut's Christoph Dreher and then with another member of Die Haut, Thomas Wydler. Bargeld's shoes were filled on the eve of the tour by, of all people, Rowland S Howard who, although he didn't know the songs, was able to jump in regardless and carry himself through the tour with aplomb.

Cave also devoted much of the year to writing his novel *And The Ass Saw The Angel*, a pastime that led him further and further into some kind of twisted Blues psyche. The overflow from this process would result in some of the American South-tinged songs on *The Firstborn Is Dead*. Within 'Blind Lemon Jefferson', 'Black Crow King', and 'Knockin' On Joe', Cave was perhaps having a tussle with himself, sifting through whatever was going on inside his mind.

That spiral did serve to ratchet up tensions among the band, with Barry Adamson becoming increasingly uncomfortable. Adamson, the band's 'black' bassist, basically 'was brought up pretty much white.' Now, though, he felt increasingly pinned down by this new foray into Black American Blues. He was uncomfortable, a situation exacerbated, he said, by drugs and negative thinking and more drugs and paranoia.

(ALBUM) *The Firstborn Is Dead*
Line-up: Nick Cave (vocals and keyboards); Mick Harvey (drums); Blixa Bargeld (guitar); Barry Adamson (bass)
8501 Say Goodbye To The Little Girl Tree
8502 Tupelo
8503 Train-Long Suffering
8504 Black Crow King
8505 Knockin' On Joe
8506 Wanted Man
8507 Blind Lemon Jefferson
CD BONUS TRACKS
8508 The Six Strings That Drew Blood
8502a Tupelo (single version).
ORIGINAL RELEASE: Mute STUMM 21, June 1985

COMMENTS: *The Firstborn Is Dead* was recorded during November and December 1984 at Hansa studios with Flood again engineering. Transplanted in soul and spirit to the grimy rot of the American Blues backwoods, many of these songs, more than any of Cave's others, perfectly capture his vision of the music that was first inserted into the American psyche, co-opted by Britain, and then recycled back to the States in the form of contemporary R&B. This still-sparse Bad Seeds line-up were fully able to create the atmosphere perfectly and, again, Bargeld's contribution is notable: his slide-playing on 'Wanted Man' and harmonics on 'Knockin' On Joe', for instance, are remarkable – here we have one of the leaders of the Berlin underground music scene, sporting leather trousers and spiked hair sounding for all the world like a latter-day Son House.

Themes of oppression and bondage, sorrow and loss dominate the album: the entire mood conveys an aura of extreme living, of being bone tired, of wanting to give up, but still having hope enough to get the words out. Awash with piano, organ and slide guitar, the album could be transplanted to a myriad of decades, diseases, lifetimes and souls. In the middle of a decade packed with vapid smiles and music devoid of much emotional context, Cave and the Bad Seeds offered work of real substance. They were also purveying alternative music that wasn't afraid to look back to music of the distant past and summon up hallowed names like Elvis and John Lee Hooker on 'Tupelo'.

'Tupelo', an extremely effective literary statement evoked with a pop sensibility and named for Elvis Presley's birthplace, is a magnificent opener and still one of the band's greatest songs. A re-invention of John Lee Hooker's classic, it is an unrelenting, exhilarating saga awash with Biblical overtones, from the deluge that preludes the song to the intonation 'The King was born in

'Tupelo'. The identification with Elvis may have backfired for Cave and he would become nearly sick to death of this song as well as being tired of being asked to explain the song's meaning to nearly every journalist he talked to. An accompanying video was directed by Die Haut's Christoph Dreher.

The cover of Bob Dylan's 'Wanted Man', an unreleased track from Dylan's 1969 *Nashville Skyline* sessions, provided another key to Cave's musical heritage. 'I love Bob Dylan,' Cave admits. 'You can forgive and forgive and forgive.' Dylan's hold over Cave and the rest of the band was indeed strong. Cave actually re-worked the lyrics to 'Wanted Man' for the album and, in order to be able to include it, had to write to Dylan for approval to release the rearranged version. With a generosity that would not be repeated until 1996, and the Dunblane charity version of 'Knocking On Heaven's Door' (which also featured revised lyrics), this permission was forthcoming but the wait, however, did delay the release of the album.

It was worth the wait. *The First Born Is Dead* received a much more positive welcome than Cave's post-Birthday Party debut. Indeed it has been described by one critic as 'one of the greatest rock and roll albums ever made'.

The American LP issue in 1985 (Homestead/Mute Records, HMS 026-2) also contains the *Tupelo* 12-inch EP – see below. The CD release then appended both sides of the 7-inch single.

(EP) Annie Hogan *Plays Kickabye*
8509 Vixo

ORIGINAL RELEASE: Double Vision DVR 9, 1985

COMMENTS: This five-track EP, featuring Cave as both lyricist and vocalist on the closing 'Vixo', was recorded between 1983 and 1985, and has been described as anything from the 'utterly abysmal epitome of art rock' to 'a superlative blending of unexpected elements and ephemeral emotion.'

Hogan, whose association with Marc Almond dated back to his Marc & The Mambas project, had already crossed paths with Cave during the Immaculate Consumptives project. Now, for her first solo release, she partnered with another of Cave's pals – journalist Jessamy Calkin, who supplied the lion's share of *Kickabye*'s lyrics. With Almond appearing under the pseudonym Raoul Revere and the addition of Jim Thirlwell credited as Clint Ruin, one of his many aliases, Siouxsie and the Banshees' drummer Budgie and fellow Mamba Gini Ball, the collective was nothing less than a super group of no-wave, new-wave propagandists.

The EP itself is difficult, artistic, egocentric and beloved by Hogan's fans; 'Burning Boats', a typical Thirlwell contribution, is an especial gem, subsequently earning a cover from Almond himself. 'Vixo', on the other hand, is not one of Nick Cave's finest moments, a shambles of discordant sound that doesn't give much pleasure.

(RADIO) *Wilde Wereld* VPRO Radio, Netherlands 19 June 1985
UNR Black Crow King
ORIGINAL RELEASE: Unreleased

COMMENTS: Nick Cave, Mick Harvey and Blixa Bargeld perform one of the new album's moodiest numbers.

(SINGLE) Tupelo
8502a Tupelo
8508 The Six Strings That Drew Blood
ORIGINAL RELEASE: Mute MUTE 038, July 1985

COMMENTS: The single version of 'Tupelo' shaved nearly two and a half minutes off its album counterpart, and worked well either way you looked at it. It was, again, a brilliant choice for a single. Perhaps more interesting, though, is a completely new and different version of 'The Six Strings That Drew Blood'. A tattered tumbleweed of a song with a twang and clatter; slow, off-kilter and languid, the song is dusty, almost incidental in its delivery, more like watching some old-timer tell a story, than spit across a stage to confront an audience.

(EP) *Tupelo*
8502a Tupelo
8402 In The Ghetto
8403 The Moon Is In The Gutter
8508 The Six Strings That Drew Blood
ORIGINAL RELEASE: Homestead HMS 029, 1985

COMMENTS: Only available in the US on the indie pioneer label Homestead, this 12-inch EP was also packaged with the US versions of *The Firstborn Is Dead*. This EP collected the singles from *From Her To Eternity* and *The Firstborn Is Dead* onto one nifty disc for the domestic market, who'd previously had to rely on imports for their Nick Cave fix.

(VIDEO) *Offair*
ORIGINAL RELEASE: unknown

COMMENTS: Legendary and seldom (if ever) seen Australian videozine. *Offair* apparently features 10 minutes of interview and live/sound check footage.

1986

As Cave's personal profile received an uplfift, personal events during 1986 saw the band receiving a setback. The first half of the year was pretty quiet for the

Bad Seeds, although Cave himself continued to be busy, spending the early part of the year in Melbourne, continuing to collaborate with John Hillcoat on the *Ghosts...Of The Civil Dead* script. Cave and Harvey spent much of December and January 1986 at Melbourne's Richmond Recorders laying out *Kicking Against The Pricks* and running up huge recording bills in the process. Studio sessions on the album were halted until later in the year, when all debts were settled and Richmond Recorders' Tim Stobart released the master tapes to the band, where they continued to record in Berlin.

Finally released in August, *Kicking Against The Pricks* was Cave's most divisive album, a collection of covers that trembled from the Bad Seeds' onslaught.

The band was still in constant flux. Barry Adamson finally threw in the towel in July. There had been a fair amount of tension within the band during the sessions for *The Firstborn Is Dead*, with Adamson in particular, becoming increasingly frustrated by the course he perceived the band to be taking. He'd had enough: the band had come into their own following the release of the first album, but the more Adamson found out about the group members themselves, as well as his own evolving sense of self, the more he knew that he needed a break – a permanent one.

In Berlin, the previous year, Adamson had been feeling very low, as recounted in Ian Johnston's biography of Cave. 'We'd played dates in Athens and then we'd come back to this oppressive atmosphere, staying awake for days on end. The pressure was on. I myself could see I was heading for a nervous breakdown and I wasn't going to let this be seen by anybody.'

So Cave, Harvey, Bargeld and Wydler soldiered on and, by September, they were augmented by the Gun Club's Kid Congo Powers and a friend of Bargeld, Roland Wolf. The ever-adaptable Harvey was now playing bass for the band.

A devastating blow fell on 7 November for Cave and Harvey, when they received word that Tracy Pew had died from injuries sustained during a severe epileptic seizure. For nearly a year and a half, Pew had been suffering from this increasingly debilitating affliction. It had recently become so bad that he'd had to drop most of his university studies to begin a round of medication.

Cave and Pew had always been close – even as the two moved in increasingly wider circles that didn't often intersect. One time they did reunite was during the Richmond Recorders sessions with Pew appearing on three songs alongside Mick Harvey and Hugo Race. But his condition had worsened and the shock of his death was to overshadow the release of the forthcoming *Your Funeral...My Trial.*

Phill Calvert had remained in close contact with Pew, and in 2005 he recalled, 'I was the only band member to attend the funeral.'

(SINGLE) The Singer
8601 The Singer
8602 Running Scared
8603 Black Betty (US Homestead single 067 only)
ORIGINAL RELEASE: Mute MUTE 47, June 1986

COMMENTS: Engineered by Tony Cohen and mixed by Flood, this single was released in both 7-inch and 12-inch formats. 'The Singer', immortalized by Johnny Cash, was kept fairly straightforward by Cave, although he infused his lyrics with his own bitter irony. The B-side, originally written and performed by Roy Orbison, doesn't quite work, in spite of the big finish: the song is over-crooned and lacks the emotional punch of some of the album's other numbers. The UK release would give the band their first UK indie hit. 'Black Betty', one of Leadbelly's most celebrated songs, finds a magnificent retelling under the auspices of the Bad Seeds. Completely stripped to just the barest bones possible, the song relies on vocals, both Cave's lead and the band's backing, as it builds and bucks to its conclusion. Not quite so much a song as some kind of exorcism, the performance marks another dramatic shift to the paths that Cave would come to tread in the future.

(The promotional 7-inch version of 'The Singer' saw the word 'fucking' edited out.

(ALBUM) *Kicking Against The Pricks*
Line-up: Nick Cave (vocals & keyboards); Mick Harvey (guitar & keyboards); Blixa Bargeld (guitar); Barry Adamson (bass); Thomas Wydler (drums).
8604 Muddy Water
8605 I'm Gonna Kill That Woman
8606 Sleeping Annaleah
8607 Long Black Veil
8608 Hey Joe
8601 The Singer
8609 All Tomorrow's Parties
8610 By The Time I Get to Phoenix
8611 The Hammer Song
8612 Something's Gotten Hold of My Heart
8613 Jesus Met The Woman At The Well
8614 The Carnival Is Over
CD BONUS TRACKS
8602 Running Scared
8603 Black Betty
SESSION outtakes
8615 Rye Whiskey
ORIGINAL RELEASE: Mute STUMM 28, August 1986

COMMENTS: This remarkable covers album included a wealth of guest musicians, with the re-appearance of Tracy Pew and Rowland S Howard amounting to some kind of Birthday Party reunion. Other guests included Cave's mother, Dawn, Hugo Race and the Berliner Kaffeehaus Musik Ensemble, orchestrated by Mick Harvey.

The album was engineered by Tony Cohen at AAV Studios in Melbourne during December 1985. More mixes were accomplished in March 1986 at Hansa, this time with Flood, Cave, Harvey and Bargeld adding to the master tapes.

Kicking Against The Pricks was a very personal album that pulled songs as disparate as the Seekers' 'The Carnival Is Over', Lou Reed's 'All Tomorrow's Parties' and even the Jim Webb classic, 'By The Time I Get To Phoenix'. *Pricks* also served to unite Nick Cave and Marc Almond for the second time – by proxy at least. Within two years, Almond would be #1 in Britain with his own rendition of 'Something's Gotten Hold Of My Heart'. *Kicking Against The Pricks*, with Cave's version of the song, managed only #89.

Very early on, Cave had planned to launch *Kicking Against The Pricks* as a double album, and during recording sessions that bumped shoulders with those for *The Firstborn Is Dead*, the Bad Seeds recorded a total of twenty-three songs for possible inclusion on this new album. The project's ultimate downsizing confined many of these to the vault, though versions of 'Black Betty' and 'Running Scared' did make it out on the flip of the 'The Singer' single. Another out-take, 'Rye Whiskey', was released as a flexi-disc with the *Reflex* magazine Volume 1, issue 10 in 1989 and the *B-sides and Rarities box set* (there is also an impromptu and truncated version of this which Cave and Harvey perform on the tour bus in *The Road To God Knows Where*).

Of the album's other highlights, 'Sleeping Annaleah', written by Mickey Newbury, is also known as 'Weeping Annaleah' and is a quirky, carnival-like version with unusual instrumentation for the band. Cave also unveiled a superb rendering of 'Hey Joe', best known from Jimi Hendrix's talismanic rendition, but based here more closely on the version recorded by Tim Rose, while the traditional spiritual 'Jesus Met The Woman At The Well' packs just enough minimal guitar backing to keep the vocals on track.

It was no surprise to see an Alex Harvey tune included on the album. Much beloved by Cave, but rarely covered once his own band was up and running, Harvey's influence on the young aspirants was finally repaid with a superbly-arranged and atmospheric cover of 'The Hammer Song' (Cave would later use the title himself with his own "The Hammer Song' on *The Good Son*).

Albums of cover versions are often perilous projects and, by and large, the band pulled it off even though Cave admitted later that it was something of an indulgence. Unlike many of these projects, *Pricks* actually came with teeth and soul: the teeth most spectacularly bared on the Velvet Underground's 'All Tomorrow's Parties', a raucous sing-along backed by big drums and bright guitar: the ghost of Reed's original is flitting through but the Bad Seeds stamp their sound all over it.

This was also an album that showcased the diverse talents of the Bad Seeds: most notably, their skill as backing vocalists. On 'Black Betty', 'Long Black Veil', 'Jesus Met The Woman At The Well' and 'The Carnival Is Over' in particular they are at their strongest, with Mick Harvey showing yet another string to his bow in the higher registers. Blixa Bargeld, meanwhile, only really sounds Teutonic because we *know* he is German: his warm, deep tones are in fact eerily reminiscent of Elvis's favourite bass vocalist on his gospel work, the legendary J.D. Sumner. It is all too tempting to think of Cave, still in the grip of Elvis, casting Bargeld in that role.

'I love singing other people's songs, and one-offs like that are great,' Cave reflected. Although a second instalment of the album could easily be accumulated from Cave's subsequent output he admitted, 'I couldn't imagine doing another *Kicking Against The Pricks,* because what you get on vinyl isn't very satisfactory for me. Not as a regular Bad Seeds album anyway. It would be more like a sneaky side project.'

(ALBUM) *Your Funeral... My Trial*
Line-up: Nick Cave (vocals & keyboards); Mick Harvey (bass); Blixa Bargeld (guitar); Thomas Wydler (drums).
8616 Sad Waters
8617 The Carny
8618 Your Funeral...My Trial
8619 Stranger Than Kindness
8620 Jack's Shadow
8621 Hard On For Love
8622 She Fell Away
8623 Long Time Man
CD BONUS TRACKS
8624 Scum
ORIGINAL RELEASE: Mute STUMM 34, November 1986

COMMENTS: The band's second album of the year, *Your Funeral...My Trial* was released on CD, and also as a double 12-inch EP on vinyl. The album was recorded at Hansa during July 1986, and engineered by Flood. Mixing took place at the Strongroom in London in August with Flood and Tony Cohen in attendance.

This album marked a much fuller sound for the band, albeit one that was punctuated by well placed open spaces and drops. Although the credits for writing split up pretty much as they always had, this album is tight and feels more of a band effort than others. This incarnation of the Bad Seeds were settling into their sound, and seemed to have a crystal clear idea of just what it was they wanted to do.

Allying itself with the best of what the late 1980s had to offer in terms of alternative music, *Your Funeral* only enhanced the band's already growing appeal in the United States. Leaving behind almost all the trappings of their past, the band were now ragged bluesmen – with a bite that appealed to an entirely new generation of the disenfranchised. Not nearly as difficult to swallow as indie peers Big Black and Sonic Youth, the Bad Seeds appealed to the same people who loved the deconstruction of the best of the American nihilists, but wanted an outlet that was more romantic,humorous, dark, but not devastating. It helped, too that one of the album's tracks – 'The Carny' – was incorporated into the cult smash movie *Wings Of Desire*.

While this eight-minute epic remains one of *Funeral*'s high points, there are several other tracks which bear witness to the skilful fusion of storytelling and sonic power that Cave had now so perfectly honed across a set's worth of songs. The music and lyrics are equally important but the telling of the story is the high point; the music a cradle of emotion to back the words, the intention, the meaning. 'Sad Waters', 'Jack's Shadow' and 'She Fell Away' are also fine examples of this.

The title track may have been inspired by Sonny Boy Williamson's 'Your Funeral And My Trial'. Like Cave, Williamson was a gifted storyteller, a bluesman with an infuriatingly unpredictable character, an embellisher of the finest degree. Cave followed suit, understated and yes, downright funereal across this song.

'Stranger Than Kindness', is a subtle and sinister Anita Lane/Bargeld collaboration, a 'love' song that is wonderfully, brutally crooned by Cave. The beautiful lyrics and unusual arrangement (layered guitars, slide, harmonics and an idiosyncratic contribution from Cave on Hammond organ) instantly signals guest authors and it seems to drift into the album and out again. It has its opposite reflection in the numbing, thunderous 'Hard On For Love', which borrows its title from a song by The Reels that was rattling around long before Cave came into his own. This is Nick Cave at his most electrifyingly lustful, a song that even overpowers the later 'Loverman'. The use of biblical imagery here is in turns hilarious and boorishly erotic but makes the song all the more powerful: 'She looks like she walked straight outta the Book of Leviticus'; 'I'm going to give them gates a shove' and much else are part of an increasingly sex-crazed litany. The build-up of vocalist and band grows all the more manic and then Cave begins yelling 'Her breasts rise and fall' before Flood brings the whole thing to a shuddering halt.

Finally, 'Long Time Man' was not only written by, but is laid out very much in the style of Tim Rose. This is one of Cave's more emotional vocal performances and it is, all round, a more passionate performance than any of the covers on *Kicking Against The Pricks*. It is another indicator of his fascination with doom-laden tales of the South, with the protagonist looking mournfully ahead to life in jail having just gunned down his wife.

Your Funeral... My Trial remains a considerable achievement, especially in the light of continuing personnel changes and Cave's pretty chaotic lifestyle. A bootleg video from this time shows Mick Harvey playing tunes from the album on the piano, displaying (and praising) Cave's gift for melody, something that is all too often overlooked. However, it also shows The Cramps' just-drafted Kid Congo Powers painfully learning the ropes and features a hilarious encounter between the German interviewer and Cave in the back of a car where the journalist's perfectly tame and polite questions drive Cave into a fit of paranoia. But that is not to say that this was behind another track from these sessions which made it out on a single (LYN 18038) sold only at Cave's October, 1986, concerts....

(SINGLE) Scum
8624 Scum
ORIGINAL RELEASE: Lyntone LYN 18038, October 1986

COMMENTS: An out-take from the *Your Funeral* sessions, this flexi-disc was sold at Bad Seeds' concerts in October 1986, and came with a free poster featuring tongue-in-cheek resumes of the band members, penned by Jessamy Calkin.

'Scum', is a withering tirade directed at the UK music press – either *en masse* or, more specifically, at Antonella Black, Barney Hoskyns and Mat Snow…or so it is said. All three had managed to offend Cave's sensitivities in recent years. Unfortunately, Cave himself was not going out of his way to discourage the abuse, scorn and/or sensationalism that his presence now seemed naturally to provoke. With his own focus frequently disrupted by substance abuse, how could the press *not* comment endlessly, not on what the band were doing, and how they were doing it, but upon just how fucked up Cave was during his interviews. It was a predictable and gratuitous approach, of course, but, with Cave's image now so tied to drink and drugs it was also somewhat wearily understandable.

(TV) *The Tube*, UK 14 November 1986
UNR The Singer
ORIGINAL RELEASE: Unreleased

COMMENTS: Still riding the waves of popularity sparked by 'The Singer', this studio playback version was featured on Channel 4's *The Tube*.

1987

1987 proved to be something of an off year for the Bad Seeds, even as Cave continued to shape *And The Ass Saw The Angel,* putting it through draft after draft, preparing it for publication. At the same time his drugs problem was coming to a head. The band themselves were in the studio, putting together what would become *Tender Prey,* but recording was a slow, lugubrious process and only came in fits and starts at best.

Neither did Cave tour this year, preferring instead to play a number of one-off shows. But there was still time for some remarkable performances around Europe. Ljubljana, Stockholm, Athens, Vienna, and Novellara and Torino, Italy, would each receive some amazing gigs, with Cave previewing two of the songs scheduled for the new album: 'Sugar Sugar Sugar' and 'City Of Refuge', at the final gigs in Italy at the end of November.

Elsewhere however, the year was pinpointed by the band's shambolic, and frankly, pretty pissed state. Gigs were cancelled or cut short, and by the end of the year, they had a manpower shortage as Kid Congo Powers jumped ship to tour with his old buddies in the Gun Club.

At least one highlight of the year came on 15/16 August, 1987, when Cave and The Bad Seeds joined Crime And the City Solution, Swans, Die Haut, The Fall and Butthole Surfers to play shows in Hamburg and Bonn, Germany, under the Kings Of Independence bill.

Despite being an absolute cavalcade of stars, however, the event was pockmarked by disaster when the band's manager and festival coordinator,

Jeanette Bleeker, oversold the event by twice the capacity allowed. The relationship, already strained, was rendered even more fraught.

Cave also spent some of the year shooting films – first up was Wenders' *Wings Of Desire* in February, when the band not only filmed the footage for their cameo, but entered Hansa Ton Studios with Flood for an all new recording of 'From Her To Eternity' specifically for the film. October, meanwhile, saw Cave in Australia, attending shooting in an old, abandoned factory in Melbourne, of John Hillcoat's still-gestating *Ghosts...Of The Civil Dead.*

He also teamed with Mick Harvey, Barry Adamson and Thomas Wydler at London's Trident Studios to record songs with Anita Lane on her first solo LP, *Dirty Sings.*

(SESSION) Original soundtrack *Wings Of Desire*
8701 From Her To Eternity
ORIGINAL RELEASE: Mute Records IONIC 2, August 1988

COMMENTS: Nick Cave was drawn into Wim Wenders' orbit after the German director heard 'The Carny', show-stopping centrepiece of the *Your Funeral...My Trial* album. He had long been a fan of Cave's music, and this song seemed tailor-made for his newest film project: he contacted Cave and invited him to contribute both music and a cameo role to the production – 'The Carny' was lifted directly from the album. In the film, we see Sollveig Donnmartin, the soon-to-be jobless trapeze artist pick up the *Your Funeral ..My Trial* LP, with Cave staring from the cover, and listen wistfully to his atmospheric tale of the doomed circus troupe, and at the end of the film, the same version is played in the club, with Cave reading from a lectern. 'From Her To Eternity', however, was completely re-recorded at Hansa, in February 1987. (It would appear both on the album soundtrack and, somewhat less appropriately, as a bonus track on CD reissues of the original *From Her To Eternity*.)

Cave recalled: 'I did a couple of songs... and he asked me if I wanted to appear in the film as well.'

The film itself revolves around the universal truths of humanity and love, the story of an angel who desires only to shake the bonds of immortality in order to love a woman, finely wrought against the backdrop of a divided Berlin.

The audience become voyeur to the drama that plays out on the screen and Wenders wanted to capture that essence, the rush of real time, the anticipation of union. And, in its own way, rock 'n' roll is the one vehicle which does capture the brutal truth of being human and being in love, the aural compliment to a dark slide into bliss. And, Wenders knew, there were only two bands who could provide the soundtrack to this.

In and around a score by Jürgen Kneiper (with additional contributions from Laurie Anderson), Cave and the Bad Seeds joined fellow Australians Crime and the City Solution on a Berlin soundstage to turn in some of the most memorable rock performances ever captured on film. Appearing as house bands in a cavernous club, where angel becomes flesh and blood, Cave and Crime subtly embodied and mirrored the action on screen within the honesty of their own performances.

Across two scenes and over two songs, while humanity is the putative focus, the music steals the scene. Wenders captured the raw honesty of Crime's 'Six Bells Chime' and the brutal truth of Cave's 'From Her To Eternity' with perfect clarity. And, although the musicians were only indeed 'playing a part,' their very presence in the film was enhanced by the actions around them, somehow making them more real and, thereby, further blurring the lines between musician and actor, between reality and realism. And, in accomplishing that magical fission, Wenders captured two great and unequalled sequences in rock film, proof that the genre doesn't have to be a long barrage of sound. It needs only to transcend that mythical fourth wall, even if just for a moment.

(SESSION) *And The Ass Saw The Angel*
8702 Mah Sanctum
8703 Lamentation
8704 One Autumn
8705 Animal Static
ORIGINAL RELEASE: Compilation *Smack My Crack*, Giorno Poetry Systems GPS 038, June 1987

COMMENTS: As the year progressed, Cave continued to work on his novel, alone in Berlin and also with Crime And The City Solution's Bronwyn Adams in July in Hamburg. Cave, however, already had enough material ready to publicly preview.

Recording at Trident Studios, London, the previous autumn, Cave produced four spoken word performances of passages from the book; these have now appeared in manifold guises, but were originally issued under the overall title *The Atra Virago*, on the Giorno Poetry Systems LP *Smack My Crack*. Material from Swans, Butthole Surfers, Diamanda Galas, Einstürzende Neubauten, Tom Waits and William Burroughs was also showcased on the collection.

Separated into four individually-titled tracks, this session would then be included on the free 12-inch single (Mute 12 STUMM 52, 1988), packaged with the initial pressing of the *Tender Prey* LP. The same performances would also appear as bonus tracks on the Japanese re-issue of the album, and be included as part of the semi-bootleg Italian *Nick Cave Man Or Myth* book/mini CD combo package in June 1995, and that's before the full *And The Ass Saw The Angel* theatrical presentation saw CD release a decade later.

(TV) *Kinofest* Germany Recorded 19 June 1987, broadcast February 1988
UNR The Singer
UNR From Her To Eternity
UNR Scum
ORIGINAL RELEASE: Unreleased

COMMENTS: The *Wings of Desire* premiere, at *Kinofest* in Berlin. This raucous press event saw the band totally out of control – scaring the pants off everyone in attendance, bar Wim Wenders, apparently. But an even more raucous event occurred prior to this, the 13th June, when the band were invited to appear at the Bundesfilmpreisverleihung, a prestigious event which had a guest list full of the great and the good, including the West German Minister For Culture. Once the Bad Seeds had been treated to a pre-performance round of tequilas, the audience of dignitaries were, in turn, treated to a gloriously shambolic display wherein Mick Harvey played his bass horizontally, Nick Cave disappeared, non-band members appeared from nowhere to insult the audience and Blixa Bargeld made an impromptu and highly unwelcome speech.

(LIVE) Knopf Music Hall 15/16 August 1987
8706 Stranger Than Kindness
8707 Saint Huck
ORIGINAL RELEASE: *Kings Of Independence* VHS Studio K7 K7 001, 1989

COMMENTS: This VHS release includes very raw and rough live concert footage of Nick Cave And The Bad Seeds performing at Jeanette Bleeker's *Kings Of Independence* festival. The quality is really rather lamentable, a flaw that extends to the other bands showcased on the same tape: however peer through the murk and you discover Cave at the nostril-flaring peak of his self-destructive stick insect phase.

(ALBUM) Compilation *Gigantic*
8704 One Autumn
ORIGINAL RELEASE: MMTRDO, 1987

COMMENTS: Cassette available only with *Melody Maker* featuring Cave reading another of the Trident Studio extracts from *And The Ass Saw The Angel.*

1988

This was the year of the big bust. The substance abuse that had been building for much of Cave's career finally reached its pinnacle when the singer was arrested for possession of heroin in January, and again the following month. By September, he was in rehab, emerging with a new album that signified yet another break in style. It was a new era for Cave, and for the Bad Seeds too.

After Cave's brush with the law in February in Melbourne, he stuck close to home, spending the first third of the year in Australia, gigging sporadically, completing *Tender Prey*'s final mixes with Tony Cohen. He was also recording the seemingly never-ending soundtrack for *Ghosts…Of The Civil Dead* with Mick Harvey, Blixa Bargeld and Anita Lane during the last two weeks of March.

By April, Cave was back in Berlin, living with Christoph Dreher, struggling with addiction, and severely straining his friendship with the Die Haut luminary. Relocating to London, Cave continued to indulge his appetite for excess, at the expense of his relationship with Tony Cohen. Cohen, fed up with his own addiction, and tired of the lifestyle, left his post as the band's sound engineer in July, returning home to Australia to kick his own habit. He was replaced with Victor Van Vugt.

Cave made his first court appearance in London on 1 August to answer charges for the year's earlier heroin possession. To avoid jail, and determined to clean up, he entered rehab, emerging at the end of September.

From rehab to the road, Cave and the Bad Seeds amped up their promo tours for the new album, landing in New York City in December for interviews, before heading back to England to record 'Helpless' for the Neil Young *Bridge* tribute album.

(EP) Anita Lane *Dirty Sings*
8801 I'm A Believer
8802 Lost In Music
ORIGINAL RELEASE: Mute MUTE 65, June 1988

COMMENTS: This four-song EP features two Cave contributions, the confessional beat patterned 'I'm A Believer', co-written with Lane, and a cover of Sister Sledge's 'Lost In Music', on which he plays organ. The former, which uses the thrum of drums to drive the movement forward, between musical interludes, provides an intense backdrop to what is essentially a piece of spoken word poetry.

All four songs from this EP would be included as bonus tracks on Lane's 1993 solo LP, *Dirty Pearl*.

(SINGLE) The Mercy Seat
8803 The Mercy Seat
8804 New Day aka New Morning
8803a The Mercy Seat (full length) —-12-inch single
8803b The Mercy Seat (video mix) –12-inch single
8701 From Her To Eternity (1987 film version) – CD single
8502 Tupelo (7-inch version) – CD single
ORIGINAL RELEASE: Mute STUMM 34, June1988

COMMENTS: Death may not be the end, but for those resigned to death – nay, wanting the bright stain that death brings – it is only the beginning. This morbid, sex-singed tale of a condemned man destined to fry in the electric chair (The Mercy Seat of the song title), set to a relentlessly rising intense wall of guitar noise, not only sheds by fire an old shell in the shape of Cave, but anticipates the resurrection of the man himself within a new context, a new guise, a new era. Christ-like, felonious, the death seat is the mercy seat; death is the culmination of everything, and there is no fear. The speaker desires nothing but the obliteration that flames will bring – the electric stink of death, the release of the soul. Murder or suicide, what dies has made his soul right before God.

Given the year Cave was having, it's perhaps no wonder his inner psyche distilled itself in such a fashion. The song would remain a touchstone of sorts for

Cave, remaining a staple of the Bad Seeds live sets for many years, even as other songs dropped silently into the past. It was clear that Cave was undergoing a massive transformation: he had truly become a major songwriter – this was a song of unreal power, a stream-of-consciousness *tour de force,* hailed as a classic at the moment of its release and signalled what his band were now capable of.

The 7-inch single was backed by 'New Day', an early version of 'New Morning'. The 12-inch single coupled the A-side with the video mix of 'Mercy Seat'. It was a completely different mix, with guitar and a cavalcade of sonics, with a completely different push, and emphasis that took away from the overall sound and allowed the images that filled the screen to take the spotlight, alternating shots of the band in red hues, and Cave, the condemned man, in black and white in a cell.

(FILM) *Dandy*
8805 City Of Refuge
ORIGINAL RELEASE: Black Sun Flower, 2001

COMMENTS: German director Peter Semple's *Dandy* began filming in Berlin in April 1986, in an attempt to capture the energy of the city's vibrant underground avant-garde scene in film and music. Both Nick Cave and Blixa Bargeld take a prominent part in the film, which also included performances from Einstürzende Neubauten, Nina Hagen and Die Toten Hosen.

Shot in both black and white and colour stock, Cave's part was highlighted by two notable performances – an acoustic version of 'City Of Refuge', and a reading of a poem – 'The Moon'.

The film was premiered at New York City's The Tunnel on 24 June, 1988 and became an underground favourite – gleefully pirated but never officially released. Until recently, when Sempel, disgusted with the trade in his film, particularly on eBay, took action, self-releasing it through his own website in an effort to thwart bootleggers.

(SINGLE) Deanna
8806 Deanna
8807 The Girl At The Bottom Of My Glass
ORIGINAL RELEASE: Mute MUTE 86, September 1988

COMMENTS: 'Deanna' borrows from the traditional 'O Happy Day', which was incorporated into live versions of the song. It was, for a long time, the closest to a pop single that Cave ever came, with its lively tune and organ, and swerves towards doo-wop. Cave's lyric suggests a commonplace love story till the listener realises that he's also talking about a regular murder accomplice. 'The Girl At The Bottom Of My Glass' is a hard-edged blues 'love' with the kind of rough backing vocals used later on 'Jack The Ripper'.

(ALBUM) *Tender Prey*
Line-up: Nick Cave (vocals & keyboards); Mick Harvey (bass); Blixa Bargeld

(guitar); Kid Congo Powers (guitar); Roland Wolf (keyboards); Thomas Wydler (drums).

8803 The Mercy Seat
8808 Up Jumped The Devil
8806 Deanna
8809 Watching Alice
8810 Mercy
8811 City Of Refuge
8812 Slowly Goes The Night
8813 Sunday's Slave
8814 Sugar Sugar Sugar
8804 New Morning aka New Day
CD BONUS TRACKS
8803b The Mercy Seat (video mix)
ORIGINAL RELEASE: Mute STUMM 52, September 1988

(EP) *And The Ass Saw The Angel*
8702 Mah Sanctum (from Book 2, Ch. V, pp. 115-116)
8703 Lamentation (from Book 2, Ch. VI, pp. 122-123)
8704 One Autumn (from Book 2, Ch. X, pp. 136-137)
8705 Animal Static (from Book 3, pp. 193-194)
ORIGINAL RELEASE: Mute Records, 12 STUMM 52 only available with first copies of LP *Tender Prey*. These tracks re-issued with extra music in 1999.

COMMENTS: *Tender Prey* was cobbled together from sessions that spanned August 1987 through January 1988, with mixing an ongoing concern through April. When released, finally, in September, the first five thousand copies of the vinyl pressing included a limited edition 12-inch single (P STUMM 52) comprised of four spoken word tracks, 'Mah Sanctum', 'Lamentation', 'One Autumn', and 'Animal Static', culled from the Trident sessions the previous year.

Tender Prey can be seen as the culmination of Cave's work reflecting his own musical vision of the blues and the American South, with the Bible's imagery still very much in play. It was about love and death and sex and wistful longing, about Jesus Christ and John The Baptist and judgement for all men...or perhaps for just one man in particular. Although *Tender Prey* was never one of Cave's favourite albums, representing as it did a very fractured time in his life, nor a particularly strong seller, the press received it well for the most part. His gifts as a storyteller were recognised as much as his lifelong love of religious iconography was lampooned and his drug escapades were hinted at.

The sessions were painfully slow, with recording seriously hindered by Cave's drug use. Songwriting, too, was stilted. At one point, Cave even considered resurrecting the Boys Next Door live staple 'Joyride' for the project, though ultimately the idea was set aside. It was not a time the band remembers fondly. Cave, who had never made a secret of his indulgence with sundry chemicals, was out of control, unable to pull his weight in the studio, as the drugs and attendant court dates took their toll. Finally, with the threat of possible imprisonment looming, Cave agreed to check into rehab in August, 1988.

Touring for *Tender Prey* (with the Bad Seeds augmented once again by Gun Club alumni Kid Congo Powers) was scheduled to start a mere four days after Cave re-emerged into the world, newly clean and somewhat unsure of what his life would be like without the comfort of drugs.

The album itself kicks off with 'The Mercy Seat', already established as a classic. With its venomous Old Testament imagery ('an eye for an eye, and a tooth for a tooth') closely followed up in 'Up Jumped The Devil', the feeling a long-time follower of Cave might get is that he is still enamoured of the extreme tenets of The Birthday Party, and in this album there are real echoes of the primal chaos and confusion of that band. This feeling is quickly dispelled by the appearance of 'Deanna', even more so by 'Watching Alice'. This mournful, sharp little vignette is something of a cross between Leonard Cohen and Lewis Carroll, featuring a Euchrid Eucrow-like personality watching his beloved from afar. It's a lugubrious but compelling number that almost seems to lurch into self-parody with the closing refrain: 'It's so depressing, it's true.'

'Mercy' is, in truth, equally despairing but, again, it is all totally compelling. Thomas Wydler's funereal drum patterns and a circling piano motif of real menace is where the song is rooted, the perfect background for Cave's story of impending doom, augmented by the Bad Seeds' vocals and brilliantly-executed bridge featuring of all things on a Nick Cave record, bass harmonica.

The howl of the harmonica is to the fore again, signalling 'City of Refuge'- as is the Old Testament. If 'Mercy' was a story of impending doom, this song is a howl from the depths of damnation, with some of Cave's most Gothic lyrics for years. Like 'Deanna', this one quickly became a live favourite with its relentless build-up and Grand Guignol singalong chorus.

A spoken-word intro clears the way for 'Slowly Goes The Night', perhaps the most unusual song on this album. Cave wakes in his boots and clothes, cursing that his $500 suit is slashed and then deeply intones 'Lover, lover, goodbye'. We're treated to Cave the spurned lover, the 'French look' Tom Jones, with backing vocals from the Bad Seeds that could have been lifted from the soundtrack of a hip Sixties film. Even recorders feature on this track, and this is probably the only Nick Cave original with such a sixties sound.

'Sugar Sugar' is another of these sinister love songs that Cave was so adept at in this time, a world away from the sensitive, reverential love songwriter of recent years. With Cave, the act of courtship seemed to require a sense of menace too and here, Cave holds up bloodstained sheets, 'the tokens of your virginity'. But a final surprise is in store, though, with 'New Morning', a song of redemption which had become the traditional impassioned closer for his live sets.

1989

Cave's 1989 live schedule also took him to the Brazilian city of São Paulo, where he met and fell in love with fashion stylist Viviane Carneiro. He subsequently relocated to São Paulo, Brazil, to live, work, and write.

The change of surroundings gave Cave a wholly new perspective. 'Everywhere you looked,' he enthused, 'there was something strange and wonderful and magical,' and the songs he was now writing would reflect that dynamism.

Cave, continually busy outside the direct confines of his band, had reason to celebrate in 1989, as *And The Ass Saw The Angel* was published and garnered critical accolades in the UK press in August. The dense, convoluted and disturbing book, marked Cave as a serious literary contender, matching wits and style with any number of schooled authors, giving the post-modern face of contemporary fiction a fresh voice. Indeed, many of Cave's performances throughout the year were literary readings. This year also saw the UK premiere of *Ghosts...Of The Civil Dead* at London's ICA Cinema at the beginning of May, with the soundtrack hustling onto the racks two weeks later.

1989 saw the Bad Seeds embark upon their fourth large tour of the United States, an eighteen-date outing that was documented by Uli M Schüppel in tour film *The Road To God Knows Where*.

By Autumn, with the year's touring done, the band – now comprising Cave, Bargeld, Harvey, Kid Congo Powers and Thomas Wydler – returned to Brazil to work again on *The Good Son*. Tapes in hand, Cave and Bargeld decamped to Trionus Studios in Berlin to mix the album with Flood and Shannon Strong. Strong, otherwise known as Bambi Lee Savage, got her start with the Denver-based Punk band Pagan Cowboys in 1985, before relocating first to London, then to Berlin where she was a freelance engineer at Hansa during a successful career that saw her record U2, Mick Harvey, and Anita Lane, and work closely with Daniel Lanois.

Cave himself wrapped up the year in Berlin, coming back nearly full circle, fleeing no longer, but once more at home in his adopted city, a new man, a clean man, an artist with a career that would soon be bigger than even he'd probably ever imagined.

(FILM) *The Road To God Knows Where*
ORIGINAL RELEASE: Mute/BMG 790475, December 1990
COMMENTS: See appendix two (Videos and Visuals) for details.

(RADIO) *Musicview #46* 'Radio's Weekly New Music Magazine' US
8901 Deanna
8902 Up Jumped The Devil
ORIGINAL RELEASE: North American promo

COMMENTS: An interview is joined by a pair of session performances within the syndicated *Musicview* series of programmes. CDs of this broadcast were produced for distribution among US radio stations; there it was joined by the starkly titled *Nick Cave The Interview* (Enigma E PRO – 172), a 27-minute interview recorded in New York City at Sun City Studios in December 1988, with Rockpool's Reyne Cuccuro.

(RADIO) *Snap* KCRW Santa Monica, California 3 March 1989
UNR The Mercy Seat
UNR 500 Miles
UNR Oh, I Love You Much Too Much
UNR Helpless
UNR The Carny
UNR Sunny
ORIGINAL RELEASE: Unreleased

COMMENTS: Long heralded as one of the United States' finest venues for alternative music, KCRW had a long standing policy of capturing evocative 'in session' sets from the era's premiere acts. Nick Cave and the Bad Seeds were no exception. Hinging on *Tender Prey*'s 'The Mercy Seat', the set was most interesting for the songs built around it. They included an odd, mainly instrumental take on 'The Carny', acoustic and incomplete with Cave adding his vocal timbre occasionally, as he and the show's host enjoy a little repartee. Skirting the traditional '500 Miles', the band offered up a tongue-in-cheek version of the AOR nightmare, 'Sunny', as well as a version of Neil Young's 'Helpless', which the band themselves had already recorded a little more reverently for *The Bridge* tribute album.

(ALBUM) Original soundtrack *Ghosts...of the Civil Dead*
8903 The News
8904 Introduction – A Prison In The Desert
8905 David Hale – I've been a Prison Guard since I was 18 years old
8906 Glover – I was 16 when they put me in prison
8907 David Hale – You're danglin' us like a bunch of meat on a hook
8908 Pop Mix
8909 Glover – We were united once
8910 David Hale – The day of the Murders
8911 Lilly's Theme ('A Touch Of Warmth')
8912 Maynard Mix
8913 David Hale – What I'm tellin' is the truth
8914 Outro – The Free World
8915 Glover – One man released so they can imprison the rest of the world

ORIGINAL RELEASE: Mute IONIC, May 1989

COMMENTS: Spring 1989 finally saw the release of John Hillcoat's *Ghosts...Of The Civil Dead*. The original soundtrack, composed and performed by Nick Cave, Mick Harvey and Blixa Bargeld also featured Anita Lane. Engineered by Ted Hamilton and compiled by Victor Van Vugt, the spoken word interludes cover movie dialogue. The quartet was able to provide some very striking and disturbing music for the film, which is used sparingly but is highly effective and memorable. Limiting themselves to just a few instruments such as tin whistles, a harmonica and the guts of a piano (no guitars), and utilising Anita Lane's ethereal voice, this was the most chilling kind of chamber music, with the echoes of Ennio Morricone that they had hoped for.

The film is a portrait of a brutal Australian prison regime and its effects on its high-risk inmates who turn on both their oppressors and themselves. The claustrophobic atmosphere is superbly evoked and the final rebellion is graphically violent: the film is genuinely shocking and thought provoking – but a film written by John Hillcoat and Nick Cave had limited appeal to critics and public alike. Indeed, the more popular press decried it as convoluted, sloppy and too hard to follow. Nevertheless, Cave's role as the maniacal Maynard is still his most successful cinematic foray thus far. His time on the screen doesn't get anywhere near half an hour but it is memorable: he invested his character with just the right mixture of evil sarcasm and naked aggression to make him stand out from all the other killers.

(ALBUM) Die Haut *Headless Body In Topless Bar*
8916 I Just Dropped In To See What Condition My Condition Was In
ORIGINAL RELEASE: What's So Funny About Records SF83, May 1989

COMMENTS: Cave embarked on this collaboration with Die Haut – a project which also included contributions from Kid Congo Powers, Anita Lane and Mick Harvey. Cave was a featured vocalist on 'I Just Dropped In To See What Condition My Condition Was In', written by Mickey Newberry. The song never proved a hit for the composer, but did give American Country musician Kenny Rogers his first major hit, masquerading as twanged out psychedelia in 1968, and would subsequently be recorded by a host of other Country stars, among them Willie Nelson and Wayne Perkins. And then Die Haut got hold of it.

A version of The Lonely Ones' 'Sad Dark Eyes', with Mick Harvey singing vocals, was also featured.

Die Haut had made only a small impression with *Burnin' The Ice,* and this new album would prove to be a difficult project. Split between instrumental and vocal tracks that featured the above assortment of musicians, *Headless Body In Topless Bar* feels like two very different albums. The instrumentals are unformed, lacking in scope – with the exception of Cave's track and Lane's other efforts. The finished project was greeted with bewilderment from critics and fans alike.

Engineered by Tony Cohen and mixed by Flood, the album was recorded at Hansa Ton Studios during 1987. Cave's track was released just prior to the Die Haut album on the *Deutschland Strikes Back Vol 1* compilation in March.

(BOOK) *And The Ass Saw The Angel*
ORIGINAL RELEASE: Black Spring Press Ltd. ISBN: 0948238038, 24 August 1989

COMMENTS: Cave's first novel finally made its London debut in August, as a snazzy 272 page hardcover. Its publication let Cave prove to many dubious critics that literary genius wasn't merely confined to the dusty halls of academia.

Cave brought his own gifts of lyric and poetry to the prose, to create the gritty world of the boy Euchrid, and the valleys and dark shadows of the fictional deep south where he lives. Packed with biblical references, blues and folk imagery and a profound understanding of the mythology of the backwoods hillbilly culture, *And The Ass Saw The Angel* was a gruesome tale, an often difficult read. Nevertheless, the book revealed the gestating state of Cave's musical mind, with elements of *Henry's Dream* and *Murder Ballads'* 'Crow Jane' already coming into play.

Cave was justifiably proud of his achievement. Many literary people essentially wrote off the novel, he explained, insisting that, 'because I was a musician, I couldn't be a serious novelist as well. It was very satisfying for me to have the last laugh on them. In the UK alone, *And The Ass Saw The Angel* sold over 15,000 hardcover copies, a remarkable feat for anyone – let alone a musician. It shocked and surprised everybody how well it sold. Including me. Obviously they were nearly all bought by fans, but still, to sell that many books on the first time out was very enjoyable. I even bumped Martin Amis off the "Book Of The Year" in one magazine.'

In addition to *And The Ass Saw The Angel*, Cave would release three lyric books. The first, *King Ink* (Black Spring Press, May 1988), was a collection of works that included most of the lyrics Cave had recorded with The Birthday Party and the Bad Seeds, as well as assorted prose pieces, short plays – five of which detailed the legend of Salome – and lyrics written, but not recorded.

King Ink II (Black Spring Press, March 1997) continued where the first volume left off, again including a wealth of lyrics for film, those commissioned by other artists as well as an illuminating article about the language of the Bible. Finally, in April 2001, Penguin books published *Nick Cave Complete Lyrics*.

(ALBUM) Compilation *The Bridge*
8917 Helpless
ORIGINAL RELEASE: Caroline CAR LP5, August 1989

COMMENTS: A Neil Young tribute album, *The Bridge* was a benefit organized to raise awareness and funds for Young's Bridge School, founded to create a safe and sympathetic enclave to educate children afflicted with severe physical and speech handicaps. It was a predicament from which one of the Young's own children suffered, and needless to say, the school was very near to his heart. Young's wife, Peggy, founded the Bridge charity and this endeavour culminated in both a two-day live music event in Mountain View California in mid-October 1989, and a tribute CD.

Although Cave didn't participate at the live shows, he and the Bad Seeds did contribute a beautiful version of 'Helpless' for the album, one of the best cover versions the band has done. The band truly caught the spirit of the original, but also lent it a new air of desolation: the warm, afflicted harmonies of the band's backing vocals and the searing slide guitar motifs that criss-cross the song combining wonderfully with Cave's heavy, resigned vocal. Of a highly variable collection, which also included the Pixies and Sonic Youth, Nick Cave and the Bad Seeds' was perhaps the most successful and certainly the most studied and thoughtful.

1990

Cave had spent a good part of the previous year touring *Tender Prey*, sandwiching many readings from *And The Ass Saw The Angel* into the band's rare down times. As the seasons turned, so did Cave's attention – to his next album. Mixes had already been completed for *The Good Son* in Berlin, but returning from a particularly packed schedule and still newly sober Cave felt dominated by the city where he had been comfortable for so many years. Berlin had lost its appeal, it was time to move on. London still was a chamber of horrors, and Cave had now fallen in love with São Paulo, and also with Viviane Carniero, the young woman with whom he would settle down and have a son, Luke in 1991. More together than he had been in years, Cave seemed to have decided to embark on a new phase of his career, indeed, his life.

Brazil was good to Nick Cave, a slow city filled with people he liked and who let him be, even though he was feted there. Studio engineer Victor Van Vugt, who would partner with Cave on his next album, explained, 'When Nick went to record *The Good Son*, he was a star in Brazil. For Nick, this was incredible.'

'Brazil is like America', Cave remarked, 'in that it's totally out of control. The people have no control of what's going on there and they're living in some pretty hideous times. But somehow, they've managed to rise above that. I sound twee, and it's only alright for me to say it because I'm not Brazilian, but they seem to be able to transcend the political and economic nightmare they're going through by virtue of the sort of people they are. They are an incredibly spirited, lively race of people.'

Following the April release of *The Good Son*, the band launched a massive fifty date worldwide tour. This time out, however, they'd be breaking in two more freshmen as Kid Congo Powers again departed to rejoin his Gun Club cohorts, leaving the door open for White Buffaloes' Conway Savage and The Triffids' Martyn P Casey to join the fold.

These were important additions to the band, both of them providing a certain subtlety in their playing which was going to be the way forward for the band as they limited the bludgeoning sounds of old.

Throughout the year, despite the band's heavy tour schedule, whenever Cave took time out, he'd retreat back to São Paulo, and his world of reading and writing. Music was, for the most part, on hold for the time being as Cave settled into the role of family man.

(TV) *Night Music TV* US 29 January 1990
UNR The Mercy Seat

UNR Hey Joe
ORIGINAL RELEASE: Unreleased

COMMENTS: Out on the prowl doing advance promos for the band's new album, Cave and Harvey hit the Big Apple for this late night music show. This brief set was recorded by the duo, accompanied by *Night Music TV*'s own house band.

(SINGLE) The Ship Song
9001 The Ship Song
9002 The Train Song
ORIGINAL RELEASE: Mute MUTE 108, March 1990

COMMENTS: The first single pulled from *The Good Son,* 'The Ship Song' was a taster for what Cave had in store. Backed by 'The Train Song', both were subdued affairs, longing, haunting, smooth and suggested a more mature style developing. Cave was writing in a gentler, more measured way on the whole, and without the bite and spite that dominated past releases.
'The Ship Song' would prove popular with band and fans alike, appearing on numerous compilation albums at the time. The song would also be heavily covered – indeed racking up more versions than any other of Nick Cave's songs, as musicians like Gene, Concrete Blonde, Immaculate Fools, and Heather Nova took his words to their own hearts. Live versions from Ed Kuepper and Pearl Jam were not unheard of either, although neither ever laid the song to tape.

(RADIO) *Nozems A GoGo* VPRO Radio Netherlands 14 March 1990
UNR The Mercy Seat
UNR The Ship Song
ORIGINAL RELEASE: Unreleased

COMMENTS: Cave and Harvey performed a brief acoustic radio session for a show well established as a lovely catch-all for some of the world's greatest alternative acts.

(RADIO) Vara 2 Meter Session, Netherlands, Recorded 21/03/1990 broadcast 24/04/1990
UNR Sad Waters
UNR City Of Refuge
UNR The Good Son
9003 The Mercy Seat
ORIGINAL RELEASE: 9003 on compilation *10 Jaar 2 Meter Sessies,* Sony Music Radio Records 487259-2, 1997

(TV) *Onrust,* VPRO Television, Netherlands 8 April 1990
UNR The Mercy Seat

UNR The Ship Song
UNR Foi Na Cruz
UNR The Weeping Song
UNR The Ship Song
ORIGINAL RELEASE: Unreleased

COMMENTS: Another acoustic performance.

(TV) *Megamix,* France 14 April 1990
UNR The Mercy Seat
ORIGINAL RELEASE: Unreleased

(ALBUM) *The Good Son*
Line-up: Nick Cave (vocals & keyboards); Mick Harvey (bass); Blixa Bargeld (guitar); Kid Congo Powers (guitar); Roland Wolf (keyboards); Thomas Wydler (drums).
9004 Foi Na Cruz
9005 The Good Son
9006 Sorrow's Child
9007 The Weeping Song
9001 The Ship Song
9008 The Hammer Song
9009 Lament
9010 The Witness Song
9011 Lucy
JAPAN BONUS TRACK
9002 The Train Song
ORIGINAL RELEASE: Mute STUMM 76, April 1990

(EP) *Acoustic Versions*
9012 The Mercy Seat
9013 City Of Refuge
9014 Deanna

ORIGINAL RELEASE: P STUMM 76 with early pressings of LP

COMMENTS: Recorded and engineered in Berlin and Brazil, some early LP pressings came with a free 7-inch single, *Acoustic Versions* that collected three tracks; 'The Mercy Seat', 'City Of Refuge' and 'Deanna', recorded between May 1989 and January 1990. The EP proved to be a hip little number, and would be re-issued on CD in Australia in 1994 as *Stripped* (Mute/Liberation/Mushroom, PRD94/84). There was also a CD single used to promote the band's then-upcoming *Let Love In* tour, and given away free with every purchase of a Nick Cave And The Bad Seeds album

Much of the material that comprised *The Good Son* had common themes with *And The Ass Saw The Angel* and these would be revisited in *Henry's Dream* too. Cave was able to pinpoint the processes that were going on: 'When I was writing the book, I know a lot of songs developed from it. I have a very lyrical way of writing, and very song-like way of writing. And I think it works the other way around – ideas for the novel came out of ideas for the songs. I think they probably scratch one another's back.'

The Good Son was a bit of a radical departure album for both Cave and the band. Departing from his normal modus operandi, for the first time ever, Cave and the band recorded demos of the songs they intended including, using these to lay down the structure of the album and round it out. Cave had trepidations regarding how this new record would come across once the final mixes were done. But, still, he also knew that he had taken his lyrics and the very fabric of the music itself to a completely different level. Influenced by the culture and people of São Paulo, *The Good Son* is less an album for fans, but an album for Cave himself, with many of the songs conceived and written as he wandered through the streets of that city.

Songs like 'Lament' and 'The Weeping Song' have a perceptible Latin swing to them and the instrumentation, the gentler rhythms and the abundance of strings on this album give it a flavour totally different to any previous Nick Cave and the Bad Seeds album.

It would have been a risky move for many. There are few musicians who are comfortable enough to tinker with their formula and record such a selfish set. However, this was fast becoming a habit for Cave, born within the confines of *Kicking Against The Pricks*, furthered here, to finally culminate the one-two punch of *Murder Ballads* and *The Boatman's Call*.

Remember, Cave was operating in the structure of a new decade, dancing in between the Glam metal revival of the new rock breed, the embryonic crunch of grunge and the absolute miasma of the coked-out 80s glitterati. It was puzzling, then to have this album land in the laps of people who wouldn't know what, if anything, to make of it. It was a gamble that would ultimately succeed, although when copies first hit the streets, it looked for a while like *The Good Son* would be a deal-breaker.

However the lukewarm critical reception could not diminish the power of this album. In fact, many critics revamped their impression of the songs once they saw Cave perform live during the ensuing tour. English reviewer Alan Brown would write, 'This was a show to shame the sourest of old sceptics.' Cave had finally come into his own.

From the reverential hush of 'Foi Na Cruz', the lush melancholy of 'Sorrow's Child', to the eerie power of 'The Weeping Song', Cave and the band succeeded in creating some spellbinding songs. The lyrical portraits are lush, the piano and strings sweeping, the mood uplifting yet sad, in the way empty streets are in twilight. There are edgy moments in 'The Witness Song', 'The Hammer Song' and 'The Good Son', but these too, are somehow subdued and a version of the latter song on the *Live Seeds* album illustrates just how restrained the band as a whole were on *The Good Son*. In style, this album owes a debt to Leonard Cohen more than any other: the fact that Cohen himself released songs like 'The Stranger Song', for instance, make this an obvious comment to make but it is also there in the gentle, courtly manner of the album.

Both 'The Ship Song' and 'The Weeping Song' were accompanied by a couple of the best videos that Cave had been involved in. In 'The Ship Song', Cave is white-suited at a piano, surrounded by girls in ballerina dresses with the Bad Seeds humming nearby (a shot from this was used as 'The Good Son' album cover). 'The Weeping Song' has Cave and Bargeld playing their Father/Son duet, rowing a rickety boat across a dustbin-liner sea and belting out the chorus in pin-striped suits while doing a slow shuffle together. Cave later said how they resembled 'two gay German businessmen' in this film.

It was released on 16 April, ghosting in to the Top 50, rising to #47 on the British chart. Those sales were probably helped along by the inclusion of the acoustic set, but Cave had rustled up a new fan base on the back of *Tender Prey*.

(TV) *The Late Show,* UK 11 June 1990
UNR Cindy, Cindy
UNR The Weeping Song
ORIGINAL RELEASE: Unreleased

COMMENTS: A rare UK television appearance.

(SINGLE) The Weeping Song
9007 The Weeping Song
9015 Cocks'n'Asses (a.k.a. The B-side Song)
8917 Helpless (UK CD Single)
9002 The Train Song (US CD Single)
9007a The Weeping Song (remix) (US Promo Mute/Elektra PROCD 8229-2)
ORIGINAL RELEASE: Mute MUTE 118, September 1990

COMMENTS: Released in various formats – 7-inch, 12-inch and CD single, not to mention a US promo set. Nick Cave and the Bad Seeds had high hopes for 'The Weeping Song'.

Deep and mournful and, with only a hint of hope, 'The Weeping Song' wove its hypnotic beats across two distinct versions. The album track was far more understated than the single remix, with some interesting percussion to while the single version had the guitars higher up in the mix and sounding more like a typical Bad Seeds track. Making the B-sides the previously released 'The Train Song', in the UK, and the *Bridge* tribute version of 'Helpless', gave Cave's newest fans a sample of the band's diversity.

For completists though, it was frustrating – leaving those poor sods to wonder just how many times they'd have to buy the same songs. But, then again, with the advent of the CD single, an entirely new way of marketing had come into vogue, and Mute were doing no less than any other label at the time.

The highlight of this single no matter what you make of the A-side, has got to be the ferocious hack job, 'Cocks 'n' Asses', also known in more demure circles (aka the United States) as 'The B-side Song,' perhaps in an attempt to thwart that country's music watchdog – the PMRC. Whatever one made of the title, though, the song itself, however, is a crazy hybrid of spritual/r&b/ electro-Gothic/experimental music.

1991

Recording through much of 1991, Nick Cave's dream of music made with scant regard for either stylistic or commercial boundaries was realised within the sessions for his next album, *Henry's Dream*; an avalanche of songs that were at once the most vitriolic, yet fragile he'd ever recorded.

Cave's finest production yet, however, came on 10 May, with the birth of his son, Luke. And, with that, Cave himself was reborn, willingly forced by the appearance of his longed-for son to look outside what had become an increasingly insulated box – once ferociously introspective and introverted, he now found himself looking at society first in São Paulo, then in New York (where the family relocated in October), utterly disgusted by the malice and degradation he witnessed there. It was an attitude that inspired his writing and he crafted a new batch of songs that were, in structure and raw energy, the complete antithesis of those on *The Good Son.*

His Brazilian sojourn ended in absolute disillusion. At first, he explained, 'it was incredible, but the last year I was there I found it very difficult. To stay in the city – I was in São Paulo, where brutality lives on your doorstep – you have to "become" Brazilian, and that meant an attitude to life I found very difficult to maintain. It was carnival…football…drinking…cocaine. It seemed to be a matter of trying to keep a smile on your face despite everything and it didn't go with my temperament. No matter how long you stay, you'll always be a gringo.'

In following this new direction, the Bad Seeds then did something they had sworn up and down they'd never, ever do – working these songs in session with an outside producer, Neil Young's most favoured collaborator, David Briggs. But whereas Briggs forced new energies and directions from the Canadian, the Bad Seeds experience proved such a disaster that the entire project was delayed (into 1992), as the group sought to salvage their own vision from the tapes.

(SESSION) Gary Lucas, September 1991
9101 And The Ass Saw The Angel
ORIGINAL RELEASE: *Improve The Shining Hour Rare Lumiere 1980-2000*, Knitting Factory Records KFW 265 28/03/2000

COMMENTS: In Rotterdam, Netherlands, at the beginning of September, Cave joined former Captain Beefheart/future Jeff Buckley guitarist Gary Lucas in the studio, to read 'The Birth' from *And The Ass Saw The Angel,* accompanied by Lucas' scattered and frenetic pickings. Unreleased for close to a decade, the track finally saw daylight on a compilation of Lucas' various other activities, a showcase for those comprehensive chops that range from Jazz and Blues to baroque rhythm.

(ALBUM) Compilation *I'm Your Fan: The Songs Of Leonard Cohen*
9102 Tower Of Song
ORIGINAL RELEASE: East West Records 9031-75598-1, October 1991

COMMENTS: Leonard Cohen, the long time bastion of alterna-rockers' most mopeish fantasies, proved to be the perfect subject for a tribute album (this one the first of two). And Cave, likewise, the perfect foil for Cohen's own twisted view of the world.

Engineered by Victor Van Vugt, the Bad Seeds' contribution to this collection was a masterful performance of 'Tower Of Song'.

Originally included on Cohen's *I'm Your Man* LP in 1988, 'Tower Of Song' was part of Cohen's 'comeback' from wilderness years where he had been dropped by his American label, just as his influence was filtering through to new generations of artists. Cave's 'Tower of Song' was deliriously powerful in its reinvention, and probably the highlight of the album. Whereas most contributors to the album – especially Lloyd Cole, REM, Pixies, and John Cale – kept their covers relatively straightforward, Cave decided to go another route, to completely let rip.

'We did an 80-minute version of "Tower Of Song." It was almost completely live, and was basically the history of music, a Blues version running into a Country version running into a Punk version into the Manchester sound, on and on and on. We were very drunk, and when it was over we edited it down with a pair of scissors. It's great, but I would never release it.' In fact, a 33-minute version of the performance has leaked out, on the *More Pricks Than Kicks* bootleg compilation (Pseudo Indie PIL08).

As for the album track, now pared down to a paltry five and a half minutes, it married the ragged slickness together into a medley that was not so much a tribute to Cohen's song itself but a rambling homage to all music, the music that moved Cave to make his own mark in the world. Rambunctious and packed with humour that would force a smile across the face of even the most jaded listener, Cave's 'Tower Of Song' teeters through rooms of late night jam sessions, guitar-picking hedonists, and the craziest assembly of musical ghosts imaginable.

(ALBUM) Original soundtrack *Until The End Of The World*
9103 (I'll Love You) Till The End Of The World
ORIGINAL RELEASE: Warner Brothers 7599 26707-2, December 1991

COMMENTS: Wim Wender's hugely disappointing, sprawling Punk-noir film may have made critics shudder, but for Cave's legions of fans, hoping to see him again paired with the inspirational director, his small role in this epic was not a let-down. The prestigious cast that Cave joined brought Solveig Dommartin, William Hurt, Max Von Sydow and Sam Neill together in one film.

The soundtrack itself was scored by Australian musician Graeme Revell and featured contributions from U2, Depeche Mode, Talking Heads, Can, and Patti and Fred Smith.

The title track, produced by Nick Cave and The Bad Seeds and Gareth Jones, is apocalyptic, filled with images of mayhem, murder, bomb blasts and turning away from God and hope in favour of the love of a woman, of fleeting emotions that are bound only to earth, that cannot be carried beyond.

Cut from its original five hours to two and a half hours, the film was shot in nine countries to the tune of some 23 million dollars. Even abridged, however, this flawed extravaganza remains too disconnected to reveal what Wenders himself tried to capture.

(FILM) *Johnny Suede*
9104 Freak Mamma's Boy
ORIGINAL RELEASE: Paramount Studios, 1991

COMMENTS: Cave once again hit the big screen, this time with a bona-fide role as Freak Storm, in Tom DiCillo's black comedy stinker, *Johnny Suede.* In a humorous cameo, singing DiCillo's 'Freak's Mamma's Boy', Cave attempts to help out Brad Pitt's would be rock and roller Johnny Suede. A dual US/Swiss production, the film took shape from DiCillo's one-man show, becoming a modern fable, a deconstructionist's dream of teenage chutzpah. Well, it would have been, if deconstructionists had a sense of humour.

It was a role that made Cave sour about the whole film-making process, at least until the beginning of 1993, and it was not too much celebrated by his fans, who expected more, perhaps, from their idol than this.

For his part, Cave explained that 'basically, I'm just dabbling with varying success. My acting is painfully bad. Any role they give me has to be very unchallenging. Things like *Johnny Suede...*I just wander around wearing a foot-high white wig and that's about it. *Johnny Suede* put me off being in a film for a long time.'

1992

Cave and the Bad Seeds jumped straight back into the swing of things with what some would call their most audacious effort to date – *Henry's Dream.* This year also brought one of the most poignant moments of Cave's recent career when a virtual Birthday Party reunion was staged at the London Town & Country Club on 1 September. A Bad Seeds show was interrupted first by a guest appearance from Shane MacGowan; and then by Cave announcing 'I'd like to give you a history lesson.' With Rowland S Howard and Mick Harvey representing The Birthday Party, and Martyn P. Casey standing in for the deceased Tracy Pew, the audience was regaled with versions of 'Wild World', 'Dead Joe' and 'Nick The Stripper'. The latter track, together with a Bad Seeds performance of 'Jack The Ripper' subsequently appeared on an NME exclusive live album, *Viva Eight* (NME VIVA 8).

(SINGLE) Straight To You
9201 Straight To You
9202 Jack The Ripper (LP version)
9203 Blue Bird
9204 Jack The Ripper (acoustic version)
ORIGINAL RELEASE: Mute MUTE 140, March 1992

COMMENTS: The first single culled from *Henry's Dream* proved an ample taster for what was going to be on offer.

'Straight To You' is a lament about endings. Slow and sweeping, with just enough guitar hooks and organ to keep the mood from being completely suicidal, was this new endeavour going to be an autobiographical one? Apparently, things were not going well in Cave's personal life, and if 'Straight To You' carried a positive message, 'Jack The Ripper' did the complete opposite.

The A-side at least hints at redemption and reconciliation, 'Jack The Ripper', is its complete antithesis. Deep and dark and dangerous, violent and brutal, the relationship within the song is vitriolic, devoid of love, filled with unspeakable pain…and perhaps just a little overwrought with its butcher knives, buckets, vipers and fists. The accompanying video was released across two distinct cuts, the 'blood version' interspersing shots of bloody surgical instruments in between the original's already dark frames. If there was any question that Cave was undergoing the destruction of his own relationships then, he was explicit some time later, explaining that 'I wrote "Jack The Ripper" for my ex-wife. Not for her, about her.'

An acoustic version of that song, included on a limited edition 7-inch single, left the quietly subdued 'Bluebird' to round out the bitter bile on the CD. A beautiful song, answering the call of someone's stomped upon heart.

With just these three songs, it was clear that Cave was again shifting his sound, and would use this new album as an opportunity to get some things off his chest.

(ALBUM) *Henry's Dream*
Line-up: Nick Cave (vocals & keyboards); Mick Harvey (guitar); Blixa Bargeld (guitar); Martyn P Casey (bass); Conway Savage (keyboards); Thomas Wydler (drums).
9205 Papa Won't Leave You Henry
9206 I Had A Dream, Joe
9201 Straight To You
9207 Brother, My Cup Is Empty
9208 Christina The Astonishing
9209 When I First Came To Town
9210 John Finn's Wife

9211 Loom Of The Land
9202 Jack The Ripper
FRENCH CD BONUS TRACK
9204 Jack The Ripper (acoustic version)
9203 Bluebird
9212 What Can I Give You?

ORIGINAL RELEASE: Mute STUMM 92, April 1992

COMMENTS: *'Henry's Dream* was a fucking nightmare to make', Cave said.

However, even with that brusque statement, no-one could deny that Cave was onto something good. Part of the problems he associated with *Henry's Dream* stemmed from the fact that, for the first time, the band brought an outsider into the studio, turning their sound over to someone who ultimately had complete disregard for their creative vision. That man was David Briggs. David Briggs had been producer on Neil Young's landmark albums, such as *Tonight's The Night* and *Everybody Knows This Is Nowhere*. His association with another uncompromising and innovative artist suggested that this was an inspired choice, but the band's frustrations with him were often kept from public knowledge.

At the time of release, Cave confessed to being pleased with the album, if not completely satisfied with the process. 'I'm not normally one to say things like this, but I'm really happy with this one. It surprised me, how powerful it came out, how much is going on in there. We used an outside producer for the first time, and – well, he had a very different way of working than we do.'

The band had, according to Cave, 'been making records for so long we thought we were too old to be bothered with that sort of thing, but the record label thought it might be a good idea, so we finally decided to try.'

Cave spent an evening going through his record collection looking for 'the producer who I felt was the least producer-like producer I could find. I came up with David Briggs. You listen to the Young albums, and they sound like there is no producer. They're extremely raw, and they are what they are – great songs performed in great ways.

'As it turned out, that's basically the way David feels a record should be made, which is very different to the way we do things. Our records are far more complex, there's a lot of overdubbing going on, a lot of riding the phasers and pulling out sounds, a lot of orchestration that we do in the mixing stage, which David was not at all interested in. So in the end, we took what we considered to be a quite undynamic sounding record and remixed it our own way.'

The bulk of the album was recorded at Sound City in Van Nuys, California over November and December 1991; two final tracks, 'Christina The Astonishing' and 'Loom Of The Land' were cut at Dreamland Studios in Bearsville NY.

The resultant *Henry's Dream* is a meeting of the minds; the Bad Seeds' attention to detail fighting it out with the raw, live sound from which Briggs had made a career.

'Where he came into his own,' Cave continued, 'was in pushing us to the limits. He forced us into some very spirited performances, whereas in the past, some of the members would do it right the first time and others would say, "we can overdub later". David was totally against that sort of thing, and that's what I felt was so great about working with him.'

Cave needn't have worried. The album proved to be a smashing success, well received and more than merely baffling to the critics, many of whom were beginning to wonder if, perhaps, Cave was transforming, fulfilling fans' very hopes that he'd become their own messiah. Messianic complexes aside, however, what remains is that Nick Cave and The Bad Seeds were marching blithely to their own agenda. There was nothing else on earth that sounded like this in 1992 – the year that grunge catapulted the screech of guitars and the ragged tatters of flannel fully into the mainstream. Nowhere else was there a sound quite so sophisticated, so brutally honest, so complex.

Finally released in April, 1992, *Henry's Dream* emerged an album of stories, intense vignettes that have the capacity to make the skin crawl. Two outstanding tracks are 'Papa Won't Leave You, Henry' and 'I Had A Dream, Joe', raucous numbers which, while they may betray Briggs' rock influence, also have some of the best elements of the band too. In 'Papa Won't Leave You, Henry', for instance, they are able to take a stunning detour into a nightmare soundscape that brilliantly mirrors the narrator's descent into chaos. That they are able to do this in the middle of what is essentially a singalong is a hallmark of a band's skill and mastery. Indeed, throughout the album, and sometimes in spite of Briggs, the atmospheres that they convey are unique and it's hard to think of many other bands achieving them. 'Christina The Astonishing' (the miraculous tale of an Italian saint), 'Brother, My Cup Is Empty' and 'John Finn's Wife', especially, are richly textured songs that do haunt the listener – quite the opposite of the rock 'n' roll immediacy that Briggs was attempting.

Henry's Dream became Cave's biggest hit yet, reaching #29 in the UK It was also a portent of things to come. The religious overtones that are threaded through the album are unmistakable as Cave sings of redemption, of faith, of blessings, all twisted through some bright eye, some oracle of love. But this religious ecstasy is not just of the Bible, not always. It stretches far further than that, into the depths of the human soul, of the joy of love, the brutal agony of letting go of...a woman, of dreams, of faith, of the very love that binds us together.

And it was fitting, too, that such an opus was available in a wealth of releases. Some copies of the album were accompanied by a colour print of Anton Corbijn's stylized cover art. Australia packaged the album in a box that included a three-track promo cassette, with the limited edition adding a t-shirt and poster to the pack.

France, meanwhile, included an otherwise unavailable 'Jack The Ripper' CD single (Mute/Virgin SA3252) with early copies of the album, that included the acoustic rendering of the 'Ripper', as well as 'Bluebird' and an unreleased track, 'What Can I Give You?' The latter was an early, working version of 'Faraway, So Close!', and remained generally unavailable until it was rounded up for the *B-sides & Rarities* collection in 2005 – with that album's liner notes confessing, 'the origins of this... version, with a new set of lyrics by Cave, are now lost in the mists of time.'

Another French promo album sampler contained regular album versions of 'Papa Won't Leave You, Henry', 'Straight To You', 'Brother, My Cup Is Empty' and 'The Loom Of The Land' (Mute/Virgin SA3252).

And for any Stateside press not yet in the loop, a massive promo package was put together (Mute/Elektra PR-8593) that included the CD, both the 7-inch and CD 'Straight To You' 7-inch singles, a copy of *And The Ass Saw The Angel*, an Electronic Press Kit VHS, and a 12-inch poster of the *Henry's Dream* album cover.

(LIVE) Paradiso, Amsterdam, 2 June 1992
9213 I Had A Dream, Joe
9214 The Mercy Seat
9215 The Good Son
9216 Tupelo
9217 Deanna
9218 Jack The Ripper
9219 In The Ghetto
9220 New Morning

(LIVE) Paradiso, Amsterdam, 3 June 1992
9221 The Ship Song
9222 The Carny
9223 Papa Won't Leave You, Henry
9224 The Weeping Song
9225 From Her To Eternity
ORIGINAL RELEASE: 9214-25 *Live At The* Paradiso VHS, Mute Film/BMG Video 74321 12160, 3 November 1992; 9213-15, 9221-22 on single Mute MUTE 148, September 1992

COMMENTS: Having already decided that the next Bad Seeds' album would be a live set, the tape recorders were out throughout the band's European-and-beyond tours until well into the new year, not only stuffing the archive with sufficient material for a dozen new albums, but also an ample stockpile of B-sides as well. Unlike many acts, however, who would then tease them out over any number of singles, the Bad Seeds decided to dump a busload off at once – five excellent performances here backed the 'I Had A Dream, Joe' 45. (These same tracks were also issued in Japan as part of the *European Tour 92* package, accompanied by a booklet of photographs excerpted from Peter Milne's forthcoming *Fish In A Barrel* – Alfa records, ALZB-12).

Mining the same source, the end of the year then brought the in-concert VHS *Live At The Paradiso* – this set proved to be one of the band's most electrifying. Recorded by Victor Van Vugt and edited by John Hillcoat, the 57-minute performance is just glorious. Long gone are the ragged days of old, replaced instead by stunning live material that was studied and still packed with energy.

(TV) *Late Show With David Letterman* US 23 July 1992
UNR I Had A Dream, Joe
ORIGINAL RELEASE: Unreleased

COMMENTS: You know you've made it when you get on the late night talk shows.

(RADIO) KCRW Santa Monica US, *Morning Becomes Eclectic* 12 August 1992
UNR Jack The Ripper
UNR Lucy
9226 God's Hotel
UNR The Mercy Seat
UNR New Morning
ORIGINAL RELEASE: *Rare On Air Live Performances Vol 1* Mammoth Records MR 0074-2, 1994; remainder unreleased.

COMMENTS: Committed to providing listeners with a well rounded sampler of the best in new music, the public radio station KCRW in Santa Monica, California has been a long time champion of Nick Cave's music: the daily *Morning Becomes Eclectic* show, meanwhile, is as close to a 'John Peel Session' as recent American radio has come, and the compilation of the same name served up some of the best performances of its day. John Cale, Beck and Tori Amos are among the other acts showcased.

(LIVE) Berlin Tempodrom, 24 August, 1992
9227 Truck Love
9228 Pleasure Is The Boss
9229 Sad Dark Eyes
9230 Little Doll
ORIGINAL RELEASE: – *What's So Funny About....* 40156982940-2, November 1993; all on VHS *Sweat*, Triple X 51184-3 (US) 1993

COMMENTS: Cave reunited once more with Die Haut for their 10th anniversary performance at Berlin's Tempodrom on 24 August, 1992, an event subsequently released on both CD and VHS, and essentially shaping up as a live interpretation of the band's forthcoming *Head On* studio LP (although Cave himself wouldn't appear on that disc).

(SINGLE) I Had A Dream, Joe
9206 I Had A Dream, Joe
9213 I Had A Dream, Joe (live)
9214 The Mercy Seat (live) 12-inch
9215 The Good Son (live)
9221 The Ship Song (live) 12-inch
9222 The Carny (live) 12-inch

ORIGINAL RELEASE: Mute MUTE 148, September 1992

COMMENTS: While the plain old single for 'I Had A Dream, Joe' was completely straightforward, the real nuggets were to be found on the 12-inch and promo CD singles, in the form of five remarkable live performances taken from the band's Paradiso show in Amsterdam on 2 and 3 June. Across old songs and new, Cave and the Bad Seeds are wound tight, slick and powerful, although Cave sounds a little ragged on 'The Mercy Seat.'

(LIVE) Town & Country Club, London, 1 September 1992
9231 Jack The Ripper
9232 Nick The Stripper
ORIGINAL RELEASE: Compilation *Viva! Eight*, *NME* VIVA, February 1993

COMMENTS: To celebrate the 40th anniversary of the *New Musical Express*, a series of concerts was staged at London's Town And Country club from 1 through 8 September, with all proceeds from the fete donated to the Spastics' Society.

Nick Cave and The Bad Seeds kicked off the event on the 1st, the show mentioned before that would subsequently go down in legend as the first and (so far) only Birthday Party 'reunion', albeit one that was condensed into a three song 'history lesson', with Rowland S Howard recreating his lead guitar from so long ago.

Two songs from the show were included on the *NME*'s accompanying CD, available by mail order, with The Birthday Party sequence represented by 'Nick The Stripper' ('Dead Joe' and 'Wild World' remain in the vault). That was joined by the more recent 'Jack The Ripper', to provide a delightful duality between old and new.

(SINGLE) What A Wonderful World
9233 What A Wonderful World
9234 Rainy Night In Soho
9235 Rainy Night In Soho (demo)
9236 Lucy
9237 Lucy (version #2)
ORIGINAL RELEASE: Mute MUTE 151, November 1992

COMMENTS: One of Cave's most potent collaborations, as he unites with Pogues' vocalist Shane MacGowan across a cover of the old Louis Armstrong chestnut 'What A Wonderful World' for a Christmas 1992 release. With a 7-inch version released in the US through Sub Pop (Mute handled the 12-inch and CD versions), this beautifully ramshackle and sluggish performance is backed with two tracks, Cave performing the Pogues' 'Rainy Night In Soho', and MacGowan returning the compliment across Cave's 'Lucy'. Two versions of each song would appear across the accompanying range of releases.

(TV) *Later....with Jools Holland*, UK 12 November 1992
UNR Lucy
UNR Rainy Night In Soho
UNR What A Wonderful World
ORIGINAL RELEASE: Unreleased

COMMENTS: Backing up the release of their single, Cave and MacGowan drop by the BBC to perform the a- and B-sides in suitably iconoclastic fashion.

1993

Nick Cave And The Bad Seeds started their year in January, performing at Australia's mammoth Big Day Out Festival alongside Iggy Pop, Beasts Of Bourbon and Sonic Youth.

Having decided that they were mightily displeased with the finished studio version of *Henry's Dream*, the group shut themselves into Atlantis Studios during February to play with the hours of tapes they'd recorded during the previous year's tours. The idea behind this session was, of course, to create the killer live album that would give fans a *real* taste of how the band had wanted the album to sound; indeed, how they'd been performing the songs in the live arena for months.

After completing the mixes for this forthcoming album, Cave and his family relocated to London, where he again partnered with Wim Wenders, writing two new songs to be included on the *Faraway, So Close!* soundtrack; and by June, he was back on the road with the band, this time for a handful of shows in Europe. For the first time, too, the band travelled to Israel, to play a show in Haifa, to discover that they were absolutely huge.

As much as Cave was enjoying the present fruits of his labours, however, he was already looking toward the future, writing the songs that would become *Let Love In*. And, by September, the Bad Seeds were back at Townhouse Studios, with Tony Cohen back in tow, to begin recording this next set in the weeks before their next European tour commenced. After a minor diversion which saw Cave jump ship to help Die Haut celebrate their tenth anniversary, the sessions wrapped up in Melbourne at the end of the year.

(SESSION) Australian Country Songs tribute album, January 1993
9301 There's No Night Out At The Jail
ORIGINAL RELEASE: *B-sides & Rarities*

COMMENTS: The first truly major discovery within the *B-sides* collection, this version of Australian Country star Chad Morgan's jailhouse lament was recorded while the band was mixing the *Live Seeds* album, for inclusion in a forthcoming collection of local folk songs. That album never materialised and, whereas other recordings from the same session (demos of 'O'Malley's Bar' and the proto-'Red Right Hand' 'Where The Action Is') would eventually see service, 'There's No Night Out' apparently languished forgotten until Mick Harvey was finally asked about it in 2004. 'It was recorded in about ten minutes, and mixed in about five,' he shrugged.

(ALBUM) *Live Seeds*
9302 The Mercy Seat
9303 Deanna
9304 The Ship Song
9305 Papa Won't Leave You, Henry
9306 Plain Gold Ring
9307 John Finn's Wife
9308 Tupelo
9309 Brother, My Cup Is Empty
9310 The Weeping Song
9311 Jack The Ripper
9312 The Good Son
9313 From Her To Eternity
9314 New Morning

ORIGINAL RELEASE: Mute STUMM 122, September 1993

COMMENTS: This ambitious live set was recorded during Bad Seeds' shows in Europe and Australia during 1992 and 1993. The final mixdown was masterminded by the Bad Seeds and Tony Cohen at Melbourne's Atlantis Studios in February. The CD was released with a slim volume of black and white photos, shot during the tour by Peter Milne. The photos would then reappear, on 14 October, as part of Milne's much larger book of this tour, *Fish In A Barrel*.

While *Live Seeds* covered a few highlights from the band's recent past, most of the album was given over to new versions of the songs on *Henry's Dream*. Cave was still fuming over the various production problems he now admitted had plagued the recording of that album, and used *Live Seeds* to take care of those indiscretions, essentially releasing an album that sounded like the band had originally envisioned the package. 'It shows how the songs could've sounded if they had been recorded properly,' he explained.

And, as good as *Henry's Dream* sounded, the recreation of these songs on tour made it obvious, with a little bit of hindsight, that he was absolutely correct. The slick production and smooth sonics of the CD aren't the best representation of the fire that Cave and the band could bring to their songs – something that they had, by now, mastered in the live arena, sounding more passionate and positively theatrical across 'Papa Won't Leave You, Henry', 'Brother, My Cup Is Empty', and 'John Finn's Wife', than ever they did in the studio.

A brooding take on 'The Mercy Seat', now Cave's signature song, is an especial treat, here slowed down with piano and muted percussion allowing Cave to sit on stage and spin his tale before the band reaches an unerring crescendo.

Also of note, is a cover of 'Plain Gold Ring', from the late 1950s, a song by Nina Simone, known for her eclectic canon of songs, from old Negro Spirituals and Bob Marley songs to the French Chanson of Jacques Brel. Never considered one of Simone's gold standards, Cave and the band re-work it wonderfully: the song is built up delicately, with only a hint of menace until the band explodes, with Cave screaming and Bargeld weighing in with an ear-splitting, one-chord 'solo' – a moment of pure outrage.

(ALBUM) Compilation *Faraway, So Close!*
9315 Faraway, So Close!
9316 Cassiel's Song
ORIGINAL RELEASE: EMI EMI 8 27216 2, September 1993

COMMENTS: Wim Wenders' disappointing sequel to the 1987 smash *Wings Of Desire, Faraway, So Close!* picks up the story of the angel Cassiel, once again surveying Berlin, this time with a new partner – Nastassja Kinski – an angel called Raphaela who replaced Damiel, now human. As Cassiel observes the changes that have occurred in the intervening years, not many of them for the better, he, too, leaves his wings to take human form. Unfortunately, the film that showed so much promise didn't capture the same breathtaking beauty as its predecessor. Looking undeveloped and rushed, *Faraway, So Close!* served only as a follow-up, and failed to make a mark of its own.

The soundtrack itself fared a little better, but not much. Featuring an original score composed by Laurent Pettigrand, and mixed by Gareth Jones, the soundtrack again partnered Wenders with a familiar assortment of musicians: Laurie Anderson, U2, Lou Reed... Cave appeared in this instance without his Bad Seeds. He added Barry Adamson on timpani for 'Cassiel's Song' and contributed two songs including a re-working of the earlier 'What Can I Give You?'. But somehow, even these two tracks are disappointing. At a time when Cave was ceaselessly raising the bar of his own creativity, his performances here are remarkably flat, making some wonder if Cave operated far better with the members of his band, than he did when striking out on his own.

(SESSION) *And The Ass Saw The Angel* – theatrical version
9317 Sleepy River Piano
9318 Doghead
9319 Pa's Traps
9320 Cosey's Lullaby
9321 Sanctum
9322 The Hobo Church
9323 Sleepy River Swoon
9324 God
9325 Euchrid On The Run
9326 Beth's Sleepy River
9327 Doghead Revisited
9328 Angels
APPENDED TO CD RELEASE
8702 Mah Sanctum
8703 Lamentation
8704 One Autumn
8705 Animal Static
ORIGINAL RELEASE: Mute EUCHRID1CD, 1999

COMMENTS: 1993 saw Mick Harvey, Ed Clayton-Jones and vocalist Katy Beale commissioned to produce music for a theatrical adaptation of Cave's now-ubiquitous *And The Ass Saw The Angel*, a production that was finally staged at South Melbourne's Napier Street Theatre in October. A CD combining the music with the four spoken word extracts previously released alongside *Tender Prey* was issued in 1999.

Probably only interesting to die-hard fans, the disc emerged as a two-fisted combo of spoken word and very lightly accentuated music. Lacking the visuals to enhance the music, however, the score falls horribly flat in places. *Ass*, then, becomes nothing more than an oddity to file away and remember you have.

1994

For Nick Cave, 1994 was a professional watershed, awash with peripheral cries of complete sell-out as he and the band embarked on that year's alternative behemoth, Perry Farrell's Lollapalooza. How exactly did Nick Cave and The Bad Seeds fit into it?

In the massive shake-up of musical mores that rocked America as the 1980s were shattered by the sonic explosions of the 1990s, the advent of Lollapalooza filled a void, brought music to the masses and used the medium to fulfil founder Perry Farrell's overly ambitious dreams. He conceived Lollapalooza not simply as the greatest American festival, but as the ultimate. In so doing, he also became an unwitting participant in the great passing of the mantle, as the exploding tatters of his own Jane's Addiction bowed down to the emergence of the denim denizens of Grunge.

Lollapalooza's origins dated back to Spring 1991. Jane's Addiction were still in the throes of a massive tour. It was a gig with no signs of ending in the foreseeable future, and, truth be told, Perry Farrell was getting cranky. He'd been touring non-stop with his band for years now, and he was tired. But the bookers never stopped booking, the promoters never stopped promoting... only when it became painfully apparent to all that Farrell had reached the end of his tether did anybody sit back. Farrell recalled being told he could do 'whatever I wanted. [They said] "We're giving you the license to do with your tour whatever you want".'

What he wanted was a tour that brought together every arena of art that he considered worthwhile. He wanted stages full of multimedia extravagance, music that spanned generations and genres, rest areas, food stalls, body piercing, and information booths. He wanted every opinion in the world to converge into one massive travelling circus, to take its message to the mobs. He wanted a Lollapalooza.

By 1994, Lollapalooza was the healthiest four-year-old in the land, the excitement building from the moment Farrell announced the new year's line-up, then sat back to laugh while the world debated his choices.

This year was no different. By January he had already sewn up a line-up that stretched from the twin poles of George Clinton and P-Funk to Nick Cave and the Bad Seeds, with Punk japesters Green Day thrown in the middle. Inevitably, such extremes raised many an eyebrow, but the addition of the Smashing Pumpkins certainly calmed a few nerves, and the invitation to Nirvana settled everyone.

Of course, Nirvana would not make it to the party in the end, but the remainder of the bill was settled, for better or for worse. As Cave quickly realized, 'Lollapalooza was really the most destructive thing I've done in my career. This, in a way, really damaged our band. It destroyed some of our love for our own music. I never wanted to do it. [But] the pressure was so great, that we relented in the end.'

He played the shows, of course, and admits that, while he didn't really like the whole festival, he did meet lots of wonderful people within the bands on tour. It was that, he insists, which kept him going throughout the gruelling routine; that, and the knowledge that on the successful back of *Henry's Dream,* the band inched their way closer to hyper-drive. The ensemble was fast becoming a viable commercial outfit and this realization fed into the sessions that spawned another bridge album for Cave – *Let Love In*.

(FILM) *Arisha, The Bear And The Stone Ring*
ORIGINAL RELEASE: 1994

COMMENTS: Short and exceedingly obscure Wim Wenders film with music by Nick Cave And The Bad Seeds.

(RADIO) *Mark Radcliffe Show* UK 14 – 25 March 1994
UNR Do You Love Me?

King Ink in Paris, 1985. (Stills Press Agency / Rex Features)

King Ink in Berlin, 1985. (Bleddyn Butcher / Rex Features)

Performing with the Bad Seeds, 1986. (Fotex / Rex Features)

Cave signing And The Ass Saw The Angel. (Nils Jorgensen / Rex Features)

Cave with Shane MacGowan and Mark E. Smith, January, 1989.
(Bleddyn Butcher / Rex Features)

A portrait from the Tender Prey *era.* (Bleddyn Butcher / Rex Features)

Live in the 1990s. (Fotex / Rex Features)

With PJ Harvey on The White Room, *1996.* (Richard Young / Rex Features)

With Kylie Minogue, Brixton Academy 1996. (Brian Rasic / Rex Features)

At the piano, 1997. (Bleddyn Butcher / Rex Features)

Live in Hamburg, 2001. (ActionPress / Rex Features)

With Susie Bick at Tate Britain, 2001. (Richard Young / Rex Features)

Nick Cave, 20th/21st Century Renaissance Man. (Everett Collection / Rex Features)

UNR Nobody's Baby Now
UNR Loverman
UNR I Let Love In
UNR St Andrew broadcast
UNR St Christina broadcast
UNR St Lawrence broadcast
UNR St Cecilia broadcast
ORIGINAL RELEASE: Unreleased

COMMENTS: With *Let Love In* now just weeks away, the Bad Seeds dropped by the BBC studios to record a quite remarkable session, previewing four of the new songs before Cave alone settled down to four readings from *Butler's Lives Of The Saints*. These were broadcast separately, one a night, between 22-25 March 1994.

(SINGLE) Do You Love Me?
9401a Do You Love Me?
9316 Cassiel's Song
9402 Sail Away
9401 Do You Love Me?
9403 Do You Love Me? (Part 2)
9401b Do You Love Me? (edit)
ORIGINAL RELEASE: Mute MUTE 160, March 1994

COMMENTS: The first single from the forthcoming *Let Love In* LP created a firestorm of interest and collectable edition. In addition to the regular 7-inch issue, the single was also pressed on silver vinyl for a limited run of 1000 copies.
'Do You Love Me?' was a sparkling slab of storytelling, backed with the Bad Seeds' trademark organ and pure sex appeal of Bargeld and Harvey's guitars, a love song of the finest order. It was backed on the CD single with another airing for 'Cassiel's Song' (from *Faraway, So Close!* and the somewhat lesser charms of the album out-take 'Sail Away'). 'Sail Away' was also included on a CD gifted to subscribers of the Japanese Fanzine *Ich Bin Ein Enzym.*

(TV) *Later...with Jools Holland,* UK 14 April 1994
UNR Red Right Hand
UNR Thirsty Dog
ORIGINAL RELEASE: Unreleased

COMMENTS: Always an arena for interesting performances, the band once again stepped on Holland's stage to present these two songs.

(ALBUM) *Let Love In*
Line-up: Nick Cave (vocals & keyboards); Mick Harvey (guitar); Blixa Bargeld (guitar); Martyn P Casey (bass); Conway Savage (keyboards); Thomas Wydler (drums).

9401 Do You Love Me?
9404 Nobody's Baby Now
9405 Loverman
9406 Jangling Jack
9407 Red Right Hand
9408 I Let Love In
9409 Thirsty Dog
9410 Ain't Gonna Rain Anymore
9411 Lay Me Low
9403 Do You Love Me? (Part 2)
ORIGINAL RELEASE: Mute STUMM 123, April 1994

COMMENTS: Produced by Tony Cohen and The Bad Seeds, *Let Love In* remains one of Cave's greatest triumphs. The band's sound soared to a level befitting the majesty of the songs, aided by a veritable wealth of guests. Rowland S Howard and Beasts Of Bourbon's Tex Perkins adding backing vocals to 'Do You Love Me?' and the Triffids' David McComb added his own voice to 'Lay Me Low'. The album marked the first time, too, that Dirty Three's Warren Ellis stepped up to the plate with his violins, adding unplumbed depths to 'Do You Love Me? (part 2)' and 'Ain't Gonna Rain Anymore'.

The album was a set of staggering proportions, becoming the perfect addendum to the songs on *Henry's Dream,* in as much as they softened that album's cruelty and supplanted it with the pain and longing of love. Very straightforward, Cave shoots from the hip on this one. Indeed, *Let Love In* is the album with which Cave says, 'I learned that you don't necessarily have to squeeze words out of yourself and twist them around constantly and obsessively like I do.'

Let Love In is a dissection of that most basic and often base of human emotions, opened up by Cave's lyrics and carved into beautiful, sculptural tones by the Bad Seeds.

Intense, haunting, heartbreakingly beautiful, this album was a turning point for Cave, as he left behind some of the crash and bang of days past for a more ethereal sound. It was an album that touched nearly everyone who came into contact with it. It made new fans of people who pretty much didn't know what Cave and the Bad Seeds had been up to for the last decade. And anyone who tried vainly picking *Let Love In* apart was disappointed. This was something that couldn't be ignored. Indeed, it scythed its way straight to the soul.

Much of the album's strength was drawn from the sheer weight of preparation that went into it. Cave explained, 'Before we actually recorded, we knew we had six or seven good songs, and before I started writing, there was a large backlog of musical ideas sitting behind me.' It was easy, then, for producer Tony Cohen to come in and pick up with the band when the time came to lay down the album. After so many years with the Bad Seeds, it was second nature for Cohen to step in and immediately see just where the band were headed, and then act accordingly.

Again, the contribution of the Bad Seeds cannot be underestimated here.

Conway Savage and Martyn P Casey were already an integral part of the band but both came to the fore on this album. Savage's light and melodious touch on the piano is given more of an outlet and Casey had matured into a bass player of sophistication and strength and in future it would not be unusual to find a song like 'Do You Love Me?' hinging round one of his inventive bass lines. He drives a song like 'Loverman' too, another stupendous love song with Cave at his most passionate, while the band create a truly awe-inspiring cacophony. Sandwiched between these two monsters is the tender (and cruel) 'Nobody's Baby Now', which has one of Cave's most beautiful lyrics and a fine melody.

Arguably, the album's centrepieces are 'Red Right Hand' and 'I Let Love In', both glorious creations. 'Red Right Hand' is one of Cave's most stylish songs, a jaunty but supremely sinister work, led by Casey's bass and the Hammond organ, but punctuated by some sublime guitar work and skilful percussion. 'I Let Love In' is a song of rare grandeur that has faint echoes of Morricone within, but also features some of Blixa Bargeld's most atmospheric and beguiling guitar lines. Perhaps outstripping all of these songs, though, is the hugely ambitious reprise of 'Do You Love Me?', dominated by the magical violin of the Dirty Three's Warren Ellis, soon to become indispensable to Nick Cave and the Bad Seeds.

Recorded at Townhouse Studios in London during September 1993 and mixed in Melbourne that December, the album's appearance in April 1994 proved a commercial watershed for Cave, reaching #12 on the UK charts. In America, though, the mainstream was still out of his grasp, although *Let Love In* did bring him out of obscurity to be crowned king of the alternative underground. Helped along by Lollapalooza, it became hip to like Nick Cave. And, although the year's tours may have damaged Cave's love of his craft, audiences, it seemed, couldn't get enough of the lean besuited spectre.

(SINGLE) Nobody's Baby Now
9404 Nobody's Baby Now
9408 I Let Love In
ORIGINAL RELEASE: Mute/Elektra PRCD 8959, 1994

COMMENTS: US only promo with insert of Lollapalooza dates.

(TV) *MTV's Most Wanted* US 23 June 1994
UNR I Let Love In
UNR The Mercy Seat
ORIGINAL RELEASE: Unreleased

COMMENTS: But most wanted by whom?
(SINGLE) Loverman
9405a Loverman
9412 B-side

9103 (I'll Love You) Till The End Of The World – limited edition picture disc
+ Australian single
ORIGINAL RELEASE: Mute MUTE 169, July 1994

COMMENTS: Although 'Loverman' didn't reach the charts, the song packed as much power as any of Cave's past singles; open to myriad interpretations, but at its core, a simply exquisite, dangerously daring devotion.

Live, it was transformed; playing to the audience, Cave substituted the key lyric 'murder' for 'molest,' to portray virtue in the face of pain. Cave may have been writing stories for himself by now, but he also certainly knew what his fans wanted, expected, to hear. Fans may have flocked before, but 'Loverman' brought forth a new wave of Gothic girly-girls, clutching CDs, and in their world, promoting Cave to the status of Elvis.

The single's B-side, the aptly titled 'B-side', was a nineteen-minute opus of 23 improvised snippets of music that Nick Cave and The Bad Seeds recorded directly onto DAT tape over the last two years in the studio. A self-indulgent selection of junk (one that echoed the construction of 'Tower Of Song), the performance nevertheless provided a tantalizing glimpse into a part of the band's process rarely witnessed by anyone on the outside. Cobbled together by Mick Harvey and David McQuarrie in Germany and Australia, the 'song' featured contributions from Rowland S Howard, Tom Stern and Gallon Drunk's James Johnston.

The snippets are as follows: 'God's Hotel'; 'Do You Love Me?'; 'Sugar-Coated Place Called Love'; 'Kiss Me In The Morning'; 'Nobody's Baby Now'; 'A-side'; 'B-side'; 'C-Side'; 'Loverman'; 'Born To Be Your Loverman'; 'Take The "O" Out Of Country'; 'Jangling Jack'; 'Sex Appeal'; 'Where The Action Is'; 'Blow That Babe Away'; 'I Let Love In'; 'Dadaladaladaladawn'; 'Thirsty Dog'; 'Man Of Steel'; 'It's A Crazy World'; 'Ain't Gonna Rain Anymore'; 'Sweet Maria'; 'Lay Me Low'; 'Vanilla Essence'; 'Do You Love Me? (Part 2)'.

(TV) *Late Night With Conan O'Brian* US, 9 August 1994
UNR Red Right Hand
ORIGINAL RELEASE: Unreleased

(LIVE) Lollapalooza, Houston, Texas, 19 August 1994
9413 What A Wonderful World
ORIGINAL RELEASE: Compilation *Loss Leaders Revisited*, Warner Brothers PRO CD 7795, 1995

COMMENTS: This nifty promo-only compilation CD, available in a limited run of just 3,500 copies, features Nick Cave and The Flaming Lips performing 'What A Wonderful World'. The same performance would also be included on the Flaming Lips' for-friends-only *It's A Hellfire Christmas* compilation and remains, sadly, unreleased to the general public.

(SINGLE) Red Right Hand
9407 Red Right Hand

9414 That's What Jazz Is To Me
9415 Where The Action Is
ORIGINAL RELEASE: Mute MUTE 172 , October 1994

COMMENTS: The third single to be pulled from the album is backed by one-and-a-half new tracks, 'That's What Jazz Is To Me' and (reprised from 'B-side') 'Where The Action Is', both were recorded in Berlin, again direct to DAT tape. As they had with 'B-side', Mick Harvey and David McQuarrie later edited and fiddled those tapes into their finished form at Studio 301 in Sydney.

Both B-sides were completely improvised numbers – screw-arounds in the studio. 'That's What Jazz Means To Me' hinges on splayed piano, and a rather gormless 'Jazz' improv organ over which Cave spouts and beats and lays down a cool rap. One can almost imagine the snapping of fingers and black berets nodding in time to the song's off-kilter beat. 'Where The Action Is', on the other hand, is a slightly sinister amalgamation of 'Red Right Hand' and a noodling, free-form composition.

For collectors, this single was released in a limited edition run of just 2000 copies on 7-inch blood red vinyl.

(FILM) *Jonas In The Desert*
ORIGINAL RELEASE: 1994

COMMENTS: Cave turned his attentions back to acting, briefly, for a quick role in Peter Sempel's *Jonas In The Desert,* bungee-jumping while 'Christina The Astonishing' plays over the shot. The song repeats in full later on. Also appearing are bits of 'Blind Lemon Jefferson' and 'Wild World', while Cave, Bargeld and Kevin Coyne are credited with composing the score. The German/US split production, filmed in both black and white and colour, was created over nearly a decade and provided an in-depth documentary of Lithuanian filmmaker/poet Jonas Mekas.

(TV) *Poetry Nation* UK 6 October 1994
UNR Infant Sorrow
ORIGINAL RELEASE: Unreleased

COMMENTS: Nick Cave reads the William Blake poem on this BBC production.

(TV) *September Songs,* Canada 1994
9416 Mack The Knife
9417 Mack The Knife (version #2)
ORIGINAL RELEASE: 9416 unreleased; 9417 on Various Artists collection *September Songs: The Music Of Kurt Weill*, Sony Classics SK 63046, August 1997

COMMENTS: This Emmy-winning Canadian documentary, running just 89 minutes and directed by Larry Weinstein, was an affectionate portrait of German theatre icon Kurt Weill. As opposed to straightforward documentary, the film offered up a number of performers covering in song and spoken word some of Weill's best loved work, among them PJ Harvey, Lou Reed, Elvis Costello and Nick Cave, covering that old familiar chest-beater 'Mack The Knife' in a fashion poised somewhere between the pure pop of Bobby Darin and the undiluted malice of the Psychedelic Furs' earlier versions. A slightly different cut, version #2, would appear on the *September Songs* tribute CD in 1997.

1995

With the band joined by Jim Sclavunos (a member at one time or another of The Cramps, Congo Norvell, Sonic Youth and Teenage Jesus & The Jerks), *Murder Ballads* would consume much of the year, despite the fact that many of the album's songs had gestated during the sessions for the previous album and the tours that followed.

This wilfully extreme album, which seemed to have been a long-cherished project, saw Cave surprise many with his latest choice of collaborators. The appearance of Shane MacGowan in all his ragged glory was predictable but juxtaposing him with two women from opposite ends of the musical spectrum – Kylie Minogue and PJ Harvey – was something that nobody was prepared for.

Cave would be romantically linked to both women during the next two years and, as the rumour mill churned, speculation of his private life at times threatened to overshadow musical masterpieces he and the band were turning out.

(LIVE) Dirty Three – Brisbane Zoo, Australia, January 1995
9501 Running Scared
ORIGINAL RELEASE: Anchor & Hope AHX01S, 1998

COMMENTS: Cave joined the Dirty Three onstage at this show, for a version of 'Running Scared' that was subsequently released on *Sharks*, a highly sought after and exceedingly rare CD single sold during the Dirty Three's 1998 tours.

(ALBUM) Original soundtrack *Batman Forever*
9502 There Is A Light
ORIGINAL RELEASE: Atlantic 7567-82759-2, June 1995

COMMENTS: Despite Cave's reluctance to continue on in the popular glare of the mainstream spotlight, he did contribute a song, 'There Is A Light', to the *Batman Forever* soundtrack. With music by Talk Talk's Tim Friese-Greene, and additional guitars from James Johnston, the song was recorded at Maison Rouge and Rubbery Studios in London.

With a readily marketable stack of acts on the soundtrack, Massive Attack, Seal, U2, PJ Harvey and the Flaming Lips among them, the album had a good showing in the charts, reaching #5 in the US. That feat thrust Cave even further into the spotlight, firming up a position he still continued to insist, made him uncomfortable.

'I'm sure there's some terrible karmic debt I'll have to pay for doing that, waiting around the corner. I don't feel I've ever done something I've not wanted to do, for money in my career, except the Batman thing.'

It was Greene who roped him, presumably kicking and screaming, into the project, calling up Cave one day and asking if he would co-write and sing on one song. Cave agreed – 'I'd always wanted to work with Tim.' But he scarcely gave the partnership a chance. 'I called him back 25 minutes later,' Cave revealed, 'and said "it's a pile of shit, but it's written".'

Indeed, 'There Is A Light' has a dark, alternative vibe that's far more in keeping with the soundtrack's intentions than with Cave's own inclinations – and that was precisely what the album's masterminds required. Besides, how hip it was to have Cave and Tim Friese-Greene – himself at the peak of his own, highly atmospheric career, following his production credits on Catherine Wheel's stunning *Chrome* and *Ferment* albums. Furthermore, while the song itself was unquestionably humdrum, it would certainly have been interesting to pair Friese-Greene with the Bad Seeds in the studio, just to see what could have come of it. In the event, their only other known collaboration fell within the remit of another soundtrack, 1997's *Mojo*, for which they co-wrote the title track.

(SINGLE) Anita Lane
9502 The World's A Girl
9503 I Love You…Nor Do I
9504 Bedazzled
ORIGINAL RELEASE: Mute MUTE 177, June 1995

COMMENTS: Cave contributed two tracks to Anita Lane's latest release, a three-track single produced by Flood, with instrumentation from Mick Harvey. Of these, 'I Love You…Nor Do I' is a not-too-serious send up of Serge Gainsbourg's classic duet with Jane Birkin, 'Je T'Aime' – although the original was far better, with Lane's vamping in particular sounding overwrought and just plain silly. 'Bedazzled', on the other hand, is positively spectacular; smoother, far more believable and, though it is sacrilegious to say so, at least the equal of Peter Cook and Dudley Moore's fabulous original.

(SINGLE) Where The Wild Roses Grow
9505 Where The Wild Roses Grow
9506 The Ballad Of Robert Moore And Betty Coltrane
9507 The Willow Garden
9508 Where The Wild Roses Grow (Bargeld vocal)
ORIGINAL RELEASE: 9504-06 on Mute MUTE 185, October 1995; 9507 on *B-sides & Rarities*

COMMENTS: And so it begins. Cave's master plan to distance himself from his own, growing reputation as a mainstream softy, backfired horribly with the success of this first single from the forthcoming *Murder Ballads*. Nick and Kylie, Kylie and Nick – the image of the two standing side by side was hard to come to grips with. But still this now immortal single made the UK Top 20, aided by a memorable performance on *Top Of The Pops*, and an hysterically characteristic UK media campaign which highlighted the accompanying video. Australian actress turned singer, Kylie Minogue, after all, was a figure of wholesome delight in the eyes of the British press, and the sight of Cave stoving in her head with a rock, and then caressing her corpse as it lay in a snake-infested pond, was too much for even the doughtiest tabloid hack.

The song itself was a triumph, a grisly, gristly ghost story ripping Catherine and Heathcliff off the moors and into the river, covered with shadow and moss – and remained so a decade later, following the release (on *B-sides & Rarities*) of the band's original version of the song, with Blixa Bargeld laying down the guide vocal that Minogue would follow.

But, in light of Cave's recent comments to the contrary, one does have to ponder precisely how 'uncommercial' it is, recording a duet with one of the hottest female artists in Britain at the time. Cave himself admits that following the *Top Of The Pops* performance, he was stopped in the street by a child demanding his autograph!

'You have to believe me when I say this,' Cave implored later, 'but we had absolutely no idea "Wild Roses" would be a hit, nobody did. We thought it would be one of the world's great flops.' The fact that Kylie had never had a flop in her life obviously hadn't crossed anyone's mind. Cave had never had a hit. Presumably the two would simply cancel one another out.

He continued, 'I truly believe that I'm able to carry on doing what I'm doing because (*Batman Returns* presumably notwithstanding) I haven't done things in a cynical way. I think my fans, the ones who really like what I do, and have done for a long time, trust that what I'm doing is for the right reasons. If they hear that I'm doing something that raises an eyebrow, they can trust that it's gonna be alright...like the Kylie thing, for example.

'I see myself as being in the tradition – and I'm not saying I'm as good as these people or whatever...the tradition of those very lyrical individualists who exist outside of the mainstream of what's going on, Leonard Cohen, Peter Hammill, Marc Almond...sometimes they seem to be relevant, and other times they're hopelessly irrelevant to what's going on.' Right now, Nick Cave was relevant. But despite all the evidence, the Lollas and Batmen and Batears and all, he hoped he wouldn't remain so for long.

Of the single's B-sides, 'The Willow Garden', sung by pianist Conway Savage, was little more than an early version of 'Where The Wild Roses Grow', leaving 'The Ballad of Robert Moore and Betty Coltrane' (featuring Gallon Drunk's Terry Edwards on sax) to round out the package. It was, of course, an up-tempo rollicking murder ballad that would have been well at home on *Murder Ballads* but ultimately lacked the grizzly punch of some of the album's stronger touchstones, most notably 'O'Malley's Bar' and 'Stagger Lee.' This ballad would remain a B-side only, until 2005 when it was re-released on the *B-sides & Rarities* compilation.

(TV) *Top Of The Pops* UK 5 October 1995
UNR Where The Wild Roses Grow
ORIGINAL RELEASE: Unreleased

COMMENTS: Duet with Kylie Minogue. The pair would repeat their *TOTP* performance the following week – same song, different version.

(TV) *Nulle Part Ailleurs*, France, 6 October 1995
UNR Where The Wild Roses Grow
ORIGINAL RELEASE: Unreleased

(TV) *MTV's Most Wanted*, USA, 13 October 1995
UNR Where The Wild Roses Grow
UNR Death Is Not The End
ORIGINAL RELEASE: Unreleased

COMMENTS: Live performance with Kylie Minogue and Shane MacGowan.

1996

Although the early release of 'Where The Wild Roses Grow' proved to be by far the most commercial thing Cave had yet done, helped in part by multiple performances of the song with Kylie Minogue at shows and on television, the critical firestorm still kept Cave in a bit of a temper, as he followed through on his *Let Love In* era threats of releasing what he perceived to be the least commercial thing he could ever do: a collection of murder songs which had been kicking around in his head for years. Gigging was still a priority and Cave and the Bad Seeds, which now included occasional appearances from Dirty Three's Warren Ellis, punctuated the year with a number of stellar shows – July's Quart Festival in Norway among them.

By 1996, Cave had been delivering his socio-sexual polemic for close to two decades, at the same time as constructing a protective layer of fan-dom which surely takes his pronouncements more seriously than he ever has. You need only follow the twisted turns to which he has subjected his muse to understand that; either that, or he really is the self-defeating, self-destructive, and ultimately self-immolating SOB whom doomed Gothic consumptives have dreamed he was. *Murder Ballads,* was something like an answer to such prayers. Whatever cloak he wore, live the band were unbeatable, and shows during this year reflected their playfulness, as now Mick Harvey stood in for Minogue to duet with Cave on 'Wild Roses', though Kylie herself did turn up to a few Australian shows.

(LIVE) Big Day Out, Australia, January 1996
9601 Red Right Hand
9602 Where The Wild Roses Grow

9603 The Mercy Seat
ORIGINAL RELEASE: *Ritual Habitual* VHS, Polygram Video PVA 1232, 1996

COMMENTS: This two-hour film, highlighting moments both on and backstage from 1996's Australian Big Day Out Festival, features live footage from the band's set plus backstage footage filmed by Nick Cave.

(ALBUM) *Murder Ballads*
Line-up: Nick Cave (vocals & keyboards); Mick Harvey (guitar); Blixa Bargeld (guitar); Martyn P Casey (bass); Conway Savage (keyboards); Thomas Wydler (drums).
9604 Song Of Joy
9605 Stagger Lee
9606 Henry Lee
9607 Lovely Creature
9505 Where The Wild Roses Grow
9608 The Curse Of Millhaven
9609 The Kindness Of Strangers
9610 Crow Jane
9611 O'Malley's Bar
9612 Death Is Not The End
JAPAN CD BONUS TRACKS
9506 The Ballad Of Robert Moore And Betty Coltrane
9507 The Willow Garden
9613 King Kong Kitchee Kitchee Ki-Mi-O

ORIGINAL RELEASE: Mute STUMM 138, January 1996

COMMENTS: Multiple releases heralded the arrival of *Murder Ballads* at the beginning of 1996. Regular and limited edition digipaks were available in the UK; in Japan, the album had the singles' B-sides as tracks. Not to be outdone, Mute also issued two different four-track promo samplers, the first with 'Where The Wild Roses Grow', 'Lovely Creature', 'Death Is Not The End', and 'Henry Lee' (Mute RCD 138); the second featuring 'The Curse Of Millhaven', 'Stagger Lee', 'Henry Lee' and 'Death Is Not The End' (Mute PCD Stumm 138).

Cave had been drafting the songs that comprised the album for quite some time, indeed, many took their initial gestation during the sessions for *Let Love In*. Cave recalled that 'I went into another studio and worked away on quite a few of these songs. I took the tape home and I really liked the way it sounded. I abhor the mixing process. I don't have the patience for it, so I find myself going off and doing something else.'

Refuting his now growing reputation as an alternative Leonard Cohen, Cave continued, 'I really didn't want anything more to do with my problems. The idea was really to make a record where I could stand outside of it... and just write a lot of stories. The idea that it would be a record of murder ballads has been around for years with us. It's been around since the beginning of the Bad Seeds.' And the songs on *Murder Ballads* are full of good, clean, wholesome fun.

'[We wanted to] make a record for our fans...' Cave's masterplan, if he was to be believed in interviews at the time, was to have this album flop. He expected *Murder Ballads* to fail, and in so doing, take some of the newly directed spotlight off the band.

'The record was intended to kind of cut the wheat from the chaff,' Cave insisted. 'I thought our popularity was kind of getting a bit out of control with *Let Love In*. I don't want to be very popular. Basically, we tried to make an extremely difficult record, which would turn a lot of people off us. We tried to make kind of like a Bob Dylan's *Self Portrait*.... But of course it didn't happen that way.' He even included a Dylan track on the set, *Down In The Groove*'s 'Death is Not The End', roping in a host of friends and band mates to give the song a remarkably twisted 'We Are The World' feel – laughing about that song later, Cave singled out Blixa Bargeld's contribution. 'He sounds like Peter Lorre.'

And still, the masterplan disintegrated. *Murder Ballads* was a wonderfully morbid and humorous collection of beautiful, evil little songs. In spite of the grimness and gore that permeated every groove of the record, this album would give Cave his highest chart position ever, reaching #8 in February. His desire to reclaim obscurity had spectacularly backfired.

But this is not to say that the album gained widespread approval. Indeed, some sections of the press were far from enamoured of the project. *Mojo*, in particular, were disparaging, saying that as a whole, it could be called *Nick Cave Has Lost It*.

Mixing the traditional murder ballads with his own take on death songs, Cave constructed a seamless montage of gruesome ends and twisted lives. Part morality play, part cautionary children's chapbook, part true crime case file, the songs on *Murder Ballads* evoked the best of the Blues and traditional folksong, mixed with the finest of Cave's own stash of stories.

While nearly every song from the album was an unerring masterpiece in and of itself, there were several tracks in particular that rose a cut above the rest. The bleakly ethereal 'Lovely Creature' was made far more mysterious thanks to Mick Harvey's wind organ, and Katharine Blake's otherworldly backing vocals, the meandering tempo proving that a song didn't need to be of epic length to impart an epic story. The lyrics themselves harken back to the grizzly old ghost tales ('King Henry', 'Tam Linn') most recently heard during the late 1960s/early

1970s electric folk revival.

'The Curse Of Millhaven', meanwhile, saw the band take a different approach entirely. Built upon Warren Ellis' violin and accordion, and Jim Scalvunos' tambourine, the song drops any pretence at sleepy storytelling, to instead become a rich gypsy folk tale – backed by the band's ubiquitous organ of course. With backing vocals courtesy of the (deliberately misspelt) Moron Tabernacle Choir (the band and friends), the song chronicles the confessions of fifteen-year-old Lottie who lays proud claims to having grim-reaped her way through the entire town. Perhaps if she'd had Prozac a little sooner....

'O'Malley's Bar,' too, is a wonderfully horrific butcher's list of atrocities that stretches out across three dozen verses, yet the stomach-turning rendering of the traditional 'Stagger Lee' surpassed even this. Long burned and buried within the mythology of America's deepest south, the 1895 slaughter of the wicked pimp Lee Shelton (over a hat) has been recounted in story and song almost from the moment the incident occurred. Shelton – Stack Lee, Stagolee and Stagger Lee, as he is variously nicknamed – promptly became a folk hero, with his misadventures provoking some wildly varied retellings from Bob Dylan, Cab Calloway, the Grateful Dead and Tina Turner, to name just a few.

But Cave's unearthing of the song and its hero also stands as a deliberate throwback to a stage in his own band's history that they themselves had now outgrown; though nobody could have realised it, the whole album was intended as a final farewell to a style of music, and a twisting of folklore, that they had excelled in.

Mute would precede the album's release with the promo interview disc *Murder Ballads: The Interview* (Mute CAVESPEAKCD1) a forty-minute interview by Jessamy Calkin. Questions are on a booklet, answers are on the disc.

(SINGLE) Henry Lee
9606 Henry Lee
9613 King Kong Kitchee Kitchee Ki-Mi-O
9614 Knoxville Girl
ORIGINAL RELEASE: Mute MUTE 189, February 1996

COMMENTS: The album's second single proved to be just as memorable as its predecessor. Indeed, this moody duet with PJ Harvey eclipsed 'Where The Wild Roses Grow' with its subtlety. Roses may have been slick, but 'Henry Lee' was gravely beautiful, sweetly mournful. With a focus that lay on vocal harmonies, the band crafted gorgeous music for the song, but let it lie in the background, with Conway Savage's piano and Thomas Wydler's brushed drums in particular adding a soft hush to the proceedings.

That PJ Harvey and Nick Cave had exquisite chemistry is obvious – a fact played out in the tenderness of the video, and even in the gorgeous photo of the two that graced the single's cover. The personal relationship that lay behind that twining, of course, added further frisson to the visual images; and, while Cave has rarely spoken publicly about their relationship rock history has long since raised their love story to such mythological levels that, like those other star-crossed liaisons into which our idols have thrown themselves (Mick and Marianne, Rod and Britt, Brett and Justine), it probably means more to us, the public, than it did for the lovers themselves.

'King Kong Kitchee Kitchee Ki-Mi-O', meanwhile, again utilized the tongue-in-cheek talents of *Murder Ballads'* Moron Tabernacle Choir to grubby up and dirty down this somewhat lasciviously rendered retelling of the traditional 'Froggy Went A Courting'. Recorded specifically as a B-side, a third track, 'Knoxville Girl', toned the mood down somewhat, a down home, countrified number that numbered just two performers, Cave and James Johnston picking an acoustic guitar. Not bad, but it was interesting to see this newest working relationship more firmly cemented.

(TV) *The White Room* UK 24 February 1996
UNR Stagger Lee
UNR Henry Lee
ORIGINAL RELEASE: Unreleased

(RADIO) *Mark Radcliffe* UK 26 February 1996
UNR Henry Lee
9615 O'Malley's Bar (part 1)
9616 O'Malley's Bar (part 2)
9617 O'Malley's Bar (part 3)
9618 O'Malley's Bar (reprise)
ORIGINAL RELEASE: *B-sides & Rarities* , March 2005

COMMENTS: Although part 1 of this sprawling performance was originally released on a freebie cassette given away with the July 1996 issue of *Vox* (VOX RAD 9799), it was not until the appearance of *B-sides & Rarities* that it received a complete airing. It was a crazy performance, a little ragged but, in its own way, even better than the studio version, sounding more like a guy spouting the most absurd braggadocio than the slick production of a classic album cut.

(TV) *Nulle Part Ailleurs* France 29 February 1996
UNR Stagger Lee
ORIGINAL RELEASE: Unreleased

(ALBUM) Compilation Songs *In The Key Of X*
9619 Time Jesum Transeuntum Et Non Riverentum
9407 Red Right Hand
ORIGINAL RELEASE: Warner Brothers 9 460799-2, March 1996

COMMENTS: 1996 saw the *X-Files* become the year's greatest TV hit – a cult favourite that smashed all the boundaries between the dork of sci-fi and hipper mainstream culture. It was a triumph. The compilation/soundtrack album for the show collected songs from a varied pool of artists, including Cave and his 'Red Right Hand', from the *Let Love In* LP.

But there was more kids, there was more. This was the beginning of the era of the *hidden track*. Back up the disc seven minutes before Mark Snow's title music and find track zero – an original composition by Cave and The Dirty Three, 'Time Jesum Transeuntum Et Non Riverentum'. Or, if your Latin's a little rusty, Cave pretty much spells the happy little title within the song; 'dread the passage of Jesus, for he does not return.' With Cave's spoken word and Ellis' haunting violin, the song may not have pleased *Files* fans, but it was sure to please Cave's and Ellis': it's a beautiful bridge between the two bands.

Unfortunately, CD technology of the time did not always allow listeners to locate the track – a flaw that also befell releases by the Astronettes and the Adverts. Dismayed by this turn of events, Cave resurrected the performance for inclusion on *B-sides & Rarities*. However, this still left fans to try and find the Dirty Three's own version of the *X-Files* theme which was similarly hidden away.

(RADIO) *The Proms* UK 28 July 1996
UNR The Flesh Made Word
UNR Into My Arms
ORIGINAL RELEASE: Unreleased

COMMENTS: A BBC Radio 3 broadcast featuring one of Cave's 'lectures' together with a preview of a new song 'Into My Arms'. 'The Flesh Made Word' is an illuminating and beautifully written piece, part-memoir, part-treatise. Cave looks back on the darkest days of The Birthday Party and seems to make a clear distinction between that era and the one he is now in: 'I closed the Old Testament and opened up the New.' Even to people that were familiar with his work may have been surprised here, about his depth of feeling for Christ and God, and it was clear that there was more to come.

(ALBUM) Tex Perkins *Far Be It From Me*
9620 Two Wrongs
ORIGINAL RELEASE: Polydor 533 062-2, July 1996

COMMENTS: One of Australia's most beloved contemporary Blues and Country musicians, Tex Perkins had already created a niche for himself within the confines of The Cruel Sea and Beasts Of Bourbon. *Far Be It From Me* marked his solo debut. Cave co-wrote 'Two Wrongs'.

(LIVE) Lollipop Festival, Sweden, 26-27 July 1996
9621 Rainy Night In Soho
ORIGINAL RELEASE: Lollipop 96 SIBBAN Waxegord 002, 1996

COMMENTS: A two-day festival, in Lida Friluftsgard, just outside Stockholm, Sweden, the Lollipop festival, like its American brethren, brought together some of the year's greatest. Cave and The Bad Seeds were joined by acts as varied as the

Dirty Three, Maria McKee, Prodigy, Bob Dylan, the Hellacopters and Black Grape.

Much of the show was recorded, and a promo CD was manufactured, featuring highlights of various performers' sets – Cave donated an airing for his favourite Pogues song. The resultant disc was scarcely available to the general public, although 10 lucky festival-goers would subsequently receive one, via a convoluted on-site competition.

(ALBUM) Barry Adamson *Oedipus Schmoedipus*
9622 The Sweetest Embrace
ORIGINAL RELEASE: Mute STUMM 134, September 1996

COMMENTS: After leaving the Bad Seeds in 1987, Adamson returned to one of his most beloved passions and began writing music that would fit within the confines of film, whether there were frames to be found or not. Following his successful 1989 debut, *Moss Side Story,* Adamson made the leap to conventional film scoring during the 1990s, contributing to *Gas Food Lodging,* and *Delusion* among others. In 1996, though, he returned to the moody noir that had informed his own work with *Oedipus Schmoedipus,* essentially creating a score for a film that didn't, and wouldn't, ever exist. And with the likes of Pulp's Jarvis Cocker and Nick Cave on board to co-write and sing a couple of tracks, Adamson's noir-beat took a most delightful turn. 'The Sweetest Embrace' is a finely-crafted collaboration, arguably the best Cave has been involved in as it highlights the best facets of both artist: Adamson's endless invention as a composer and Cave's direct emotion.

(ALBUM) Current 93 *All The Pretty Little Horses*
9623 All The Pretty Little Horses
9624 Patripassian

ORIGINAL RELEASE: Durto 030 CD, October 1996

COMMENTS: Cave was a featured vocalist on Current 93's *All The Pretty Little Horses* and, if Cave had been longing for a return to obscurity, well, this was definitely the way to go.

The album was the centrepiece of founder David Tibet's *The Inmost Light* trilogy and remains that band's finest ever set. The title track, a long familiar lullaby, is exquisitely off-kilter English, something that Current 93 did so well, and Cave's participation on such a faithful rendering, his voice a reassuring contrast to Tibet's own sibilant whisper, was comforting. Cave's other contribution was a spoken word litany recited over the ghostly chorals on 'Patripassian', a mass for the divine, or the divinely lunatic.

(ALBUM) The Witches *Undercover*

9625 Shivers
ORIGINAL RELEASE: NMC 201772, 1996

COMMENTS: A remarkable coup for this Israeli band, as they resuscitated the Boys Next Door's 'Shivers', and then persuaded Cave to lend some vocals: possibly the first time he'd thought about the song since 1979 (sadly his largess did not extend to the video clip though he would turn up in the Dirty Three's 'Everything's Fucked' video from 1996).

(ALBUM) Original soundtrack *To Have And To Hold*
9626 To Have And To Hold
9627 The Jungle Of Love
9628 Candlelit Bedroom
9629 Luther
9630 A House In The Jungle
9631 Delerium
9632 The River At Night
9633 Mourning Song
9634 Romantic Theme
9635 Snow Vision
9636 Rose
9637 The Clouds
9638 Noah's Funeral
9639 The Flight
9640 Kate Leaves
9641 We're Coming-The Riot
9642 Murder
9643 The Red Dress
9644 I Threw It All Away
9645 To Have And To Hold End Titles
9646 Gangster Bone

ORIGINAL RELEASE: Mute IONIC 15, October 1996

COMMENTS: Recorded at Melbourne's Sing Sing studios in November 1995, the Cave/ Bargeld/Harvey-composed soundtrack to John Hillcoat's latest film, stands as one of their most adventurous extra-curricular collaborations, with the album enhanced by the appearance of the legendary Scott Walker, for a dynamic Barry Adamson-arranged version of Bob Dylan's 'I Threw It All Away'. Walker, the definitive rock recluse had only recently returned to the music scene with his momentous and mind-boggling *Tilt* album – so this collaboration tends to overshadow the rest of the album, which is a shame.

Set in Papua, New Guinea, Hillcoat's movie of love bordering on obsessive and mindless violence was well cradled by the score – which, in turn, really doesn't make much sense on its own; the music and effects need the humid backdrop of jungle and love to set the stage. The casual Cave fan probably won't think much of it, and nor will anyone who hasn't actually seen the film. But it remains a marvellous score, and would be something of a shock to anyone who bought this after 'Where The Wild Roses Go'.

Cave would be involved in two other movie projects during 1996, playing a pimp in Michael Hausman's *Rhinoceros Hunting In Budapest*; and submitting himself to an interview – by a film-maker without any questions – in Malga Kubiak's *Baby Trouble Hole*.

1997

With Warren Ellis now a *de facto* Bad Seed, the band set about making an album that established Nick Cave as an artist of major stature. *The Boatman's Call* was above all else, a mature work with mature themes. There was a slow, stately pace to all the songs, rigidly adhered to throughout the album, as were the themes of love addressed to different women. People either loved or hated it. The press loved it, mostly; hard-core fans loved it, and new fans loved it. But, beneath all that love there were grumbles, and one reviewer despised the album so much that he used his copy of the promo cassette to keep his window propped open.

(SINGLE) Into My Arms
9701 Into My Arms
9702 Little Empty Boat
9703 Right Now, I'm A Roaming
ORIGINAL RELEASE: Mute MUTE 192, January 1997

COMMENTS: Those that hadn't caught Cave on tour for the past few years were in for a mighty surprise as his latest single appeared on the racks at the end of January 1997. Backed by sparse piano and bass alone, Cave stripped the Bad Seeds out of the mix altogether. Gone was the jangle and the roaring passion of old, to be replaced by a man who sounded as if he was singing from his heart to an audience of one.

This new sound was heralded by many as the big breakthrough they'd been waiting for. The band had been regaling audiences with songs that would eventually shape the forthcoming *The Boatman's Call* for several years now. 'Into My Arms' itself was a live staple that could be dated back to 1995, while it was also previewed at the BBC radio *Proms* the previous year.

Ubiquitous on radio over the next few months, 'Into My Arms' was included on the soundtrack to the 1997 film *Zero Effect*, although it would be most poignantly rendered when Cave sang it on 27 November, at friend Michael Hutchence's funeral.

Cave and Hutchence had met in London and had become close friends. 'Michael was a good friend of mine. We liked each other very much, but we came from different places musically, obviously, and I think we both understood that, and we didn't go into each other's music all that much. He was a very beautiful guy with a generous spirit, and he was very honest about things to me, and I appreciated that.'

(ALBUM) *The Boatman's Call*
Line-up: Nick Cave (vocals & keyboards); Mick Harvey (guitar); Blixa Bargeld (guitar); Martyn P Casey (bass); Conway Savage (keyboards); Thomas Wydler (drums); Warren Ellis (violin); Jim Scalvunos (percussion).
9701 Into My Arms
9704 Lime Tree Arbour
9705 People Ain't No Good
9706 Brompton Oratory
9707 There Is A Kingdom
9708 (Are You) The One That I've Been Waiting For?
9709 Where Do We Go Now But Nowhere?
9710 West Country Girl
9711 Black Hair
9712 Idiot Prayer
9713 Far From Me
9714 Green Eyes
CD BONUS TRACKS JAPAN
9703 Right Now, I'm A Roaming
9702 Little Empty Boat
SESSION outtakes
9715 Sheep May Safely Graze
9716 Opium Tea

ORIGINAL RELEASE: Mute STUMM 142, February 1997; on *B-sides & Rarities*.

COMMENTS: When Cave was asked if the album was any good, his answer was tart. 'Is it any good? I don't know what people are interested in, and I don't care, to be honest. I wanted to concentrate on making the sort of record I've been wanting to make for many years, which is a record which is slow from beginning to end, a slow, melancholic record, which is very sparse, very raw and beautiful. And I think I've done that.'

Recorded during July 1996 at London's Abbey Road Studios, Cave and Flood mixed the album that September. Coming off the heels of *Murder Ballads'* lukewarm press, this new album wasted no time in endearing itself to nearly everyone who heard it. Early reviews were glowing. America's *All Music Guide* gushed, 'the music is direct, yet it has many textures, from blues to jazz, which offer a revealing and sympathetic bed for Cave's best, most affecting songs.

The Boatman's Call is one of his finest albums, and arguably the masterpiece he has been promising throughout his career.'

Reversing the theme of Peter Hammill's 1976 album *Over*, which chronicles the end of a relationship, *The Boatman's Call* tells the story of a relationship budding to bloom, as 'Into My Arms' amply illustrates. The mood created with the songs was almost painfully intimate, as a Mute press release explained, 'a [blend of] the spiritual with the sensual, using religious imagery to reflect the glories of personal love to affirm religious belief.'

With the Bad Seeds' unique sound all but relegated to the sidelines, despite full band participation, the songs hinge heavily on Cave's own voice, light washes of piano and Warren Ellis' violin. Not at all commercially driven, *The Boatman's Call* appears to be an album for Cave alone; emerging more a solo effort than a Bad Seeds album.

Digging deeper into his Biblical iconography than ever before, Cave pulls so many religious images to the fore ('Brompton Oratory', 'There Is A Kingdom', 'Far From Me') that one can almost hear Bob Dylan's Born Again-era *Saved* spinning on some lonely turntable. Indeed, like Dylan before him, Cave had not only earned the luxury of recording as and what he pleased, he clearly revelled in that freedom. Illustrating just how much extra material was recorded during these sessions, *The Boatman's Call* outtakes would appear across two sets of single B-sides, and on 2005's *B-sides & Rarities* collection.

Stunningly produced, lushly arranged and starkly evocative in the stripped-down simplicity that hallmarks songs like 'Idiot Prayer', 'Lime Tree Arbour' and 'Where Do We Go Now But Nowhere?' it can be argued that *The Boatman's Call* is the sound of Cave enjoying his finest hour; open, empty, rich and naked, it is a volume of poetry set to music.

This is a beautiful album, 'a logical conclusion,' explained Cave, 'of the music we've been making for years.' Yet he also acknowledged, 'I've always thrived on my audience throwing their hands up in the air in exasperation. I think that people who genuinely understand what I do, and what I've done, will not be surprised at this record. If people have gotten to me through the *Batman* record, then I apologise.' But really, if people had gotten to Cave through *Batman*, then anything before or after would have been a shock – especially given the similarity of the two records' titles.

With the prayerful delivery of 'Into My Arms' setting the stage for what was to follow, Cave explored themes of love and loss more fully, and more honestly, than ever before. Indeed, the marvellously moody 'West Country Girl' and hollow 'Black Hair,' are twinned together in what would appear to be a homage to PJ Harvey. Take away any supposed personal invocation, however, and these songs are universal touchstones for anyone who has ever loved.

Of course, not everybody who encountered the Boatman was impressed, with those who needed Cave to hit them with noise and furore only the most sorely disappointed. Cave, too, was aware that whispers in the shadows insisted that this was an album he should have left unreleased, but countered by insisting, 'it's the first record I've been able to listen to and actually enjoy, as opposed to finding a myriad of faults within it.'

Furthermore, several of the most obvious criticisms of the record could be dismissed by simply listening to it. The obvious under-employment of the Bad Seeds, for example, is obviated by the deeply personal nature of the music, and, besides, their support is often crucial regardless: Casey's bass on 'Into My Arms' and 'Lime Tree Arbour,' Warren Ellis's accordion on 'Black Hair', the collision of bass and Savage's piano on the simply stunning 'Idiot Prayer', Ellis's violin and Jim Sclavunos' percussion throughout. All show a sense of economy and lightness that contrasted beautifully with Cave's emotional outpourings, making it an exquisite exercise – and master class – in minimalism.

Of course, a sombre tone was maintained throughout, in the music and lyrics, and getting used to the slow pace also frequently made one overlook the strength of the melodies. 'People Ain't No Good', 'Far From Me', and 'Are You The One That I've Been Waiting For?' are all great tunes.

Cave continues, 'It's a very human record and, despite the key players, it's a record that's very much about normal pain and normal life. A lot of what I was singing about was going on as I was making this record. The actual feelings that I've been left with, due to the relationships being talked about, have been leaked to the record in some way.'

Cave promised that the tours to support the album would be as stripped down as the songs themselves were – even older songs, he warned, would be peeled back, to stand 'more in keeping with this album. We would keep everything low and slow.'

Seven years on, that lowness and slowness remained appealing to many. 'People Ain't No Good' would appear not only on the *Shrek 2* soundtrack (Geffen B0002557-12) in 2004, but also as incidental music on Showtime's provocative show *The L Word*.

Once again, a promotional interview disc was produced (Mute CAVESPEAK2), while Mute's Australian wing also produced the very deceptively titled *The Boatman's Call Australian Tour Nov/Dec 1997* – a title that simply screams 'oh my God, there's a new live album I've never heard of!' at you. Unfortunately, it rounded up nothing more exciting than the non-album B-sides from the associated singles.

(RADIO) *The Peter Curran Show*, UK, 24 February 1997
UNR Into My Arms
ORIGINAL RELEASE: Unreleased
COMMENTS: A spartan performance on London's GLR.

(TV) *Nulle Part Ailleurs*, France, 4 March 1997
UNR Into My Arms
ORIGINAL RELEASE: Unreleased

(TV) *Recovery*, Australia 5 March 1997
UNR Into My Arms

ORIGINAL RELEASE: Unreleased

(TV) *Willemsens Woche*, Germany, 24 April 1997
UNR Brompton Oratory
ORIGINAL RELEASE: Unreleased

(TV) *Live & Loud*, US 18 May 1997
UNR Into My Arms
UNR Brompton Oratory
UNR West Country Girl
UNR Far From me
UNR The Carny
ORIGINAL RELEASE: Unreleased

COMMENTS: This live performance for *MTV* was dominated by *The Boatman's Call*, but also found room for one old time favourite, a rearranged take on 'The Carny'. A shortened version of the session was rebroadcast by the network on 12 April as *In Tune Concert*, pointlessly cutting 'West Country Girl'.

(SINGLE) Are You The One That I've Been Waiting For?
9708 (Are You) The One That I've Been Waiting For?
9717 Come Into My Sleep
9718 Black Hair (Band Version)
9719 Babe, I Got You Bad
ORIGINAL RELEASE: Mute MUTE 206, May 1997

COMMENTS: This touching weepie was a satisfactory second single, although the greatest point of interest lies in the full band version of the hitherto unadorned 'Black Hair'.

(LIVE) Royal Albert Hall, London, 19-20 May 1997
9720 Lime Tree Arbour
9721 Stranger Than Kindness
9722 Red Right Hand
9723 I Let Love In
9724 Brompton Oratory
9725 Henry Lee
9726 The Weeping Song
9727 The Ship Song
9728 Where The Wild Roses Grow
ORIGINAL RELEASE: *Live At The Royal Albert* Hall, Mute (LCDMUTEL4), October 2001

COMMENTS: Recorded across two Royal Albert Hall shows on 19 ('Brompton Oratory' and 'Wild Roses') and 20 May, 1997, this live set was added as a bonus disc to the 2001 reissue of the 1998 *Best Of* set. It captures the live show of the era, unplugged and naked, in all its glory, with both new and old songs touchingly rearranged to match the moods of the current album in stark contrast from *Live Seeds*.

(LIVE) Liss Ard, Skibbereen, West Cork, Ireland, 4-5 September 1997
9729 People Ain't No Good
9730 Dead Joe
9731 Black Hair
9732 Into My Arms
ORIGINAL RELEASE: *The Garden's Voice* and *Lending The Garden A Voice* benefit discs.

COMMENTS: Appearing alongside Tindersticks, Nick Kelly, Pat McCabe, Spiritualised, the Dirty Three, Lou Reed, John Martyn and more, Cave's performances over the two nights of Liss Ard were spread across these two obscure releases, with 'Into My Arms' (recorded at the second night, with Mick Harvey on guitar) and 'Dead Joe' (recorded the previous evening) featuring on both. The promo CD *Liss Ard Volume One* (Edel 0039602) also features 'Dead Joe', 'Black Hair' and 'People Ain't No Good', though these are the regular studio versions only.

(TV) *The Great Hunger: The Life And Songs Of Shane MacGowan*, UK 4 October 1997
UNR Rainy Night In Soho
ORIGINAL RELEASE: Unreleased

COMMENTS: A sixty-minute BBC documentary profile. Six years later, Cave would appear within another MacGowan documentary, Sarah Stone's *If I Should Fall From Grace: The Shane MacGowan Story*, although his contribution was restricted to an interview.

(TV) *World Food Day*, Italy 26 October 1997
UNR Into My Arms
ORIGINAL RELEASE: Unreleased

COMMENTS: This concert, marking World Food Day, was a Benefit for the observation of the founding of the Food and Agriculture Organization. Headquartered in Rome, the annual event is marked by keynote speeches, special football games and a massive telecast of bi-continental concerts. Cave performed 'Into My Arms'.

(ALBUM) Mick Harvey *Pink Elephants*
9733 I Love You, Nor Do I
ORIGINAL RELEASE: Mute STUMM 157, October 1997

COMMENTS: Mick Harvey, who should be lauded as one of the hardest working men in the music business, had continued to work with the Bad Seeds and Crime And The City Solution, while carving out his own, very different solo career. 1997 brought his two Serge Gainsbourg tributes, *Intoxicated Man* and *Pink Elephants*, with the latter reuniting Cave, Lane and Harvey to record an all new version of 'I Love You, Nor Do I' – and a vast improvement on their earlier take it turned out to be, emerging far less histrionic, and a lot more orchestrally informed.

(ALBUM) Original soundtrack *Mojo / Soho*
9734 The Big Hurt
9735 Mojo
ORIGINAL RELEASE: EMI 7243 8 235302 7, 1997

COMMENTS: The Italian release of the *Mojo* original soundtrack found Cave and Gallon Drunk performing two songs for this re-working of sorts of the Jez Butterworth play. 'Mojo' was written by Nick Cave with Tim Friese-Greene, and emerges a vast improvement on the last collaboration. 'The Big Hurt' was formerly a hit for the Walker Brothers.

(ALBUM) Original soundtrack *Scream 2*
9407a Red Right Hand
9407b Red Right Hand
ORIGINAL RELEASE: Capitol December 1997 US / Premier 8219112 April 1998 UK

COMMENTS: The second instalment in Hollywood's latest teen scream phenomenon, the soundtrack to *Scream 2* featured a plethora of hip alternative bands, and that included, of course, the nearly omnipresent 'Red Right Hand'. As a bonus, the song was also granted a new twist, as a DJ Spooky remix manipulated its atmospheres, while leaving the basic heart of the number untouched – a restrained effort in a field that all too often demands bombastic abuse.

While it probably did something for the kids, it didn't come close to touching the original, here becoming as banal as the movie was. The film itself, meanwhile, used yet another alternate version of the song.

1998

Nick Cave And The Bad Seeds continued on from where they'd left off the previous year. 1998 saw the band on the European festival circuit during the first half of the year, and when that wrapped up, they headed Stateside to tour the US. Cave was even busier with a handful of solo shows.

In the middle of all this Cave embarked on a major schedule of promotional work for the May release of *The Best Of Nick Cave And The Bad Seeds*.

(TV) *Later...with Jools Holland* UK 8 May 1998
UNR Do You Love Me?

UNR Nobody's Baby Now
ORIGINAL RELEASE: Unreleased

(RADIO) *Keith Cameron Show* UK 11 May 1998
UNR Brompton Oratory
UNR Into My Arms
UNR Lime Tree Arbour
9801 The Mercy Seat
ORIGINAL RELEASE: 9801 on compilation *The Carve-Up* – Loose Recordings EXFM1, August 1999. Remainder unreleased.

(TV) *The Late Late Show* Ireland 15 May 1998
UNR Into My Arms
ORIGINAL RELEASE: Unreleased

COMMENTS: The release of the album prompted Cave and the Bad Seeds out onto the promotional circuit, turning in some exhilarating performances that captured (but rarely improved upon) the mood of the album. The two older songs that crept in – the Keith Cameron take on 'The Mercy Seat,' and a tremulous 'Do You Love Me?' for *Later* – offered advance warning of how Cave was stripping bare his older material, to blend it in with the new, a new process that cynics might compare to the once pernicious practice of 'colourising' old films in the hopes of making them seem more contemporary. Only in reverse.

(RADIO) *The Black Sessions* France 19 May 1998
UNR Lime Tree Arbour
UNR I Let Love In
UNR Stranger Than Kindness
UNR Red Right Hand
UNR Nobody's Baby Now
UNR Do You Love Me?
UNR Into My Arms
UNR The Ship Song
UNR The Mercy Seat
UNR Brompton Oratory
ORIGINAL RELEASE: Unreleased

COMMENTS: This heady, hefty session featured a juggled line-up, with James Johnston replacing Blixa Bargeld.

(TV) *Talk Music* UK 24 May 1998
UNR Red Right Hand
UNR From Her To Eternity
ORIGINAL RELEASE: Unreleased

(ALBUM) Compilation *Au Royaume De Tricatel*
9802 Goodbye Marylou
ORIGINAL RELEASE: France 1998

COMMENTS: This compilation album features Nick Cave covering Michel Polnareff's 'Goodbye Marylou'...in French. Polnareff, the eccentric French popster, first made waves in the mid-1960s with his debut single, 'La Poupée Qui Fait Non', a song that hit the top of the French charts, paving the way for an extremely successful pop career (Saint Etienne later turned in a gorgeous cover of that number).

Produced by Bertrand Burgalat, Cave's performance is what it is – Cave's French is not the best, the song's not bad but overall, it falls short of the cult status it's achieved. The song would appear on many compilations, including 1999's *A Tribute To Polnareff* (Bis Records France 520995 2 PM 806), and that might be the one you want to pick up, including as it does further contributions from Pulp, Marc Almond, Saint Etienne and Peter Hammill.

(ALBUM) Fuji Rock Festival '98, Tokyo, 1 August 1998
9803 From Her To Eternity
ORIGINAL RELEASE: *Fuji Rock Festival In Tokyo*, Polydor POCP – 7341-2, 1998

COMMENTS: A double CD was compiled from this mammoth festival on the slopes of Japan's most famous mountain. Cave's performance, in keeping with the remainder of the tour (and the tapes thereof) was dedicated in the main to the new album. An almost frighteningly spartan rendition of 'From Her To Eternity,' however, evinced the undiluted power of the show, and certainly highlights this collection.

(TV) *The David Letterman Show*, US 11 September 1998
UNR Into My Arms
ORIGINAL RELEASE: Unreleased

(LIVE) Vienna, 29 September 1998
UNR Love Song
ORIGINAL RELEASE: Unreleased

COMMENTS: From the stage to the screen to the lecture hall? On 29 September, 1998 Cave was invited to give a workshop/lecture to students at Vienna's Akademietheater. The product of this effort was the unreleased 'Love Song,' written by Cave and his students and then performed with Cave on piano. The song can be sourced on the Duende bootleg.

(ALBUM) *The Words Of The Wise*
9804 Intro to *The Gospel According To Mark*

ORIGINAL RELEASE: Canongate CAN CD 0000, October 1998

COMMENTS: Free CD with *Etcetera* magazine from Books Etc. in October 1998. Cave reads from his intro to the recently published new edition of *The Gospel According To Mark*. Some music from *Ghosts...Of The Civil Dead* also appears. (Cave would repeat this reading for BBC Radio 4 later in the month.)

That Cave had dabbled extensively in the morass of modern and historic Christianity was no surprise to anyone who'd been following his career. Iconography and scripture had been well woven into his lyrics for years, coming through stronger still with the publication of *And The Ass Saw The Angel*. By the end of the 1990s, though, even he had to laugh a little not only at the God-like status bestowed upon him by his followers, but at the sheer ridiculousness of his own proclamations. 'I always feel like David St. Hubbins from *Spinal Tap,* giving his views on God and religion.' As for what those views were, he admitted that he may not believe in the virgin birth, may not believe in the resurrection – but does 'believe that Jesus was an enigmatic and heroic person, and a great thinker.'

(TV) *Roy & HG's Planet Norwich*, 8 October 1998
UNR Into My Arms
UNR Interview
ORIGINAL RELEASE: Unreleased

1999

And The Ass Saw The Angel had now been kicking around for nearly a decade, with readings cut to CD and Cave's own appearances well documented. Indeed, this thick volume had seen a number of reissues during the 1990s and, with the decade ending, the book was to receive yet another one, joining Cave's two *King Ink* (1988 & 1997) lyric books on the shelf.

1999 would also allow Cave to expand his horizons when he was appointed curator of that year's Meltdown Festival, which, since its inauguration in the early nineties, had rapidly become one of the outstanding annual cultural events. Staged on London's South Bank, and running from 2nd July for two weeks, Cave and long-time friend Mick Geyer were solely responsible for selecting both the events and performers for the massive festival of music, film, art and photography. Rumour has it that Cave was taken by surprise by the speed with which himself and Geyer had to put the whole thing together, but both responded magnificently to put together a diverse and challenging range of artists.

It was predictable that some of the Bad Seeds would be on the bill too, but the event was none the worse for that. Conway Savage, a highly skilled songwriter in his own right, played a sparkling solo set and the inimitable Blixa Bargeld came up with an inspirational and entirely improvised spoken word evening, called Rede (Speech in German), captivating an audience for nigh-on two hours with only a voice effects pedal for company. Beginning the evening with a jocular query ('Has anyone seen *Mamma Mia* yet?'), he went off on a miraculous exposition of music, science, philosophy and anecdote. Possibly the highlight of the Bad Seeds' contribution, though, was the appearance of Warren Ellis's Dirty Three at the Queen Elizabeth Hall. These three amazing musicians blew the audience away with the sweeping melancholy and grand passion of their music and Warren Ellis unveiled once again his madcap humour and goofy charm, regardless of his peculiar habit of spitting on stage. This intoxicating performance was followed by renditions of the music of the legendary Estonian minimalist composer, Arvo Pärt – Cave's favourite composer by far. The heavily spiritual and cerebral style of pieces like 'Fratres', 'Tabula Rasa' and 'Speigel im Speigel' were the perfect counterpoint to The Dirty Three and it was truly an inspired bill by Cave.

Cave was rumoured to have missed out on three musical legends for the festival. Bob Dylan, Johnny Cash and Scott Walker all demurred for various reasons (Walker instantly declining, but also putting his name forward as curator for Meltdown 2000). But there were a couple of coups. He coaxed cult icon Lee Hazlewood out of one of his regular retirements to play a rapturously received set, supported – in another bit of inspired casting – by the Harry Dean Stanton Band. To have the grouchy composer of Cave's first single there was certainly a fitting gesture, and a fascinating one – uncompromising, resolutely uncommercial and totally self-willed, it was suddenly easy to see Hazlewood as Cave's closest spiritual forebear in music.

The composer of another song Cave had covered, Nina Simone, also made one of her last-ever concert appearances at this Meltdown. In this instance, Cave saw it fit to walk on stage himself to introduce the ailing Simone who, like Hazlewood, was as grouchy as ever, but still produced a powerful and beautiful array of music – making it one of the most emotional evenings at any Meltdown festival. Less emotional was a hilarious bill, dubbed 'Australia Evening', where the singular talents of Rolf Harris, Barry Humphries and Kylie Minogue were brought together.

Cave himself played a number of times and shared the stage with the Bad Seeds in a hastily arranged night at the Royal Festival Hall. Despite this, the band produced yet another memorable show and it was surprising and invigorating to see them open in this hallowed hall with a blistering version of 'Long Time Man' and close the show with an equally forceful 'St Huck'.

All in all, the 1999 Meltdown was deemed a great success and the role of curator seemed ideal for Cave who had, after all, *always* been a man of wide cultural experience and taste. Music aside, he surprised no one by screening Carl Dreyer's *Joan of Arc*, but less predictable was Alexander Mackendrick's *Sweet Smell of Success*, the celebrated Broadway exposé with Burt Lancaster and Tony Curtis. There were art and photography exhibitions and a special evening celebrating the work of Samuel Beckett (an old favourite Cave had discovered back in Berlin) where Cave pulled off another coup by getting Beckett's greatest interpreter, Billie Whitelaw on to a stage for the first time in years. This was the first time she had ever done a talk of this kind, where she introduced the extraordinary and seldom-seen film of *Not I*. Whether he was hanging in the foyer with a host of luminaries and the Bad Seeds themselves, lurking in the wings, or roaring with laughter at Bargeld and Ellis along with the audience, it was clear that the curator's role was one that Cave relished and that he pulled off brilliantly.

(LIVE) Actor's Song Contest, Wroclaw, Poland, 14 March 1999
9901 Into My Arms
9902 Weeping Song
ORIGINAL RELASE: 9901 on Compilation *Artysci Piosenki* Luna Music LUNCD041, March 2000, 9901-9902 on second volume LUNCD/MC 059

COMMENTS: Although its billing sounds suspiciously close to certain other pan-continental musical events of dread renown... either that or some ghastly gathering of the singing thespians we know and fear, the Polish Actor's Song Contest was actually a far more sober, respectable and, indeed, impressive event, with Cave's presence lending even greater gravitas to the proceedings.

Several of the featured artists performed Cave compositions, and the ensuing *Artysci Piosenki* compilation includes 'The Curse Of Millhaven', as performed by Kinga Preis, and 'The Mercy Seat' by Krzeslo Laski. Cave himself contributed a version of 'Into My Arms', performed alongside Stanislaw Sojka.

Luna Music released a second album from the event in 2001, featuring both 'Into My Arms' and 'The Weeping Song'. Unfortunately, contractual wranglings with some of the other artists scheduled for inclusion saw the set withdrawn shortly after release.

(TV) *Songwriter's Circle* UK, recorded 12 May 1999, broadcast 9 June 1999
UNR West Country Girl
UNR Henry Lee
UNR Into My Arms
UNR The Ship Song
UNR Ship Of Fools (John Cale)
UNR I'll Stand By You (Chrissie Hynde)
UNR Sad Waters
UNR The Mercy Seat
UNR I'm Waiting For My Man
ORIGINAL RELEASE: Unreleased

COMMENTS: An uneven, but nevertheless legendary broadcast as Cave, John Cale and, possibly out of her depth, Chrissie Hynde combined for a Subterrania Club performance that invoked an attempt to re-stage the Immaculate Consumptives revue for the oldies generation.

Cave's songs dominated the broadcast, with six of the nine taken from his repertoire. However, he remained on stage for Cale's 'Ship Of Fools', and Hynde's 'I'll Stand By You', playing piano on these and on the closing (but not broadcast) thud through the Velvets' 'I'm Waiting For My Man' – a Lou Reed composition, of course, but one which Cale had readily absorbed into his own repertoire two decades before.

Cave certainly held his own against these two. Hynde appeared overwhelmed by it all anyway, but the notoriously cranky Cale seemed strangely subdued and Cave came across as by far the most interesting of the three. Bootleg copies of the broadcast do, inevitably, circulate and cannot be recommended too highly. An official release must, some day, be forthcoming.

(TV) NHK Japan, 1 June 1999
UNR The Mercy Seat
ORIGINAL RELEASE: Unreleased

COMMENTS: Performance recorded at the Greenwich Naval College UK

2000

2000 saw the Bad Seeds keep a low profile while they concentrated on recording the follow-up to *The Boatman's Call*, the album that would become *No More Shall We Part*.

(ALBUM) *The Secret Life Of The Love Song*
0001 The Secret Life Of The Love Song
0002 The Flesh Made Word
0003 West Country Girl
0004 People Ain't No Good
0005 Sad Waters
0006 Love Letter
0007 Far From Me

ORIGINAL RELEASE: King Mob KMOB 7, February 2000

COMMENTS: Another in that growing sequence of off-kilter releases, *The Secret Life* is largely consumed by two lectures: 'The Secret Life Of The Love Song', which Cave initially prepared for his participation in 1998's Vienna Poetry Festival; and 'The Flesh Made Word', which was written for broadcast by BBC Radio 3's Religious Services in 1996. The text itself subsequently appeared in 1997 within the covers of Cave's *King Ink* lyric book (Black Spring Press). These versions, however, were recorded in April and July 1999 respectively.

Five musical pieces also appear during 'The Secret Life Of The Love Song' – and, not surprisingly, they are indeed love songs. Recorded at London's September Sound studio in April 1999 with Warren Ellis, drummer Jim White and bassist Susan Stenger, they include a re-working of 'Love Letter', the song Cave composed with Bruno Pisek.

(ALBUM) Ute Lemper: *Punishing Kiss*
0008 Little Water Song
ORIGINAL RELEASE: Decca 466 473-2, April 2000

COMMENTS: German chanteuse Ute Lemper has claimed the throne as her generation's siren, one with looks that kill and an unerring knack for interpreting the music of Kurt Weill. This album is a collection of collaborations with Divine Comedy and current recordings in which she bypasses Weimar Germany and focuses instead on living, breathing, contemporary songwriters – Nick Cave, Scott Walker, Elvis Costello and Tom Waits among them. Cave does not sing or perform on the album, but did contribute the previously unrecorded 'Little Water Song'.

Co-written with Bruno Pisek, the ballad was described by Lemper herself as 'a jewel on this album. When I heard his demo cassette for the first time, with just piano and him singing, I was totally overwhelmed. The surreal text, together with a rather minimalist melody, make a real art song.'

(TV) *Tenco Awards* Italy 27 October 2000
UNR West Country Girl
UNR Henry Lee
UNR Into My Arms
UNR The Mercy Seat
UNR And No More Shall We Part
UNR The Ship Song
UNR Papa Won't Leave You Henry
ORIGINAL RELEASE: Unreleased

COMMENTS: Italy's long-running (founded in 1972) Club Tenco was founded in memory of the Italian songwriter Tenco, who committed suicide in 1967; divided into several domestic categories, the event also offers a special career award, the Premio Tenco, to world-famous artists, whose short performances are the international highlight of the event. Vinicius De Moraes, Tom Waits, Charles Trenet, Leo Ferrè, Georges Brassens, Jacques Brel, Lluis Llach, Leonard Cohen, Chico Buarque De Hollanda, Joni Mitchell and Randy Newman numbered among past participants, with Cave joining the select roster in this year.

(FILM) *Scream 3*
9407c Red Right Hand
ORIGINAL RELEASE: *B-sides & Rarities,* March 2005

COMMENTS: Yet another appearance for the old chestnut, manipulated this time by Barry Adamson, and featuring the addition of an orchestra and four entire new verses from Cave. Which doubtless explains why, although a snippet appears in the film, the accompanying soundtrack CD overlooked it altogether. The full length version was finally aired on *B-sides & Rarities*.

2001

Nick Cave was now permanently based in West London with his new wife, Susie Bick, and their nine-month-old twin boys – Earl and Arthur. Further signs of his domesticity were revealed when he told *Mojo* magazine that he now had an office, complete with an iMac, as opposed to simply toting his work around in a bag as was once his want. He called it 'sense and order', and, if anything, he seemed to want to surprise people by revealing that he had a rigid nine-to-five schedule.

His new location quickly informed his songwriting. One of the loveliest of his compositions, 'Lime Tree Arbour', from *The Boatman's Call* was 'sort of based in Holland Park. Well, it's not actually an arbour, but there are some lime trees. No loons, unfortunately. Some other wildfowl of some description, but no loons. I would say that it's a particularly beautiful song, a song set in a wooded area of contemplation.'

After so long out of the limelight, 2001 would see the Bad Seeds swing back into action, with their duties this year including their long promised return to Australia, for a six-date tour – their first in four years. Cave, too, struck out on his own, with a two-week solo tour of the US that saw him appear on *Late Night With David Letterman* on 19 March, before hitting a number of theatres in Chicago, Los Angeles, San Francisco, Seattle and Denver.

And then it was 11 September. The band had been looking forward to a mammoth US tour during September and October, but with the horrific events unfolding in New York, the entire outing was scrapped, to be rescheduled for the following year. With much of the world reeling, it was a difficult, but understandable decision. Somehow 'life goes on' simply didn't seem an appropriate response, as an official statement to fans made clear:

'In the wake of this week's tragic events in New York, Washington, and Somerset County, Pennsylvania, Nick Cave and The Bad Seeds have decided to cancel their entire North American tour previously set to run from September 18 through October 9. The band members feel that it is inappropriate and disrespectful to be performing concerts in a country that is, as described by its president and media, at war. While regretting any disappointment this causes their fans, they believe this is a time to be at home with their families. All of them extend their deepest condolences to those who have lost family or friends as a result of these reprehensible acts.'

(RADIO) *Triple J* Australia 5 January 2001
UNR Little Janey's Gone
UNR God Is In The House
UNR Love Letter
UNR And No More Shall We Part
ORIGINAL RELEASE: Unreleased

COMMENTS: A Sydney radio session introducing material destined for the forthcoming new album.

(SINGLE) As I Sat Sadly By Her Side
0101 As I Sat Sadly By Her Side
0102 Little Janey's Gone
0103 Good, Good Day
0101a As I Sat Sadly By Her Side (radio edit)
ORIGINAL RELEASE: Mute MUTE 249, March 2001

COMMENTS: Recorded at the Abbey Road sessions for the forthcoming *No More Shall We Part,* Cave seems to resemble Bryan Ferry on the bitter 'As I Sat Sadly By Her Side'. On the flip, 'Good Good Day' is a slab of wavering pop, with backing vocals from the band that don't quite fit in and a pop rock pounding that sounds a little too grown up for its own good. Elsewhere, though, Kate & Anna McGarrigle's guest vocals add warm depths to the song.

(TV) *The David Letterman Show* US 19 March 2001
UNR Love Letter
ORIGINAL RELEASE: Unreleased

COMMENTS: Cave launches his solo US tour with this late night TV appearance. Facing an audience that, for the most part, would not have known him from Adam (unless, of course, it was Adam Sandler – Cave was guesting with the big boys now), Cave elected to pull one of the friendlier songs from the forthcoming album, and turned in a gently memorable performance.

(RADIO) *Morning Become Eclectic* US 30 March 2001
UNR The Mercy Seat
UNR God Is In The House
UNR Sad Waters
UNR Papa Won't Leave You, Henry
0104 Into My Arms
ORIGINAL RELEASE: 0104 on Compilation *KCRW: Sounds Eclectic Too,* Palm Pictures 2089, September 2002

COMMENTS: Another solo performance included some old gems, with the KCRW staple's second compilation album drawing out this shimmering version of 'Into My Arms' for inclusion alongside Coldplay, Zero 7, Air, REM, Dido and Norah Jones.

(ALBUM) *No More Shall We Part*
Line-up: Nick Cave (vocals & keyboards); Mick Harvey (guitar); Blixa Bargeld (guitar); Martyn P Casey (bass); Conway Savage (keyboards); Thomas Wydler (drums); Warren Ellis (violin); Jim Scalvunos (percussion).
0101 As I Sat Sadly By Her Side
0105 And No More Shall We Part

0106 Hallelujah
0107 Love Letter
0108 Fifteen Feet Of Pure White Snow
0109 God Is In The House
0110 Oh My Lord
0111 Sweetheart Come
0112 The Sorrowful Wife
0113 We Came Along This Road
0114 Gates To The Garden
0115 Darker With The Day
SPECIAL EDITION BONUS TRACKS
0116 Grief Came Riding
0117 Bless His Everloving Heart
SESSION outtakes (WESTSIDE STUDIOS)
0118 God Is In The House
0119 We Came Along This Road
0120 No More Shall We Part
0121 Fifteen Feet Of Pure White Snow

ORIGINAL RELEASE: Mute STUMM 164, April 2001; 0117-0120 on *Westside Sessions* EP, Mute REDSTUMM 164.

COMMENTS: Recorded, for the most part, at London's Abbey Road Studios during September 2000, *No More Shall We Part* featured the same Bad Seeds line-up as *The Boatman's Call*, augmented with guest vocalists Kate & Anna McGarrigle, the Canadian sisters whose eclectic stylings placed them at the forefront of the 1970s folk boom.

A second set of sessions, at Westside Studios the following month, saw the band continue working on the new material – the fruits of these sessions, the so-called 'alternate' version of various album tracks, would subsequently appear among forthcoming B-sides, and as a stand-alone Mute promo.

Perhaps the most notable things about this work were the extent to which it was self-penned, and Cave's further development as a vocalist. The new, isolated work regime meant that Cave improved his piano technique considerably, and he was rightly proud of the fact that he could play an entire album's worth of songs without a band to help him. In fact, he acknowledged, 'I had highly arranged the whole thing before I went in, which inhibits the band. If something's already kind of complete and all they have to do is play the parts, it doesn't give them much breathing space.' That said, where rock 'n' roll had been abandoned entirely in the last album, this time, the band seemed to be making a huge effort to insert it into another deeply reflective set of songs.

Although the album is not even close to being *The Boatman's Call* revisited, many critics still wanted to see the two records conjoined as two of a kind. Cave was, as always, in metamorphosis. A full half of the album was packed with a capella intros, roars replaced by mesmerising lyrics and romantic sighs replaced with balladeering.

Cave also had the time to stretch himself vocally, more than he had for many years, and this bore fruit with tracks like 'Hallelujah' and, especially 'God Is In The House,' where he invests a complex song with real passion laced with just a smattering of tricky sarcasm.

The other key difference between No More Shall We Part and The Boatman's Call lies in the very timbre of the songs. Whereas the earlier set cast Cave as the budding or spurned lover, this was very much his Wedding Album, with the celebratory tone of that description marred only by Cave's apparent reaction to marriage: complex, difficult, even tortured. On the title track, in particular, this becomes self-evident, as the depths of a marriage are explored in such a way that the music itself appears to be in direct conflict with what should be a happy occasion.

These themes are revisited and reflected in the album's denser arrangements – which are richer and more colourful, just as the gorgeous Tony Clark painting that adorns the cover contrasts so much with Anton Corbijn's melancholic Boatman's Call cover shot.

Elsewhere, the songs startle. 'The Sorrowful Wife,' begins as a melancholy love song, bolstered by ghosts of Let Love In and augmented simply with piano and violin, before it changes completely as Cave himself dissolves into an angry cavalcade of emotion, flanked by guitar. The album is far more successful across more straightforward songs, evidenced most clearly on 'As I Sat Sadly By Her Side,' 'And No More Shall We Part' and the utterly unerring 'Fifteen Feet Of Pure White Snow,' which blends the swing-laden music and Cave's lyrics with little discord.

But, as different as this album was from its predecessor, the songs themselves continued to flow as pure, protracted poetry, and while it would be sheer hyperbole to describe this album as a complete reinvention, if you came to No More Shall We Part from the Henry's Dream/Let Love In/Murder Ballads triptych, there was little to find that was immediately recognizable. Yet Cave hadn't forgotten the past, not really, weaving the essence of Leonard Cohen into 'Hallelujah,' and echoing the essence of a disembodied Scott Walker through the outer fringes of the rest.

So, while older fans may have fallen away, unimpressed by Cave's quiet side, what makes this album coalesce so beautifully in the end is his rich imagery, and his ability to juxtapose the sublime with the mundane. And the critical reaction to No More Shall We Part was absolutely remarkable. For once, there seemed to be no carping from any quarter about this Nick Cave album. There was blanket positive coverage in the music press, extensive broadsheet interest – if there was a medium with an opinion, Cave was in it, earnestly discussing his work, his marriage and God with anyone who'd listen. How long ago seemed the ill-tempered spats he had once enjoyed with the NME!

Appended to initial 'special edition' copies of the album was a bonus CD that included two session outtakes, 'Bless His Ever Loving Heart' and 'Grief Came Riding' and a CD-ROM video track, shot at the Westside Studio session on 6 October.

Promo hunters were pleased with the Electronic Press Kit video package (MUTE IPK CD Stumm164) that included lyrics, MP3 song snippets, a photo gallery, discography, internet links, plus an interview with Cave, during which he answered some thirty questions about the album. For the rest of the masses, the label also released a limited edition box set containing the album, the bonus disc, a flyer and two postcards (Mute BCDStumm164).

(RADIO) *Radiokulturhaus* Austria 8 April 2001
UNR Long Time Man
UNR As I Sat Sadly By Her Side
UNR God Is In The House
UNR And No More Shall We Part
UNR The Mercy Seat
UNR The Weeping Song
UNR Fifteen Feet Of Pure White Snow
UNR Love Letter
ORIGINAL RELEASE: Unreleased

COMMENTS: A Bad Seeds concert in Vienna. The show was broadcast live on Austrian radio, then rebroadcast on TV four days later.

(TV) *Boxed Set* UK 12 April 2001
UNR As I Sat Sadly By Her Side
UNR Lime Tree Arbour
UNR Do You Love Me?
UNR God Is In The House
UNR Red Right Hand
UNR Hallelujah
UNR No More Shall We Part
UNR The Sorrowful Wife
UNR The Weeping Song
UNR The Mercy Seat
UNR Fifteen Feet Of Pure White Snow
ORIGINAL RELEASE: Unreleased

COMMENTS: Before a small audience a tight, live performance with a small audience.

(TV) *Later...with Jools Holland* UK 11 May 2001
UNR Fifteen Feet Of Pure White Snow
UNR God Is In The House
ORIGINAL RELEASE: Unreleased

COMMENTS: A live preview for the new single. These were charming performances, particularly for 'God Is In The House' which, of course, only featured Cave, Ellis and Harvey on guitar – but the other Bad Seeds helped out by standing beside Cave's piano like choirboys with candles aloft.

(SINGLE) Fifteen Feet Of Pure White Snow
0108a Fifteen Feet Of Pure White Snow
0118 God Is In The House
0119 We Came Along This Road
0108 Fifteen Feet Of Pure White Snow
0120 And No More Shall We Part
ORIGINAL RELEASE: Mute MUTE 262, May 2001

COMMENTS: The album's second single led off with the sweetly sombre 'Fifteen Feet Of Pure White Snow', one of the better tracks on the album, at least so far as prospective singles were concerned – and the inspiration for a magnificent video, studded with special guests, and featuring Cave with Pulp's Jarvis Cocker.
The real meat, however, lay in the shape of the Westside Studio alternates, making their public debut, although you needed to pick up both the CD and 10-inch vinyl versions to get all three – or wait a few months and buy the Australian 'Love Letters' single, which rounded up the full quartet.

(LIVE) Le Transbordeur Lyon, France, 8 June 2001
0122 Do You Love Me?
0123 Oh My Lord
0124 Lime Tree Arbour
0125 Red Right Hand
0126 As I Sat Sadly By Her Side
0127 The Weeping Song
0128 God Is In The House
0129 We Came Along This Road
0130 Papa Won't Leave You, Henry
0131 Hallelujah
0132 The Mercy Seat
0133 Into My Arms
0134 Saint Huck
0135 The Curse Of Millhaven
ORIGINAL RELEASE: *God Is In The House* DVD Mute 9224-9, August 2003

COMMENTS: See appendix two (Videos and Visuals) for details.

(RADIO) *John Peel Tribute*, UK, recorded 25 September 2001, broadcast 11 October 2001
UNR The Mercy Seat
UNR Into My Arms
UNR God Is In The House
ORIGINAL RELEASE: Unreleased

COMMENTS: Among the performances staged at King's College to commemorate veteran radio and television man John Peel's 40 years in broadcasting, the appearance of Cave was second only to The Fall among the evening's most inevitable events – Peel's kindness to The Birthday Party, at a time when nobody else gave a fig for the band, was something that had never been forgotten.

Taking the stage after Billy Bragg, thanking Peel for all he had done, and recalling some of his own memories of the DJ, Cave appeared solo at the piano, to perform three songs.

(SESSION) Original soundtrack *Winged Migration*
0136 To Be By Your Side
ORIGINAL RELEASE: Higher Octave, April 2003

COMMENTS: Working closely with directors Jacques Perrin, Jacques Cluzaud and Michel Debats, composer Bruno Coulais hoped to capture through sound, the emotion and energy of birds in flight. Exquisitely realised in this stunning 2001 documentary, sound replaced voice as the music itself became the narrative that held the birds aloft on their migratory routes.

Coulais had become aware of Cave through his performances on the French music TV show *Nuelle Part Ailleurs*. 'I was really impressed by his intelligence. He understood that the lyrics shouldn't give too much meaning to the sequence. He had to write about earth and humans, more than about birds.'

Cave explains that 'Bruno came backstage and I was handed photographic evidence of what the film was about.' The trick, for Cave, was to take Coulais' music and write a song to fit within the framework, something he'd never previously done. 'A lot of what I write, lyrically, is very much rooted in nature and natural things. And, I think, lyrically, it's very much along the lines of what I write anyway.' The resultant 'To Be By Your Side', while admittedly not one of Cave's best, still resonates with a passion that captures what both director and composer had in mind.

2002

Although Nick Cave And The Bad Seeds were rattling along quite nicely on the back of *No More Shall We Part*, Cave spent most of the year allying himself with an eclectic assortment of projects, including Pulp's Jarvis Cocker and American Country icon Johnny Cash. He also undertook what would have been unthinkable in The Birthday Party days, recording two Beatles' songs.

(ALBUM) Original soundtrack *I Am Sam*
0201 Let It Be
ORIGINAL RELEASE: V2 VVR1019412, January 2002

COMMENTS: Surely not inspired by the title of the last Pulp single, Cave contributed this Beatles' cover to the *I Am Sam* soundtrack and, one has to admit, though the Fab Four seem omnipresent in every corner of the rock world, Cave is one person who might be deemed to be immune to their influence. Where the Beatles' rendition of this stately ballad sounded hopeful and naively sweet, Cave merely sounds morose i.e. 'let it be, because you can't change a thing.' It's true enough to the original, but a pretty flat and uninspiring version. Cave worked on this track with Ian Dury's Blockheads, and they hit it off so much that Cave invited them to appear on the *Nocturama* album.

Later culled as one of Cave's own B-sides, the song would also make an appearance on *Mojo* magazine's freebie *The Score* CD.

(SINGLE) Love Letter
0107 Love Letter
0118 God Is In The House
0119 We Came Along This Road
0120 No More Shall We Part
0121 Fifteen Feet Of Pure White Snow
ORIGINAL RELEASE: Mute MUTE 284, February 2002

COMMENTS: An Australian single released to commemorate the band's latest visit to those climes (hence the 'tour edition' billing) finally serves up all four of the Westside Session versions.

(SINGLE) Pulp 'Bad Cover Version'
0202 Disco 2000
ORIGINAL RELEASE: Island/Universal CIDX 794/582 899-2, April 2002

COMMENTS: Nick Cave and Pulp's Jarvis Cocker had already shared space on the Polnareff tribute CD, but now the two musicians were brought closer together, as Cave tackled an absolutely mangled version of the classic 'Disco 2000' for the B-side of the band's 'Bad Cover Version' single – produced by another of Cave's associates, Scott Walker.

Cave told *Mojo* Magazine, 'You should have heard the other version of that song. As far as I'm concerned, they used the wrong one. We did a kind of Punk rock version, really rough, very funny, a really adolescent version, and then we also did that lugubrious waltz version which Jarvis preferred. But the Punk one was better.'

It was a cover version, it was bad in its own way, slow and not nearly as smarmy as Jarvis himself was sometimes prone to sound. But it wasn't *quite* the worst cover version imaginable…. Cocker, meanwhile, would promptly return the favour, turning up to vamp in the video for '15 Feet Of Pure White Snow' – most easily seen among the bonus material on Cave's 2003 *God Is In The House* DVD.

(TV) *Tonight Show* US 17 April 2002
UNR Fifteen Feet Of Pure White Snow
ORIGINAL RELEASE: Unreleased

(SINGLE) Here Comes The Sun

0203 Here Comes The Sun
0201 Let It Be
ORIGINAL RELEASE: V2 70720193, May 2002

COMMENTS: Once, apparently, was not enough. Having already mangled 'Let It Be', Cave now turned his attention to George Harrison's 'Here Comes The Sun', a song that has already suffered more than its fair share of deleterious cover versions though Cave fave Nina Simone made the song her own in a bittersweet elegiac take. Again, he succeeded in squeezing most of the joy from the original, but still it made for a fascinating conversation piece – particularly in Germany, where both Beatles songs were issued as a stand-alone single.

(SESSION) Olympic Studios, 28 May 2002
0204 I Feel So Good
ORIGINAL RELEASE: compilation *The Soul Of A Man*, Columbia CK 90491, 2003

COMMENTS: Written and directed by Wim Wenders, *The Soul Of A Man* was just one part of the PBS series *Martin Scorsese Presents The Blues*. Debuting at the Cannes Film Festival Premiere on 15 May 2003, the show was then aired nationally in the US on 29 September.

Cave and the Bad Seeds' pounding version of bluesman JB Lenoir's 'I Feel So Good' was recorded at Olympic Studios in London during the mixing sessions for Cave's next album *Nocturama*. Like the *Nocturama* album, it was produced by Nick Launay – reunited with Cave for the first time since the days of The Birthday Party. The Wenders project permitted Cave, for the first time, to delve fully into his long-standing fascination with American Blues. It resulted in one of the most effective moments within a multi-part series that, though noble in its intentions, sadly and unexpectedly emerged a largely turgid meandering through a series of repetitive (not to mention irrelevant) images and visions.

(SESSION) Johnny Cash
0205 I'm So Lonesome I Could Cry
0206 Cindy
ORIGINAL RELEASE: 0204 on *American IV: The Man Comes Around*, American Records 440 077 083-0, November 2002; 0205 on *Cash Unearthed*, American 024986133-2, November 2003

COMMENTS: Johnny Cash had already dabbled in Cave's music, recording a gritty cover of 'The Mercy Seat' for *American III.* Now it was Cave's turn to return the compliment.

If it was unimaginable to picture Nick Cave covering the Beatles, it was perfectly feasible for him to pair with Cash. Cave explained to *Mojo* Magazine that he was 'rung up by Rick Rubin, who asked me if I'd like to come into the studio the next day and sing a song with him and I was like "Well, YES!"'

Personally convinced that 'the difference between Johnny Cash and me is he's great, and I'm not. Deep in my heart I know that,' Cave continued, 'I put down the phone and then thought "How the hell am I gonna do this?" So I went to see Warren Ellis who was lying on his bed listening to Hank Williams. I told him, "I gotta sing with Johnny Cash, what'll I sing?" and he just points at the stereo where "I'm So Lonesome I Could Cry" was playing, and he said, "sing that," We sat down and did it in two takes. The first take, Johnny was flat. They stopped it and said, "Sorry we're gonna have to do that again," and I thought "Fuck!" So I said, "I'm flat, right?" and they said "Nope, Johnny's flat!" So Johnny turns to me and nods, "Nick, I think I might have been a bit off there."'

The session also saw the pair tackle Cash's own 'Cindy' – a song that Cave later admitted he was unfamiliar with and, consequently, a little nervous about recording, although Cash quickly put him at ease. Nevertheless, the performance would not see the light of day until the release of Cash's posthumous *Cash Unearthed* box set of latter-day rarities and outtakes.

The entire session was a moving experience for Cave, who later professed himself shocked at just how frail Cash had become. 'When Johnny arrived he looked very sick to me, very frail. But he was extraordinarily warm and extraordinarily gentle.'

Cash would die in September 2003.

2003

2003 brought a massive change within the Bad Seeds camp. It would herald, once again, a major shift in the band's direction, at the same time as marking the departure of Blixa Bargeld. Although Bargeld was a member of the band for the sessions that produced the forthcoming *Nocturama*, by the time the album hit the racks, he was gone and concentrating more fully on Einstürzende Neubauten and all his other projects.

The split, Cave said, was 'amicable and totally Blixa's decision,' a summary with which Bargeld agreed. 'This has been a very difficult decision for me, and I have spent a great deal of time thinking about it. My leaving has nothing to do with artistic or personal differences with the band; I just feel it is time to concentrate on other creative areas in my life.'

Also, in this year, Cave's elevation to the cultural elite was affirmed with an appearance on *The South Bank Show*. It was a superb overview of his career, moving from the raging turmoil of The Birthday Party, through the fire-and-brimstone early years of the Bad Seeds, and up to the more sedate and haunting songs of recent years, though it did skim over the middle period of the Bad Seeds' careers concentrating on Cave's recent years as piano-based singer-songwriter.

Cave himself talked frankly about his drug-taking, his influences (Johnny Cash, Nina Simone, John Lee Hooker), his literary inspirations (predominantly the Bible, and particularly the Old Testament) and his approach to songwriting. At one point he opined: 'For me, the great love song has within it an ache' – this was illustrated by a snippet from 'The Sorrowful Wife' He confessed of 1997's *The Boatman's Call* that 'there is an element that disgusts me', referring to the most openly and undisguisedly autobiographical songs like 'West Country Girl' and 'Black Hair', both written about Polly Harvey. Since then, he claims to be standing more 'outside' his lyrical material.

A fine supporting cast, including Will Self, Wim Wenders, *The Observer's* Sean O'Hagan and members of the Bad Seeds Blixa Bargeld and Mick Harvey, offered their own perceptive observations – O'Hagan claimed, 'I think rightly, that with the Bad Seeds the focus is very much on Cave and his lyrics, the music existing as a complementary backdrop, and Self argued that although Cave''s novel *And The Ass Saw The Angel* isn't the most gripping narrative ever committed to paper, it is however 'beautifully written'.

(SINGLE) Bring It On
0301a Bring It On (edit)
0302 Shoot Me Down
0303 Swing Low
ORIGINAL RELEASE: Mute MUTE 5468640, February 2003

COMMENTS: As funky as you can get with Warren Ellis sawing away, but dark as you could hope, Cave finally sounds like he's wandering off the increasingly adult-oriented rock path he'd been on, ready to reclaim some of his past in the form of the absolutely glorious hybrid of his future. Abandoning the simple catch of his recent piano ballads, Cave keeps his sophistication intact, but allows for a little more ragged rock and roll. It was a bridge between two worlds, between two eras, and pleasing all around. And, to herald this new age, 'Bring It On' was drawn from the forthcoming album, as if to usher the fan club alumni gently back in.

'Bring It On' marked another historical union for Cave, as he came together with The Saints' Chris Bailey for the first time, with Bailey contributing some marvellously characteristic backing vocals on the song. Cave explained, 'the chorus reminded me of a Saints song for some reason, so it seemed sort of appropriate. He can sing that sort of stuff; he's got a huge voice.' The circle was closing.

(ALBUM) *Nocturama*
Line-up: Nick Cave (vocals & keyboards); Mick Harvey (guitar); Blixa Bargeld (guitar); Martyn P Casey (bass); Conway Savage (keyboards); Thomas Wydler (drums); Warren Ellis (violin); Jim Scalvunos (percussion).
0304 Wonderful Life
0305 He Wants You
0306 Right Out Of Your Hand
0301 Bring It On

0307 Dead Man In My Bed
0308 Still In Love
0309 There Is A Town
0310 Rock Of Gibraltar
0311 She Passed By My Window
0312 Babe, I'm On Fire
JAPAN CD BONUS TRACKS
0302 Shoot Me Down
0303 Swing Low
0313 Everything Must Converge
ORIGINAL RELEASE: Mute STUMM 207, February 2003

COMMENTS: The final Bad Seeds album with Blixa Bargeld, *Nocturama* continued the group's revived relationship with Nick Launay, and found the band in fine fettle, giving the long-serving guitarist an at-times almost joyous send-off. Recorded at Sing Sing in Melbourne during March 2002, the album was as loud and dirty, desperate and fulfilling as it was quiet.

Cave told the BBC that 'I just keep writing all the time. I keep going into this place, this little room I have and writing all the time. I'm kind of afraid to stop, really. To stop, it takes such an effort to get going again – it's not really worth it, I find. And I'm not one to reflect, so I just barrel onwards, really.'

Although Cave had spent a lot of time on his own, writing the songs that would become *Nocturama*, the album itself was a full band project, recorded in 'something like seven days or something like that… I think the idea was to take some of the preciousness about the making of a record away and possibly create records more like they did in the old days, which was a faster turnaround.'

The studio seemed to be open all hours – visitors to the sessions included the late Ian Dury's old band mates, the Blockheads – Johnny Turnbull, Norman Watt-Roy, Mickey Gallagher and Chaz Jankel; their joyously raucous tones can be heard on 'He Wants You', 'She Passed By My Window' and best of all, 'Bring It On', a kicked-back rocker that allows Ellis' violin to cut gypsy folk through the verses. That song too, was augmented by the Saint's Chris Bailey, and it's his distinctive voice that gives the chorus a sing-along swing.

Conversely, songs like 'Dead Man In My Bed' may be whip-tight and very grown up, but it still roils with the energy that only the Bad Seeds could bring to the studio, even as songs like 'Right Out Of Your Hand' and 'Still In Love' ached like a deep, but healed, scar.

And that's one of the most remarkable things about this album, more purely pinpointed now, in the wake of Cave's two past albums. The band are at the forefront, and the playing feels completely free and loose – but not ever sloppy.

That ethic most definitely spilled over to the album's closer, 'Babe, I'm On Fire'. The song itself was a phenomenal finale, a rag-tag jam where Bargeld's guitar just scythed through the lyrics, and a wonderful curtain on one of rock music's most endearing partnerships. As good as the song was, though, the video was even better, an out of control fifteen-minute extravaganza that saw all of the Bad Seeds cut loose with the wit and wicked humour that is so often hidden from the public eye.

Of the shoot, Cave said, 'we've been trying to do it. I have a little bit of help…someone standing there with cards so I can read the thing. [The song is] a lot more difficult to play than it appears, to maintain a certain amount of sanity in the song, so the whole thing holds together in some form or another without completely descending into utter racket.'

But what an awesome racket it was, as band members took it in turns to skewer politicking baddies, terrorists, all manner of crazies, and most importantly themselves. 'Babe, I'm On Fire,' was the perfect closer to an album that, after the near-unanimous outpouring of support for its predecessor, returned Cave to the realms of the brutally divisive. People either loved the album, or they loved to hate it, and critical reviews ran the gamut from unmitigated ego-stroking to blistering rhetoric.

One particularly savage review appeared on the *All Music Guide* website: ' a writer on his 15th book with nothing much left to say, nothing left to do but go through the motions, phoning his performance in with a yawn. His fans should send him a message by leaving *Nocturama* (his worst record title ever) to gather dust on record store and warehouse shelves. His laziness and weak effort should not be rewarded with your hard-earned cash.'

Ouch. Now that's vitriol, although Cave responded to such musings by shrugging, 'it doesn't upset me to get a bad review. It upsets me to get a sloppy review; as long as they're well-written bad reviews, I don't really care.'

Perhaps part of the problem people had in getting their heads around *Nocturama*, then, lay in the fact that Nick Cave and The Bad Seeds had evolved to such an extent that their sound had been permanently altered. Listen to anything the band were doing through the 1980s, and again during their *Let Love In* heyday, and the sound is undeniably Bad Seeds. Now, however, with Ellis and Sclavunos and Johnston helping to shape the sound – effectively, half the band – the sound had shifted into entirely new dimensions.

Also worth noting here is that Cave had, on the two albums previous to this, produced very personal, even solitary music and used the band sparingly, appearing to be summoning them from the wings to help him when he needed them. On this album, it was clear that Cave wanted to get back into the experience of being in a band, and making a record that showcased that fact.

Of course, the album's release was somewhat overshadowed by Bargeld's departure. Even as *Nocturama* rose to #20 on the UK charts, the band itself was well aware that his leaving had delivered them into a new space; possibly revitalizing them even further than the album itself had. That said, they also needed to decide if the Bad Seeds could even continue without Bargeld's presence – and, if so, how?

As for Bargeld himself, his contributions to the album were, as always, invaluable. The old pugnacious style that had so captivated Cave at the beginning was still there, but Bargeld had also, long ago, developed a unique and understated style of guitar-playing, combining slide and feedback, that gave the songs a beautiful texture. This can be heard to best effect on 'He Wants You' where the aching strains he produces are a perfect complement to Cave's song of spiritual yearning.

The answer to the Bargeld 'problem' arrived in the form of long-standing associate and occasional collaborator James Johnston, initially drafted in for live shows alone, but quickly assimilated as a full band member. Cave admitted that he was 'the total opposite to Blixa in a lot of ways, and he's playing organ and guitar. He played with us at the ill-fated Lollapalooza and did really well there. He just hammers the stuff out. It's exciting.'

(SINGLE) He Wants You
0305 He Wants You
0312a Babe, I'm On Fire (edit)
0315 Little Ghost Song
Everything Must Converge
ORIGINAL RELEASE: Mute MUTE 290, June 2003
COMMENTS: Recorded at Sing Sing, Melbourne, in March 2002, and mixed at Olympic Studios, London in June. Even though the A-side chugs along quite nicely, the highlight of this single is, of course, 'Babe, I'm On Fire', here edited down to an utterly ridiculous three and a half minute rip. Along for the ride, but scarcely worth their bus fare, were two songs from the sessions, the mediocre 'Everything Must Converge' and 'Little Ghost Song'.

(LIVE) Pyramid Room, Helicon Mountain Studios, 20 October 2003
0316 The Kiss Of Love
ORIGINAL RELEASE: Jools Holland & His Rhythm & Blues Orchestra: *Friends 3* Radar/Rhino R2 76559, September 2004

COMMENTS: *Friends* 3 is the third volume in an on-going series of extravaganzas, wherein Holland and his band invite a party's worth of people to jam with them, record the whole thing and put it out on CD. Alongside appearances from Shane MacGowan, Ringo Starr, Eric Clapton, Ronnie Wood, Peter Gabriel and the late Kirsty MacColl (represented by a demo recorded in 1983 with Alan Lee Shaw), and many more, Cave linked with singer Sam Brown for a moving rendition of her own 'The Kiss Of Love'.

(SINGLE) Rock Of Gibraltar
0310 Rock Of Gibraltar
0314 Nocturama
ORIGINAL RELEASE: Mute 318, September 2003

COMMENTS: Despite garnering some of the most uncomplimentary Internet reviews of *any* Nick Cave song yet recorded the powers-that-be nevertheless determined that 'Rock Of Gibraltar' should become the third single from *Nocturama*, compounding the illogic of that decision by rendering it a limited edition 7-inch only, and then throwing a new song, the unreleased title track to *Nocturama* itself, on the B-side.

2004

Despite a delay that saw the long awaited, and oft-promised *B-sides & Rarities* compilation pushed back to the first half of 2005, Cave nevertheless celebrated the year by finally commencing shooting his screenplay *The Proposition*, with John Hillcoat inevitably directing.

He also turned in what stands among the Bad Seeds' most ambitious projects ever – the behemoth *Abattoir Blues/Lyre Of Orpheus*. The album's release was rendered especially poignant with its dedication to long-time friend Mick Geyer, who succumbed to cancer the very day the album was completed.

Their relationship dated back to the time when Boys Next Door were making their first tentative steps in the music business, and the friendship had endured, despite the intervening years of over-indulgence and separation by continent and circumstance. Cave and Geyer renewed their close friendship about the time of the *Murder Ballads* session, and had remained close ever since.

It was, in part, Geyer's presence, and the sadness of watching a beloved friend grow frail that produced such a manic bout of activity represented by the new album, and which saw the projected single disc ultimately flower as two distinct albums – packaged together but, according to Cave, very much intended as individual entities. Cave explained, 'by the time I wrote the lyrics for it, he was unable to read or concentrate because of the amount of drugs he was on. He was really tired, but you know he was…so you know it was kind of written without him.'

(SINGLE) Nature Boy
0401 Nature Boy (edit)
0402 She's Leaving You
ORIGINAL RELEASE: Mute MUTE324, September 2004

COMMENTS: The first single pulled from *Abattoir Blues*, 'Nature Boy' finds Cave with a freewheeling pop momentum that is startling, stunning and a refreshing surprise from the now elder-statesman of doom and gloom. It is a beautifully sung, sexually charged piece and quite possibly the most danceable song that Nick Cave and the Bad Seeds have ever recorded.

'She's Leaving You', is a complete turn-around, an absolutely stellar out-take from the *Abattoir/Lyre* sessions that, while it obviously didn't have a home on the album, is a brilliant clash of old and new. It combines the light and bright sonics of Cave's most recent past, but harks back, nearly completely, to the timbre and metre of the best of *Let Love In*, leaving one to wonder just how long this had been kicking around.

(ALBUM) *Abattoir Blues/The Lyre Of Orpheus*
Line-up: Nick Cave (vocals & keyboards); Mick Harvey (guitar); Martyn P

Casey (bass); Conway Savage (keyboards); Thomas Wydler (drums); Warren Ellis (violin); Jim Scalvunos (percussion); James Johnston (guitar & organ)

0403 Get Ready For Love
0404 Cannibal's Hymn
0405 Hiding All Away
0406 Messiah Ward
0407 There She Goes, My Beautiful World
0401 Nature Boy
0408 Abattoir Blues
0409 Let The Bells Ring
0410 Fable Of The Brown Age
0411 The Lyre Of Orpheus
0412 Breathless
0413 Babe, You Turn Me On
0414 Easy Money
0415 Supernaturally
0416 Spell
0417 Carry Me
0418 O Children

Nick Cave
& The Bad Seeds
Abattoir Blues / The Lyre of Orpheus

The new two album set.
Released October 26th

ORIGINAL   RELEASE: Mute STUMM233, September 2004

COMMENTS: Yow! After what could have been called an off-kilter period for Cave and the Bad Seeds, the band rebounded mightily with this delicious and deliciously audacious double set – a complete redemption of sorts. Divided into two very distinct albums, the opening *Abattoir Blues* disc comes through loud and proud, with the band pounding their way through the opening 'Get Ready For Love', packing the grooves with screeching guitars and a tempestuous rhythm as Cave casts off all remnants of his softer side, and simply lets it all go. And that's before the London Community Gospel Choir weighs in, for just over five minutes of pulse-raising chorus that should be completely out of place, but works just perfectly.

Where the subtle contributions of Kate and Anna McGarrigle on *No More Shall We Part* might, in all honesty, have been missed in places, there was no escape from the LCGC. Their contribution throughout, in all its brilliance, is most reminiscent of Bob Dylan's backing on *Street Legal* and the gospel work that followed; at other times, they sound for all the world like the glam-soul backing that Marc Bolan employed around the time of '20th Century Boy.' Indeed, it is in those same early 1970s that much of the album appears to be situated (if it is meant to be situated anywhere!), a mood exemplified by the use of a wah-wah pedal on 'Cannibal's Hymn.'

Occasionally, songs like 'Hiding All Away' harken back to Punked out, dirty blues, but there are more driving pop tunes here than have ever been heard on a Nick Cave LP. The deep dance beat of 'Abattoir Blues' and the buoyancy of 'Messiah Ward' and 'Let The Bells Ring' are truly infectious – pure alternative pop. For once in their careers, Cave and the band seemed to discard the raiment of gothic noir. There is a real sense that the whole band have been given their heads more than they ever were, with only Warren Ellis (in hindsight, perhaps over-used on the three previous albums) seeming subdued across *Blues*.

Lyrically, too, the album is loose, as Cave brings a sense of humour even to his musings on God, relationships, life and love, a quality that was conspicuously lacking on *No More Shall We Part*. Whether he is rhyming 'Gauguin' with 'man,' and summoning up Karl Marx and *Das Kapital* on 'There She Goes My Beautiful World' or – hilariously – telling us to praise God until you've forgotten what you're praising him for on 'Get Ready For Love,' Cave sounds just as exuberant as the band.

Indeed, as Cave told *Rolling Stone*, 'yeah, I consider myself to be first and foremost a comic writer. The way I entertain myself – especially in those long and grim hours in the office – is to write stuff I find funny. That's not to say my songs are not addressing serious concerns and things that are very meaningful to me. But a necessary part of it to me is the humour.'

'Nature Boy' keeps a frenetic pace going – slacker's hi NRG anyone? – and, as a slab of pure pop with its strangely familiar succession of stops and starts, it really does seem to be a correct, and even tongue-in-cheek rearrangement of Cockney Rebel's 'Come Up And See Me (Make Me Smile)'.

Part of the song, at least, comes from Cave's own childhood. 'Yeah, that is a lovely, little pop song [*laughs*]. The first verse, which deals with me as a child, is a true story. I was at my grandmother's place in Melbourne watching the news on TV with my father and seeing the attempted assassination of George Wallace, and I was really shaken by that because I knew it was the real thing. [My father] said, "Yes, there is that, but there are other things in the world as well," which seemed to me like a reasonable observation.'

The second album in the package, *The Lyre of Orpheus*, finds Cave in a quieter and more introspective mood, but again shot through with a brighter sparkle than his late 1990s albums. Swapping the heavy drumming for jazzier percussion, the music turns inward as it swings from the blues-based chunk of the title track to the rapier-sharp self-deprecation and tender delivery of 'Easy Money.'

Of course, it remains a total contrast to *Blues*, something that brought some consternation to the internet message boards, where reviews again proved that this album was divisive. One *Rate Your Music* member noted that '*The Lyre of Orpheus* has a few interesting lyrical moments, but the music is so muted as to add neither texture nor melody to proceedings. Most of that disc feels monochrome and dull. Disturbing developments include the departure of Blixa Bargeld and the addition of choral backing vocals. The former problem leaves almost no friction in the music.'

But, despite the sleepier swing of the songs (notably 'Breathless,' which sounds remarkably like Van Morrison), the band had a few startling riffs up their sleeves nevertheless. One may have been cuddling a cup of tea throughout the opening strains of *Orpheus*, but when 'Supernaturally' hits the ground – almost as if it were there by mistake – things shift again, the tea goes flying, and you're tapping your toes through first degree burns. A bristly flamenco-styled lament, the shouted chorus is a huge step back in time all the way back to *Henry's Dream*.

Things quickly swing back round, though, with the gentler rhythms of 'Spell,' one of the most beautiful songs on the album. The Bad Seeds create a spry but eerie backdrop of brushed drums, insidious bass and chiming guitars and keyboards (which is vaguely reminiscent of 'Red Right Hand'), while Cave's tremulous invocations and the harmonies of the LCGC combine wonderfully with Ellis' violin.

One man, two albums, trebled intentions: with *Abattoir Blues/The Lyre Of Orpheus*, Cave and the band proved yet again that, although they can throw rock riffs in with the best of them, they have very little or nothing to do with the rock world, preferring instead to keep to their own rhythms, using their forebears to inform but never direct the music. The band prefers to operate from the margins of popular culture, carving out a niche and achieving the respect without compromising their music. And it is this album which triumphantly reaffirmed the sense of drive and ambition that Nick Cave and the Bad Seeds have always had, and which always makes their music compelling.

As always, Cave and the band embarked on a lengthy series of TV performances to coincide with the album's release. One of the most inspired of these, a tremendous version of 'There She Goes, My Beautiful World,' was included (alongside offerings from The Cure, PJ Harvey and John Cale) on the *Later With Jools Holland... Even Louder* DVD (May 2005).

(ALBUM) Marianne Faithfull *Before The Poison*

0419 Crazy Love
0420 There Is A Ghost
0421 Desperanto
ORIGINAL RELEASE: Naïve Records NV 800111, September 2004

COMMENTS: Marianne Faithfull has a strong track record for collaboration, stretching back to her earliest dalliance with the Rolling Stones, on through partnerships with David Bowie, Roger Waters and The Boys, and most recently on 2002's *Kissin' Time*, which saw fruitful partnerships forged with Beck, Jarvis Cocker and Billy Corgan. Here, she repeats the process, becoming even moodier across songs written with PJ Harvey, Blur's Damon Albarn and Nick Cave.

Cave wrote the music for three songs, and backed Faithfull with a band comprising Warren Ellis, Martyn P Casey and Jim Sclavunos. 'Crazy Love' is a temperate piano-driven ballad that very softly whispers a backdrop behind Faithfull's gravelly vocals. 'There Is A Ghost', too, is performed in much the same spirit. And, although the lyrics are by Faithfull alone, the cohesion between the words and music are so beautifully entwined that the composition could just as easily fit into Cave's canon as well.

'Desperanto', on the other hand, bristles in the opposite direction entirely. It's a stomping, rousing, rockabilly, countrified, guitar-driven funk, gloriously muddy and finding Faithfull stepping far out of her usual confines, rapping out a spoken word slab of poetry that is akin to Pet Shop Boys or Jim Morrison. The rest of the band belt out the chorus in a manner that brings to mind the old call and response chants of first wave funk. But, somehow it works. And, it's nice, too, to see Cave himself step out from behind his own façade to collaborate in a way that forces him to stretch.

(SINGLE) Breathless
0412a Breathless
0407a There She Goes, My Beautiful World
0422 Under The Moon
0402 She's Leaving You
ORIGINAL RELEASE: Mute MUTE 329, November 2004

COMMENTS: Newly remixed by Nick Launay, 'Breathless' somehow manages to improve on the already exemplary album version; 'There She Goes, My Beautiful World', on the other hand, pales a little by comparison, as the editing scissors slice into this dirty, yet extremely understated, latter day fists-of-fury sing-along... with full gospel choir.

Listening to 'Under The Moon', meanwhile, it's clear why the song was left off the album; it doesn't hold a candle to the tracks that made the cut. But still, it's a sweet apologist's love song, upbeat and spry.

The 7-inch version of the single replaced both CD flips with a reprise of 'She's Leaving You'.

APOCRYPHA

APPENDIX ONE:
COMPILATIONS AND ANTHOLOGIES

This section includes all significant gatherings of both previously released and archive material, listed chronologically by release date. Various artist compilations and original soundtracks featuring individual, previously available, tracks are not included.

(ALBUM) The Boys Next Door/The Birthday Party *The Birthday Party/The Boys Next Door*
    8005 Mr. Clarinet
    8003 Hats On Wrong
    7917 The Hair Shirt
    8004 Guilt Parade
    8002 Riddle House
    8010 The Friend Catcher
    8011 Waving My Arms
    7914 The Red Clock
    8012 Catman
    8001 Happy Birthday
    ORIGINAL RELEASE: Missing Link LINK 7, November 1980

COMMENTS: With the bulk of this album recorded during two sessions – August and September 1979 and January and February 1980 – this compilation makes a nice package of the band's early singles, with the addition of the *Hee-Haw* EP tracks. The album was credited to both the Boys Next Door and The Birthday Party upon its initial release. Later pressings of the LP were credited to The Birthday Party alone.

A reissue of this collection, appended to the *Hee-Haw* EP, was released in 1988 as *The Birthday Party/Hee-Haw* (4AD CAD 307)

(ALBUM) The Birthday Party *The Birthday Party*
    8118 Release The Bats
    8119 Blast Off
    8010 The Friend Catcher

8005 Mr. Clarinet
8001 Happy Birthday
ORIGINAL RELEASE: 4AD BAD 307, June 1983

COMMENTS: This 12" EP, from 1983, was a collection of the band's 4AD singles.

(ALBUM) various artists/Birthday Party *No Worries*
8102 Blundertown
8215 After The Fire-works
ORIGINAL RELEASE: Hot WORRIED 1, 1985

COMMENTS: Compilation album of Australian bands, including future Bad Seeds' Hugo Race's 'Hellbelly'. Version of Blundertown from January 1981 sessions/12" Nick The Stripper single, with 1984's Tuff Monks single included for good measure.

(ALBUM) The Birthday Party *Best And Rarest / A Collection*
8119 Blast Off
7917 The Hair Shirt
8009 King Ink
8217 Junkyard
8211 Big Jesus Trash Can
8118 Release The Bats
8102 Blundertown
8103 Kathy's Kisses
8107a Ho-Ho
8214 The Friend Catcher
7901 Scatterbrain
7918 The Plague

ORIGINAL RELEASE: Missing Link LINK 22, 1985

COMMENTS: The Birthday Party may not have existed anymore, but that didn't stop Missing Link from riding the back of Cave's burgeoning solo success with a compilation that featured many unreleased Birthday Party outtakes and rarities – things that the band, obviously, kept unreleased for a reason.

The first half of the LP was already out in the public eye – either as singles or LP versions. Both 'Blundertown' and 'Kathy's Kisses' were pulled from the 'Nick The Stripper' single, for example. However, the last five songs, though not completely unreleased, now enjoyed their first major vinyl excursion. 'Ho-Ho' is the version that features Cave's vocals, 'The Friend Catcher' is an alternate take on the song, and had remained unreleased until this point. 'Scatterbrain' was taken from the band's Crystal Ballroom freebie single, while Tracy Pew's 'The Plague' was drawn from the 1979 *Hee-Haw* sessions.

The band was furious at what they saw as betrayal from the label that'd help launch them. Mick Harvey remembers 'Some of this material was never meant to see the light of day. It was completely Keith's idea. The cover he put together was almost like a bad joke on us, using those ridiculous old portrait photos.' Much of this material would subsequently be issued with the group's own blessing, as bonus tracks within The Birthday Party CD reissue programme.

(ALBUM) The Birthday Party *A Collection*
8119 Blast Off
7917 The Hair Shirt
8109 King Ink
8246 Junkyard
8242 Big Jesus Trashcan
8118 Release The Bats
8237 She's Hit
8103 Kathy's Kisses
8010 The Friend Catcher
8104 Zoo Music Girl
8101 Nick The Stripper
8240 Hamlet
ORIGINAL RELEASE: Missing Link SBCD 2017, 1987

COMMENTS: A straightforward anthology of the band's best-loved singles and album cuts. For even more adventurous fans and collectors, Missing Link later produced a box set, *The Definitive Missing Link Recordings 1979-82*, comprising each of the label's albums and compilations, plus a remarkably uninteresting booklet (LINK 30).

(ALBUM) The Birthday Party *Mutiny/The Bad Seed*
8308 Sonny's Burning
8309 Wild World
8310 Fears Of Gun
8311 Deep In The Woods
8322 Pleasure Avalanche
8318 Jennifer's Veil
8319 Mutiny In Heaven
8320 Swamp Land
8321 Say A Spell
8323 The Six Strings That Drew Blood
ORIGINAL RELEASE: 4AD CAD 301, 1988

COMMENTS: A CD release twinning the *Mutiny* and *The Bad Seed* EPs, appended with two outtakes.

(EP) Nick Cave And The Bad Seeds *The Good Songs*
9012 The Mercy Seat
8615 Rye Whiskey
8917 Helpless
8701 From Her To Eternity
9002 The Train Song
ORIGINAL RELEASE: Mute Sonet France SA 2110, May 1990

COMMENTS: This five-track compilation was made available via mail to subscribers of the French music magazine *Les Inrockuptibles*. Culled from a variety of sources, it offered a handy little selection of recent rarities, including the acoustic 'The Mercy Seat', the *Kicking Against The Pricks* out-take 'Rye Whiskey', the Neil Young tribute and the *Wings of Desire* 'From Her To Eternity'. The set was then completed with the recent B-side 'The Train Song'.

(ALBUM) The Birthday Party *Hits*
8010 The Friend Catcher
8001 Happy Birthday
8005 Mr. Clarinet
8101 Nick The Stripper
8104 Zoo Music Girl
8109 King Ink
8118 Release The Bats
8119 Blast Off
8237 She's Hit
8240 Hamlet (Pow, Pow, Pow)
8238 Dead Joe
8244 Six-Inch Gold Blade.
8246 Junkyard
8242 Big Jesus Trash Can
8309 Wild World
8308 Sonny's Burning
8311 Deep In The Woods
8320 Swampland
8318 Jennifer's Veil
8319 Mutiny In Heaven
ORIGINAL RELEASE: 4AD CAD 2016, 1992

COMMENTS: Once more around the block for the greatest hits of a band that never had any hits. No complaints about the actual track selection... and no surprises, either. But there was an entire generation who'd grown up in the ten years since this stuff first came out, and they deserved to base their appreciation of Cave's back pages on something more solid than their parents' misty-eyed memories. They got it.

'Six-Inch Gold Blade', incidentally, appears only on UK pressings. Obviously, American listeners didn't deserve it.

(EP) The Birthday Party *Hits*
8101 Nick The Stripper
8118 Release The Bats
8308 Sonny's Burning
8311 Deep In The Woods
8318 Jennifer's Veil
ORIGINAL RELEASE: 4AD, 1992

COMMENTS: They did, however, deserve this – a five-track promotional cassette issued in the US only, to help promote the parent *Hits* compilation. Doubtless, US radio programmers had an excellent time trying to decide which of the five cuts most merited airplay.

(ALBUM) Anita Lane – *Dirty Pearl*
8904 A Prison In The Desert
8801 I'm A Believer
8802 Lost In Music
8218 The Fullness Of His Coming

ORIGINAL RELEASE: Mute STUMM 81, 1993

COMMENTS: Although this is considered to be Lane's first album, and billed as such, *Dirty Pearl* is more like a strange compilation that traces her career in reverse. Produced by Mick Harvey with additional arrangements from Barry Adamson, and featuring all the usual suspects, this album also rounded up the entire *Dirty Sings* EP, plus one superb surprise bonus track.

Although it was nice to revisit 'I'm A Believer' and the odd Sister Sledge cover, 'Lost In Music' (plus one cut from *Ghosts... Of The Civil Dead*), as far as Cave's own history goes, what is most important was the first ever release of 'The Fullness Of His Coming', recorded during the May 1982 sessions by The Birthday Party.

Other musicians appearing on this remarkable album include Die Haut, Blixa Bargeld and Einstürzende Neubauten, Bronwyn Adams, and the Triffids' Evil Graham Lee; Flood, Tony Cohen and Victor Van Vugt were all involved in engineering the sessions.

(ALBUM) *The Boatman's Call Australian Tour Nov/Dec 1997*
9702 Little Empty Boat

9703 Right Now I'm A Roaming
9717 Come Into My Sleep
9718 Black Hair (Band Version)
9719 Babe, I Got You Bad
ORIGINAL RELEASE: Mute NICK 1, 1997

COMMENTS: This freebie sampler was given away in Australia with the purchase of any Bad Seeds CD, and was timed to coincide with the band's tour of that country. All five songs were drawn from recent B-sides.

(ALBUM) *The Best Of Nick Cave And The Bad Seeds*
8806 Deanna
9407 Red Right Hand
9201 Straight To You
8502a Tupelo
9404 Nobody's Baby Now
8619 Stranger Than Kindness
9701 Into My Arms
9708 (Are You) The One That I've Been Waiting For?
8617 The Carny
9401a Do You Love Me?
8803 The Mercy Seat
9606 Henry Lee
9007a The Weeping Song
9001 The Ship Song
9505 Where The Wild Roses Grow
8407 From Her To Eternity

ORIGINAL RELEASE: Mute MUTEL4, 1998

COMMENTS: Released both on CD and LP, this solo career-spanning collection is noteworthy for containing several so-called 'single' versions of past Cave triumphs; sharp ears may also note 'Tupelo' has been extended by around ten seconds.

A very straightforward collection, aimed directly at the legion of new fans now appearing, *The Best Of* nevertheless doffed its cap towards older supporters and collectors via the inclusion, with early pressings, of a bonus live disc, *Live At The Royal Albert Hall* (see main text for details). Other incentives included a promo only box set that included the album, an interview disc, and the *A Short Film*, a 23 minute EPK video, directed by Sven Harding, together with a biography and discography. Apparently, at this project's outset, Cave asked the band (himself included) to come up with a definitive list of titles to be pooled for the final selection. In the event, Mick Harvey was the only person that came up with a list at all and it is, therefore, his selection.

(ALBUM) The Birthday Party *The John Peel Sessions*
8006 Cry
8007 Yard
8008 Figure Of Fun
8009 King Ink
8114 Release The Bats
8115 Rowland Around In That Stuff
8116 Pleasureheads Must Burn
8117 Loose
8131 Big Jesus Trash Can
8132 She's Hit
8133 Bully Bones
8134 Six-Inch Gold Blade
8255 Pleasure Avalanche
8256 Deep In The Woods
8257 Sonny's Burning
8258 Marry Me (Lie! Lie!)
ORIGINAL RELEASE: Strange Fruit SFRSCD 098, 2001

COMMENTS: After several years of mere highlights from the band's remarkable BBC archive popping up hither and thither, the entire sequence was finally issued on one disc, to remind us of a time when this music was *not* an all-too-familiar adjunct to a career that is fast approaching its thirtieth birthday.

Still, in equal doses, frightening, frustrating and furious, The Birthday Party stand revealed as psychotic axe murderers when compared to virtually anything else around at the time. Even the once 'difficult' sounds of The Slits, The Fall and The Pop Group, the only other bands truly operating this far out on a limb, have now become so absorbed into what we think of as 'normal' as to sound less than startling. But the dislocation that comes out of this set, no matter where in the chronology the needle falls, remains distinct and vivid.

(ALBUM) *B-sides & Rarities*
9014 Deanna (Acoustic Version)
9012 The Mercy Seat (Acoustic Version)
9013 City Of Refuge (Acoustic Version)
8403 The Moon Is In The Gutter
8508 The Six Strings That Drew Blood
8615 Rye Whisky
8602 Running Scared
8603 Black Betty
8624 Scum
8807 The Girl At The Bottom Of My Glass
9002 The Train Song

9015 Cocks 'n' Asses
9203 Blue Bird
8917 Helpless
9226 God's Hotel
9103 (I'll Love You) Till The End Of The World
9316 Cassiel's Song
9102 Tower Of Song
9212 What Can I Give You?
9233 What A Wonderful World
9234 Rainy Night In Soho
9237 Lucy (Version #2)
9204 Jack The Ripper
9402 Sail Away
9301 There's No Night Out At The Jail
9414 That's What Jazz Is To Me
9507 The Willow Garden
9506 The Ballad Of Robert Moore And Betty Coltrane
9613 King Kong Kitchee Kitchee Ki-Mi-O
9614 Knoxville Girl
9508 Where The Wild Roses Grow
9615 O'Malley's Bar Pt.1
9616 O' Malley's Bar Pt.2
9617 O' Malley's bar Pt. 3
9619 Time Jesum Transeuntum Et Non Riverentum
9618 O'Malley's Bar Reprise
9407c Red Right Hand (*Scream 3* Version)
9702 Little Empty Boat
9703 Right Now I'm A-Roaming
9717 Come into My Sleep
9718 Black Hair (Band Version)
9719 Babe, I've Got You Bad
9715 Sheep May Safely Graze
9716 Opium Tea
0116 Grief Came Riding
0117 Bless His Ever Loving Heart
0103 Good Good Day
0102 Little Janey's Gone
0204 I Feel So Good
0302 Shoot Me Down
0303 Swing Low
0315 Little Ghost Song
0313 Everything Must Converge
0314 Nocturama
0402 She's Leaving You
0422 Under This Moon

ORIGINAL RELEASE: Mute, March 2005

COMMENTS: 'This is my favourite Nick Cave and the Bad Seeds album,' enthused Nick Cave as this mammoth project finally came to fruition, and well it might be. Twenty-plus years in the making, the actual notion of such a beast had been kicking around the Bad Seeds camp since the mid-1990s, when Mick Harvey first suggested compiling a 2CD package of all the little odds and sods that were driving collectors crazy.

The bootleggers, of course, had long since beaten them to it – indeed, the semi-legendary *More Pricks Than Kicks* collection still wipes the floor with the 'real thing' when it comes to unearthing some genuine treasures (33 minutes of 'Tower Of Song', a radio cover of 'Sunny', and so forth.) But still Harvey's notion met with general approval from his bandmates, with just one proviso: 'The general response was, "Yes, great idea. We just have to look for the right moment to do it." There hasn't been enough space where there wasn't something else imminent.'

Even its release in 2005 (having loomed over much of 2004) was 'a fairly arbitrary moment in time,' Harvey continued. But it had to happen some time. Already the original concept had swollen into a three disc package – wait any longer and nobody would be able to lift the thing up.

Generally chronological, the set follows Cave's career, for the most part, from the perspective of his B-sides and contributions to compilations and soundtracks. Mingled in among them, however, are a clutch of genuine treasures – unreleased gems like Blixa Bargeld's original guide vocal on 'Where The Wild Roses Grow', a leviathan BBC radio version of 'O'Malley's Bar', forgotten contributions to unreleased tribute albums, and so forth.

Harvey admitted, 'the quality jumps around enormously. "God's Hotel" is very rough and ready, all DI lines, radio studio, and then it cuts to "(I'll Love You) Till The End Of The World"… high production, quality song… it jumps from one thing to the next. The same thing happens with "Cassiel's Song" that runs into "Tower Of Song", which was us just hammering it straight out to DAT in the studio.' And such was the attention to detail that just two B-sides were omitted from the set: 'B-side' 'because that's not a song, it's an editing exercise;' and 'Where The Action Is', 'because it was too long and sprawling.'

Aside from the titular qualifications, there was just one essential criteria to be adhered to. 'It [had to be] a Bad Seeds recording, not a Nick Cave recording.' With the exception of Cave's Dirty Three backed contribution to the *X-Files* compilation… included because the original was hidden away at Track 0, and a lot of people missed it entirely… 'there isn't anything by Nick working with other people or by himself, it's just Nick with members of The Bad Seeds.'

APPENDIX TWO:
VIDEOS AND VISUALS

This section features only complete Cave related packages; contributions to various artist and movie productions are referenced in the main text.

(VIDEO) *Pleasure Heads Must Burn*
Nick The Stripper
Fears Of Gun
Hamlet (Pow, Pow, Pow)
Deep In The Woods
Junkyard
Dead Joe
A Dead Song
Junkyard
Release The Bats
Pleasureheads Must Burn
Big Jesus Trash Can
Hamlet (Pow, Pow, Pow)
Pleasure Avalanche
Six-Inch Gold Blade
Wild World
The Six Strings That Drew Blood
Sonny's Burning
She's Hit
ORIGINAL RELEASE: VHS IKON 7, 1988

COMMENTS: Excerpts from two live shows, at Manchester's Hacienda in 1982 (six songs) and 1983 (seven songs), are appended (the first five tracks) with two Birthday Party promo videos, and three TV performances. See the main text for details.
   The full set has since been reissued on a no-frills DVD (Cherry Red).

(VIDEO) *The Road To God Knows Where*
ORIGINAL RELEASE: Mute/BMG 790475, December 1990

COMMENTS: This documentary, shot in black and white, chronicled life on the road for Nick Cave and the Bad Seeds during their early 1989 American tour. Filming commenced on the opening night at Philadelphia's Chestnut

Cabaret on 7 February and carried through to the final show at Scream in Los Angeles on 4 March.

The film itself was treated to a world premiere screening at the Olympic Film Festival in Manchester on 29 June 1990. It proved to be very much an acquired taste, full of dark shadows, subtitles throughout (it is unclear whether this is because of the film's German origins or whether certain people are incoherent in it!) and, it must be said, a fair share of humdrum footage. It can be fascinating, though, on many counts. The closeness of a band that was still nowhere near a definitive line-up is nearly touching: linking hands and dancing before one concert, huddled together and joking in a lift, singing Hank Williams on a tour bus, with a rare glimpse of Nick Cave playing a guitar. The business-like, near-ruthless streak that they possessed is on display when they are tormenting a photographer doing a shoot just before a show; making cold and methodical deliberations on an error-prone sound engineer on tow who is doomed to be sacked and, a memorable row with a venue (obviously one of many) where Bargeld wades into the argument and pummels a hapless mixing engineer into the ground.

Inevitably, Cave becomes the star of the show with some of his encounters. With a radio show host and a driver, he shows his considerable charm and he displays a lot of patience with assorted backstage freaks, interviewers and the near-psychotic musings of a correspondent by letter. The patience wears thin with people at venues, naturally, and he storms out of one. By far the best non-music scene in the film is one where a clearly exhausted Cave is subjected to an interview and photo shoot in his hotel room. The hopelessly incoherent interview technique of the journalist and the smarmy remarks of the photographer, in what looks like (in the few minutes we see), the most disastrous interview ever, are mirrored by Cave's comical air of befuddlement at the inane questions, closely followed by boiling rage at the photographer's importuning.

The musical content, meanwhile, is often minimal – time is spent on Cave's pre-song introductions and speech, sometimes at the expense of the music, and the clips of each number that do surface – including an otherwise unavailable take on the Philly soul classic 'TSOP' (recorded, of course, in Philadelphia), a turbulent 'From Her To Eternity' and a sound checked 'Fever' – are often so brief, muffled and muddy that they really have no business even appearing in a discography. Nevertheless, there is a beautiful version of 'The Mercy Seat' recorded at the same radio session as 'Sunny', and there's a poignant 'New Morning' to close. Also, there is a powerful version of 'Knockin' On Joe', which because of the low budget, looks like it was performed in near-darkness: making the death-row song all the more dramatic, and the nonchalant way that the band stop half way through to see to an onstage problem and start again is charming and highly charismatic.

Although it can hardly be classed as a classic rock 'n' roll documentary, the director, Uli M Schuppel's stated intention of not making a film of 'musicians as exaggerated mythical figures' was realised on film. It's a brutally honest account of life on the road and it was something that Cave and the band could be proud of being involved in.

The lack of a number of complete tunes, perhaps, meant that the movie's VHS release in December 1990, was bolstered with the bonus inclusion of the videos for 'In The Ghetto', 'Deanna', 'Tupelo', 'The Singer', and 'The Mercy Seat'. In Japan, meanwhile, it was buried away within a limited edition, numbered bumper pack alongside Cave's *King Ink* lyric book, as well as the *Ghosts...Of The Civil Dead* soundtrack. (ALZB-1).

(VIDEO) *The Videos*
Stagger Lee
Where The Wild Roses Grow
Into My Arms
(Are You) The One That I've Been Waiting For?
Henry Lee
Red Right Hand
Loverman
Do You Love Me?
Deanna
The Ship Song
Tupelo
In The Ghetto
Jack The Ripper
What A Wonderful World
Straight To You
The Mercy Seat
The Weeping Song
The Singer
I Had A Dream Joe
Wanted Man
ORIGINAL RELEASE: Mute MF030, May 1998

COMMENTS: At last, the Nick Cave videos collection, and it's about damn time, people said, especially those in the United States who'd had little exposure to Cave's clips. After waiting for so many years, then, the release of this first video collection was a triumph.

Sadly sideswiped by MTV broadcasters and others of their ilk, many of the reels shot for the band's songs passed the mainstream by completely. Even in the wake of Cave's white-hot mid-1990s hipness, it seemed that kids (or, at least, TV programmers) were far more interested in the raunch and roll of any one of a handful of fifth generation Punk slobbos than the real thing.

Segmented by snatches of band commentary about the individual videos, the contents pull mostly from Cave's *Henry's Dream/Let Love In* heyday, but allow a smattering of pre and post nuggets to jostle alongside. From the classic simplicity of 1985's Mick Harvey-directed one-two punch of 'Tupelo' and

'Wanted Man,' to the low-budget, cash-squandered mess of 'In The Ghetto,' and on to the newer 'Into My Arms,' here was a band that loved the camera.

The videos become slicker and sleeker as time passes, with some of the most startling fare – 'Jack The Ripper,' 'Loverman,' and 'Do You Love Me?' – shot by filmmaker John Hillcoat. Also of note is the beautifully brutal 'Henry Lee' duet between Cave and west country ingénue PJ Harvey, a passionate come-on against a green curtain and framed only by a single camera and the murderous lyrics.

All angles and sharp planes, world-weary shoulders and lean figures, this is a band, visually, that demands to be captured on film. And whether on grainy 16mm, handheld video or state of the art digital, the end result is never a stinker.

Cave and Harvey provide nearly all the commentary here, and there are Bargeld interjections, filmed earlier in a theatre. Their commentary is consistently funny, self-deprecating and often surprising, so much so that one often wishes the interviews last longer – Cave is not afraid to say how bad a video like 'Straight To You' is, for instance.

The entire set was re-issued on DVD in 2004. It was a straight reissue of the 1998 VHS release, and that means no post-*Boatman's Call* videos, no bonus materials, no documentary footage, no DVD goodies at all. On the other hand, though, having these twenty clips under the direct control of the remote control means no more fast-forward and rewinding to watch just *this* or *that*, either.

(VIDEO) *God Is In The House*
Do You Love Me?
Oh My Lord
Lime Tree Arbour
Red Right Hand
As I Sat Sadly By Her Side
The Weeping Song
God Is In The House
We Came Along This Road
Papa Won't Leave You, Henry
Hallelujah
The Mercy Seat
Into My Arms
Saint Huck
The Curse Of Millhaven
ORIGINAL RELEASE: DVD Mute 9224-9, August 2003

COMMENTS: This nicely varied set was filmed in Lyon, France on 8 June 2001. The somewhat belated DVD release included some nice bonus features; a documentary on the recording of *No More Shall We Part,* as well as video clips for 'As I Sat Sadly By Her Side', 'Fifteen Feet Of Pure White Snow', and 'Love Letter'. Let's see you watch those on MTV US kiddies!

APPENDIX THREE:
THE ACTS OF THE APOSTLES

Nick Cave is one of those rare musicians whose associates have remained friends and excellent working partners throughout the duration of his entire career. Notwithstanding a few wobbles over the years, the core members of Boys Next Door became The Birthday Party became the Bad Seeds. It is rare to mine such golden partnerships over and over.

Each of the musicians here contributes/ed a vital part to the sound that Nick Cave and his bands have propagated. Without Bargeld, or Adamson or Ellis the bands' sound wouldn't have been what it was. These men, too, have often taken on the impossible, working within the confines of several different bands, often at the same time!

So here, then, are those talented men who have become a part of the Boys Next Door/Birthday Party/Bad Seeds legends.

A brief note.... It would be easy to fill another book with the honours and exploits of Cave's core fourteen. What follows, then, is a brief biography and selected album discography – the essential listening, if you will – for each musician.

BARRY ADAMSON

A uniquely talented musician, Barry Adamson has come nearly full circle, developing his early love of film and film scores into a vital, vibrant parallel to an already brimful rock and roll career.

Adamson, a first-rate bassist, first came into the spotlight via Howard Devoto's Magazine outfit, formed by the vocalist after he departed the Buzzcocks in 1977. Alongside John McGeoch, Bob Dickinson and Martin Jackson, Magazine was one of the very first wave of bands to emerge from the rapidly shredding Punk rebellion. Indeed, with their mix of classic Punk ethics and edgy instrumentation, Magazine helped to define the newly emergent post-Punk genre, adding a sophisticated theatrical edge to their live performance.

With a wash of keyboards, Howard Devoto continued to hone the keen politically edged lyrics with which he'd become associated. Under the influence of Adamson, though, pure Punk was supplanted by a miraculous Pangaea of sonic landscapes, intricate melodics that created as much of a visual image as the band themselves did.

Although that outfit would survive only through the middle of 1981, as members spun off and on to newer projects, Adamson was rapidly expanding his horizons, as part of Visage as well as adding his stamp to work from Pete Shelley and Midge Ure and Wolfgang Press. These associations and many others would bring him out from behind his bass to emerge as producer, remixer, collaborator and guest for a wealth of acts – a trend that continues to the present day.

Adamson had already dabbled his toes in Nick Cave's camp, of course, filling in for Tracy Pew in 1982, and as Nick Cave And The Bad Seeds coalesced around a firm line-up in the mid-1980s, Adamson found himself again handling his bass for the beautifully evolving combo. It was a stint that would last until he left the Bad Seeds in 1987, but those partnerships would continue to inform his work, both solo and in collaboration with Nick Cave.

After leaving the Bad Seeds Adamson now had the time to fulfil one of his earliest desires. With a host of classic icons percolating in his mind, Ennio Morricone, and John Barry among them, Adamson cast his eyes toward creating music that was nearly completely informed by the soundtracks and scores he'd loved. Adamson released his debut, 1988's *The Man With The Golden Arm* EP, and swiftly followed up with a full-length album, *Moss Side Story*, the following year. It was a startling panorama of sound that washed the best of post-Punk with a noir-ish tint and then added sonic electronics on top.

The soundtrack for a movie that never existed Adamson parlayed the ideals forged on this remarkable album into a new career that would see him score and contribute to numerous soundtracks, most notably for *Delusion, Gas Food Lodging, Last Of England* and *Lost Highway*.

When not working within the confines of cinematic hullabaloo, Adamson continued to record remarkable solo albums through the rest of the decade and into the new millennium. *The Taming Of The Shrewd*, *Soul Murder*, *The Negro Inside Me*, *Oedipus Schmoedipus* and *As Above So Below* may not have showered the bassist with any major commercial successes, but that was of little consequence. Adamson had carved a niche for himself, creating an impressive and critically well received array of material which placed him within a genre nearly of his own making.

By the end of the 1990s, Adamson was collaborating with Finland's Pan Sonic and the Hafler Trio to compose music for an Icelandic Choir in response to a request from Iceland's Kitchen Motors record label, in an attempt to expand and revitalize Iceland's flagging avant-garde music scene. Pan Sonic explained that 'we've enlisted the help of Barry Adamson. [We] don't know quite what will come of it, but it sounds interesting. We certainly don't have any experience with this sort of thing, but then, Barry Adamson does.'

More in the shadows than out during the beginning of the next decade, Adamson was returned for public consumption with the release of 2002's *The King Of Nothing Hill*.

The album was a masterful continuation of what Adamson had been doing all along – combining poignant narration with absolutely ethereal, rock solid cinematic sound.

SELECTED LISTENING

MAGAZINE:
1978 *Real Life*
1979 *Secondhand Daylight*
1980 *The Correct Use Of Soap*
1981 *Play (Live at Melbourne Festival Hall)*

BARRY ADAMSON:
1989 *Moss Side Story*
1992 *Soul Murder*
1993 *The Negro Inside Me*
1996 *Oedipus Schmoedipus*
1998 *As Above So Below*
1999 *The Murky World Of*
2002 *The King Of Nothing Hill*

BLIXA BARGELD

Born Christian Emmerich in Berlin, Blixa Bargeld's name has now become irrevocably twined with that of Nick Cave. However, one of his proudest and most important achievements is the founding of Einstürzende Neubauten. But Bargeld is not nearly the sum of these two, admittedly enormous, undertakings. He has had a widely panning career that has seen him work with a myriad of other performers, and cross boundaries into the realms of theatre, spoken word and film.

But, in the beginning anyway, there was Einstürzende Neubauten. Bringing that band to life in 1980, while still in his teens, Bargeld was heavily influenced not only by the DIY ethics of the Punk revolution, but also by the German Die Geniale Dilletanten movement, one that borrowed heavily from the philosophies of the Dada-ist culture.

Einstürzende Neubauten (Collapsing New Buildings), with an original line-up that included N.U. Unruh, Beate Bartel, Gudrun Gut and Alexander Van Borsig, can be given all but sole credit for igniting the industrial scene of the early 1980s. Combining the energy of Punk, a thousand shards of art rock glass was one thing, but it wasn't nearly enough for Bargeld who, alongside his bandmates, delivered a dense pounding wall of noise that clattered, roared and screeched. By using an arsenal of instruments, augmented by power tools and the ubiquitous hammer, Einstürzende Neubauten completely deconstructed conventional music, and re-invented it with a completely new pathos. It proved to be a powerful calling card.

By the time their first single, 'Fuer Den Untergang' appeared in 1980, the band had already set their sonic thumbprints on what alternative music was becoming. And, by the time The Birthday Party relocated to Berlin in 1982, it was inevitable that these two bands would forge some kind of kindred movement.

Their debut LP, *Kollaps*, was released in 1982 and, by the time they'd hit Britain's tour circuit with The Birthday Party the following year, it was evident that Neubauten were going to become the darlings of the UK press.

Bargeld and Neubauten expanded their ever widening circle the following year as Bargeld teamed with Rowland S Howard and Lydia Lunch for the magnificent *Thirsty Animal* EP. But, with The Birthday Party taking up his time, and then with the advent of the Bad Seeds in 1984, Bargeld and Neubauten were spread too thin. The band teetered on the edge of disbanding as Bargeld tried to maintain his Neubauten role while becoming a full-time member of the Bad Seeds, while Van Borsig and more recent member Alexander Hacke would split to form Crime And The City Solution with Simon Bonney and Rowland S Howard.

But Neubauten *was* still an ongoing concern. The band's stimulating *Halber Mensch* was released in 1985 and emerged an electric battering ram – a cacophony of full-blooded battery that used percussion as rhythms to back spectral melodies and the harmonic whisper of chanting vocals. It was a startling revitalization of the band's sound, which had hitherto only hinted at such powerful atmospherics. Bargeld balanced with the solo release, *Commissioned Music,* the same year. That album was a compilation of Bargeld's music scored for the film *Jahre Der Kalte*, and the stage play *Dumpfe Stimmen*.

Einstürzende Neubauten disbanded in 1989 but reformed during the 1990s, and Bargeld once again continued to work within the framework of two bands, while also becoming what amounted to a one-man art factory, balancing the work of both bands with his own strivings as an actor, both in front of the camera and behind the scenes, participating in numerous music and theatre projects, as well as touring with Die Haut in 1992 and 1994.

Bargeld was also becoming increasingly active with spoken word readings and as a participant in industry panels – most notably in 1991 when he performed a reading of Heiner Muller's *Die Hamletmaschine*. Einstürzende Neubauten provided the background music for that performance, naturally.

In 2003, Bargeld left the Bad Seeds to concentrate fully on Einstürzende Neubauten.

SELECTED LISTENING:

EINSTURZENDE NEUBAUTEN:
1981 *Kollaps*
1983 *Portrait Of Patient Ot*
1985 *Halber Mensch*
1987 *Feunf Auf Der Nach Oben Offenen Richterskal*
1989 *Haus Der Luge*
2000 *Silence Is Sexy*

BLIXA BARGELD:
1985 *Commissioned Music*

PHILL CALVERT:

Drummer Phill Calvert was an early, integral player in the evolution of Nick Cave's musical persona. Calvert, of course, got his start in the business as part of the Concrete Vultures aggregation at the Caulfield Grammar School in Melbourne in the mid-1970s.

Unlike his bandmates, though, Calvert was already a competent musician when he stepped behind the Concrete Vultures' kit. He'd been drumming since he was in grade school, and by the time he was ten, was taught by Moscow Circus drummer Les Taskin.

Calvert would stay with the band through the end of school as they transformed into the Boys Next Door, and then drove themselves ahead as The Birthday Party. But there were deep fractures from way back, with Calvert establishing himself very early on as a target for the others' ire and mirth. By the time The Birthday Party were preparing 'Release The Bats' in 1981, the relationship between Calvert and the rest of the band was obviously becoming more fraught.

As The Birthday Party continued to develop their ideal sound, it quickly became clear that Calvert's drumming, precise, rhythmic and technical, was no longer in keeping with the pure, raw sonics that his band were plying and that only added to the growing resentment. When the band relocated to Berlin, Calvert was very ungraciously dumped from the line-up; there was no German invite for him.

But Calvert himself was ready to move on, and indeed, no sooner had he put one boot out of The Birthday Party, than he was walking right back into another band. He'd caught Psychedelic Furs' frontman Richard Butler's attention and that band's manager approached Calvert to come sit in on a session.

From that inauspicious beginning, Calvert found himself to be the new drummer for the Psychedelic Furs, touring with the band during 1982 and 1983. And he'd probably have continued on, for some time at least, if he'd not gotten into a fight with the producer and band as sessions for *Forever Now* were about to commence. In the wake of that fractious incident, Calvert was fired.

London, for Calvert, was over and he returned home to Melbourne.

There he hooked up with Ian McLean, Mulaim Vela and Adam Learner who, as Scrap Museum, had recently released the 'Say Die' single. Replacing drummer Frank Borg, Calvert launched a new start as Scrap Museum became the blues rock combo, Blue Ruin.

Signed to Rampant, Blue Ruin released *Such Sweet Thunder* in January 1986, followed by *Flame* in Spring 1987. But, despite such a portentous beginning, Blue Ruin foundered in Australia, and relocated to the UK in search of an audience where they pounded pavement for a solid year, gigging and hoping for a big break. It didn't happen, and by the beginning of 1991, not long after the band released their third LP, *I'm Gonna Smile,* Calvert left.

A short stint in The Sunday Kind followed, where Calvert wielded his sticks from late 1993 through August 1995. He followed through with Sugarhips in 1998 and launched yet another project, In Vivo, in 2002. Partnered with Magic Dirt's Dave Thomas, and Have A Nice Day's Fiona Lee Maynard, the band cut an album,

Punks Like You Are A Dime A Dozen, released in the beginning of 2003.

SELECTED LISTENING:

BLUE RUIN
1986 *Such Sweet Thunder*
1987 *Flame*
1989 *Strange Things In The Corner*
1990 *I'm Gonna Smile*

IN VIVO
2003 *Punks Like You Are A Dime A Dozen*

MARTYN P CASEY

Although Martyn P Casey is now firmly linked with Nick Cave's Bad Seeds, the fluid bassist is better known to some as part of the definitive line-up of The Triffids. Formed in Perth by school friends David McComb and Alsy MacDonald, The Triffids had already made seven cassette albums, two independent singles and an EP when Casey replaced bassist Byron Sinclair in September 1982. The impact was immediate.

The *Bad Timing* EP, recorded in October and released by Mushroom Records in April 1983, had a newfound flow which strongly argued his influence. Mushroom didn't notice or didn't care for flow and let the band go shortly after the EP's release. Undeterred, The Triffids paid for the recording of their debut album, the darkly disturbing *Treeless Plain*, then arranged for its release by Hot Records, a new Australian independent.

Treeless Plain was well received locally but the band had already set its sights higher. Like many of their Australian peers, The Triffids realized they had a better chance of establishing themselves overseas. Their instincts proved astute. The band found an eager audience in Britain and, soon, the Continent, making the cover of the *NME* in January 1985. Later that year they recorded *Born Sandy Devotional*, a stunning sequence of heartsore songs of exile. When released in June 1986, it was an immediate *succes d'estime*: the band was courted by several UK majors before signing a contract with Island Records in November 1986.

In the meantime, they had recorded and released *In The Pines*, a rough-and-ready slab of powerful alt pop, in a woolshed in the southwest of Western Australia during a break in their annual tour. Before returning to England to record *Calenture*, their debut album for Island and an exotic extension of *Born Sandy*'s alienated themes, they toured the stadiums of Australia's capital cities as a package with The Saints, Mental As Anything, INXS and three other Australian bands.

They continued to gig in the Northern Hemisphere until the end of the decade, proving especially popular in Scandinavia. Their 1989 LP *The Black Swan*, a restless experimental set produced by Stephen Street, gave the band their first bona fide UK chart place. But, inventive as they still seemed to be, The Triffids were unable – or unwilling – to make a move toward a more mainstream spot: they played their last show on 14 August 1989.

Dave McComb, Alsy McDonald and Ca\sey then reconvened The Blackeyed Susans, the 'holiday band' Dave and Alsy had formed earlier in the year with original Triffid Phil Kakulas and Rob Snarski from Chad's Tree. This incarnation of the band had already folded when Casey was invited to join the Bad Seeds in April 1990. The Susans regrouped in 1992 with Kakulas returning on bass and Warren Ellis, Jim White and Graham Lee from The Triffids joining the line-up.

Casey also played on McComb's 1994 solo album *Love of Will*. Sadly, McComb died in February 1999.

SELECTED LISTENING:

1983 *Treeless Plain*
1985 *Love In Bright Landscapes*
1986 *Born Sandy Devotional*
1986 *In The Pines*
1987 *Calenture*
1989 *The Black Swan*
1990 *Stockholm*

WARREN ELLIS

The classically trained violinist was a dominant presence in a veritable treasure trove of Australian bands, including Paranoid, the Nursing Mothers and Blackeyed Susans – with whom he'd recorded 1993's stellar Leonard Cohen-esque *All Souls Alive*. However, he made his first explosive marks on the music scene within the framework of his Dirty Three aggregation.

Formed in Melbourne in 1992, Ellis teamed with Feral Dinosaurs guitarist Mick Turner and ex-Sick Things drummer Jim White and debuted his new band with a sound that captivated audiences and peers from the very beginning. Using his violin not only as the instrument had been intended, but also plying it like a guitar, like a banshee, he defined a lo-fi scratch that set the stage for a wealth of up and comers. Like the Doctors Of Madness' Urban Blitz before him, Ellis brought the violin back to the forefront, giving Alternative mopesters everywhere a new brand of music to chew.

The trio made their debut with *Sad & Dangerous* in 1994, an album of unparalled intensity that was essentially recorded as a demo. This stunning slab of pop landed the band a number of prestigious opening slots on tours for some of the era's most venerable demi-gods, Sonic Youth and John Cale among them.

By 1995, the band had inked to Touch & Go and delivered their eponymous album that same year, following quickly with *Horse Stories* in 1996, *Ocean Songs* in 1998 and *Whatever You Love, You Are* in 2000. It seemed that people just couldn't get enough of this band.

Ellis kept busy during the 1990s, too, with assorted side projects and guest spots that included appearances on Robert Forster's solo *I Had A New York Girlfriend* in 1995, and The Cruel Sea's *Three Legged Dog* and *Where There's Smoke* in 1995 and 2001 respectively.

Although Dirty Three had intended to record a snappy follow-up to their last album, the band's foray into the studio proved unsatisfying, and the group took a hiatus as members scattered to their own projects, and Ellis joined Nick Cave & The Bad Seeds for their massive 2002 world tour.

And, although Ellis has been a part of that band since, he also returned to the studio with the Dirty Three to record some of the music for the award-winning film *Amalie*, before releasing his solo *3 Pieces For Violin* on the Dirty Three's off-shoot label Anchor & Hope in 2002. A completely deconstructed series of solo violin compositions, Ellis initially wrote and recorded them for the Canadian dance group Body Of The Holy Tattoo. Ellis and the Dirty Three themselves would follow with an all-new album, *She Has No Strings Apollo,* in early 2003.

BLACKEYED SUSANS:
1993 *All Souls Alive*

DIRTY THREE:
1994 *Sad & Dangerous*
1995 *Dirty Three*
1996 *Horse Stories*
1998 *Ocean Songs*
2000 *Lowlands*
2000 *Whatever You Love, You Are*
2003 *She Has No Strings Apollo*

MICK HARVEY

Although the talented multi-instrumentalist is most firmly allied to the Boys Next Door/Birthday Party/Bad Seeds camp, there are many other side and solo projects that Mick Harvey has masterminded over the years.

Harvey's songwriting partnership with Cave has generated much dissertation and dissection, but what he accomplished on his own stands up proudly alongside his Bad Seeds output.

Aside from his solo outings, the bond forged between Harvey and Crime & The City Solution's Simon Bonney would endure across many years of fruitful collaboration. Bonney's Crime got its start in 1978, as the Boys Next Door themselves were making their own first tentative steps within the Australian music scene.

It wasn't until 1984, after the break-up of The Birthday Party, that Simon Bonney's band really came into their own. Recruiting both Harvey and Rowland S Howard from the wreckage of The Birthday Party, and adding Rowland's brother Harry to the line-up, the seminal core of Crime & The City Solution was born, followed swiftly by the group's debut, 1985's *Dangling Man* EP.

With Swell Maps' eclectic drummer Epic Soundtracks on board following the EP's release, the quintet were finally free to really let rip, illuminating some of the Alternative underground's moodier, murkier alleyways with their brand of deep pop, played marvellously on *Just South Of Heaven,* and finally realized on the exquisite *Room Of Lights* in 1986. That album, of course, featured the haunting ballad 'Six Bells Chime', a song which, when coupled with Nick Cave And The Bad Seeds' own 'From Her To Eternity', sparked one of the finest moments in rock film, as part of Wim Wenders *Wings Of Desire.*

Harvey would continue to contribute to Crime & The City Solution, now relocated to Berlin in the wake of a shuffle that saw the Howard brothers and Soundtracks remain in London, where they eventually formed These Immortal Souls. In Germany, meanwhile, Harvey and Bonney put the band back together with a new line-up that included Bonney's girlfriend Bronwyn Adams, Einstürzende Neubauten guitarist Alexander Hacke, D.A.F's Chrisio Haas on keyboards and bassist Thomas Stern. That incarnation would cut three more albums before disbanding for good in 1991, following the release of their *Paradise Discotheque* swansong.

Not content to work within the confines of two massive bands, however, Harvey struck out on his own, with a remarkably distinctive solo career that was highlighted by two masterful albums dedicated to the extensive canon of French songwriter Serge Gainsbourg, *Intoxicated Man* in 1995 and *Pink Elephants* two years later.

And, like his fellow Bad Seed, Barry Adamson, Harvey has also been bitten hard by the same cinematic bug, with some of his work collected on the 1996 *Alta Marea & Vaterland*. Aside from this, and his film work with the Bad Seeds, Harvey laid his hand in mainstream cinema as well, appearing on a number of notable soundtracks, among them *Basquiat,* and *Jay & Silent Bob Strike Back.* He returned to the silver screen in 2002, with a heady score for *Australian Rules,* Paul Goldman's examination of the cultural tension between Australians and Aboriginals.

Harvey has also guested with a number of other performers, too, working with John Parish and Polly Jean Harvey, Robert Forster, Conway Savage and Scott Walker. It's this impressive roster of projects that certainly must earn Harvey some sort of 'hardest working man in the business' award. That he has done so much is nearly unthinkable, but that everything he's tackled has been rendered with grace, talent and outstanding energy is nearly beyond words.

SELECTED LISTENING

CRIME & THE CITY SOLUTION:
1985 *The Dangling Man* EP
1986 *Just South Of Heaven*
1986 *Room Of Lights*
1988 *Shine*
1989 *The Bride Ship*
1990 *Paradise Discotheque*

MICK HARVEY
1995 *Intoxicated Man*
1997 *Pink Elephants*
2002 *Australian Rules*

ROWLAND S HOWARD

Rowland S Howard's own career has remained remarkably entwined with those of his Birthday Party/Bad Seeds cohorts. However, when he has broken away for fresher waters, the results have always been startlingly different.

Howard, of course, participated in the Simon Bonney/Mick Harvey Birthday Party off-shoot, Crime & The City Solution, staying with that band until their first big split in 1986. At that time, Howard, his brother Harry and drummer Epic Soundtracks remained in London, while the rest of Crime relocated to Berlin.

With recent relationships festering, and the realization that the band couldn't continue to move forward as it was, the trio now formed their own band, These Immortal Souls. Howard had been kicking that name around in his head since at least 1984, when he'd been loosely affiliated with the Moodists' Chris Walsh and Laughing Clowns' Jeffrey Wegener. In fact, that fragmented aggregation had gone so far as to record a series of demos, which ultimately came to naught, with other band commitments precluding any further development of that un-named project. But now, with time and space, Howard could resurrect These Immortal Souls.

Adding keyboardist Genevieve McGuckin to the line-up, the group wasted no time in getting themselves out there, and with such a stellar resume behind them, quickly landed a deal with the prestigious underground American indie SST, first debuting an EP, *Marry Me,* and then a full length LP, *Get Lost (Don't Lie)* by the end of 1987. With a large tour surrounding the release of these two gems, it seemed that Howard was on yet another fast track.

But These Immortal Souls fell by the wayside, dropping from the radar for nearly three years before returning in 1992. Now linked with Mute, the quartet released *I'm Never Gonna Die Again,* which garnered both critical and popular acclaim. The band never really got off the ground, though, and essentially disbanded when Soundtracks quit to launch a solo career – a golden but stunted affair which was cut short by his suicide in 1997.

Although These Immortal Souls was left foundering, as members moved on to other assorted projects, Howard renewed his partnership with Lydia Lunch in the early 1990s. The pair, of course, had sparked beautifully off one another when they covered Lee Hazlewood's 'Some Velvet Morning' in the early 1980s. It stood to reason, then, that anything they attempted now, would be equally as fruitful.

In 1990, Howard and Lunch wrote and recorded the absolutely smashing *Shotgun Wedding*. Produced by Foetus, the album fully realized the chemistry only hinted at on 'Some Velvet Morning'. Completely understated and surprisingly musical, given Lunch's penchant for artistic experimentation, *Shotgun Wedding* allowed Howard a fresh avenue for his own writing, while the pair turned in a A+ cover of Alice Cooper's 'Black Ju Ju' which fully restored the venerable rocker to its Punk rock origins.

SELECTED LISTENING

CRIME & THE CITY SOLUTION:
1985 *The Dangling Man* EP
1986 *Just South Of Heaven*
1986 *Room Of Lights*

THESE IMMORTAL SOULS:
1987 *Marry Me*
1987 *Get Lost (Don't Lie)*
1992 *I'm Never Gonna Die Again*

WITH LYDIA LUNCH:
1991 *Shotgun Wedding*

SOLO:
1999 *Teenage Snuff Film*

NOTABLE GUEST APPEARANCES:
1984 *Gag*   Fad Gadget
1986 *Texas*   Nikki Sudden
1987 *Dead Men Tell No Tales*   Nikki Sudden
1987 *Kiss You Kidnapped Charabanc*   Nikki Sudden
1987 *I Knew Buffalo Bill*   Jeremy Gluck
1993 *Rise Above*   Epic Soundtracks

JAMES JOHNSTON

James Johnston's Gallon Drunk was to the early 1990s what performers like Morphine and Tom Waits were to the 1980s, plying a new breed of dark and moody music, and offering a viable alternative to Grunge. A string of singles and a ream of great press in the British music mags during 1990 and 1991 led to the band's first full-length album, *You, The Night And The Music* in 1992, released on their own Massive imprint.

An album of their early singles followed, as did a superb live Peel Session release, and it wasn't long before the band jumped ship to the major Warner Brothers. And, although Johnston would be linked to the Bad Seeds as early as 1994, when he joined them for their Lollapalooza outing, he continued to keep Gallon Drunk in the spotlight with a string of albums throughout the 1990s.

Alongside these two ventures, though, Johnston dabbled in more experimental waters, most notably in 1994: teaming with fellow Drunk Terry Edwards (Butterfield 8, the Scapegoats) for *Dora Suarez,* an album inspired by author Derek Raymond's *I Was Dora Suarez.* That album featured Raymond reading from his book, backed with Johnston and Edwards' moody instrumental soundtrack.

Johnston and Gallon Drunk worked tirelessly on studio material throughout the 1990s, but also contributed music for two films, *Black Milk* and *East End.*

1998 saw Johnston again step out on his own with a new single, 'Hurricane', released under the name JJ Stone.

SELECTED LISTENING

GALLON DRUNK:
1992 *Tonight...The Singles Bar*
1992 *You, The Night And The Music*
1992 *The Peel Sessions*
1993 *From The Heart Of Town*
1993 *Dora Suarez*
1995 *The Traitor's Gate*
1995 *Camden Crawl* (live)
1996 *In The Long Still Night*
2000 *Black Milk*
2002 *Bear Me Away*
2002 *Fire Music*

TRACY PEW

Most of Tracy Pew's musical connections lay within the auspices of the Boys Next Door and Birthday Party – so much of his biographical details are to be found in the main text of the book.

After The Birthday Party disbanded, Pew returned home to Australia where he would all but disappear out of the musical fray – bar a few guest appearances with Cave, and a stint touring with The Saints during their 1984 outings.

He passed away on 7 November 1986.

KID CONGO POWERS

The erstwhile Brian Tristan and *Slash* magazine contributor Jeffrey Lee Pierce formed Creeping Ritual in Los Angeles in 1980. Ensconced in the West Coast

Punk/psychobilly scene, Creeping Ritual added bassist Brad Dunning and drummer Don Snowden to the line-up, becoming the Gun Club, named at the behest of Circle Jerks' Chris Morris.

The band took the local scene to task, becoming an outlet for songs that tackled sex, drugs, insanity, suicide and loneliness, sometimes all in one go. Gun Club's initial acceptance into the music scene was strong and gigging was de rigueur for the band. They were unable to capitalise on any early vibes, though, and with a line-up that was somewhat fluid, the first incarnation of the band collapsed not long after Powers was poached by the Gun Club's East Coast big brother, the Cramps.

Congo decamped East to join Lux Interior and Poison Ivy, who'd been regaling the Eastern seaboard with a wicked stew of drugs, depravity and ghoulish vamping since their inception in 1976.

However, his tenure with The Cramps would last just two years. He replaced founder guitarist Brian Gregory just as the band were poised to cross to more mainstream virtues via their 'Goo-Goo Muck' and 'The Crusher' singles, pulled from the absolutely devilish *Psychedelic Jungle* LP. And even though this Cramps line-up was simply majestic, they accomplished very little, primarily because the band were involved in nasty legal battles with their former record label.

He rejoined the Gun Club in late 1982, but stayed only long enough to play a handful of gigs with the band. He'd return to the fold in 1984, recording *Las Vegas Story* and joining the band on tour. The Gun Club, however, were close to shutting down. Ticket sales for the tour were disappointing and reaction to the new album was even more tepid.

Powers again decamped, this time taking Gun Club bassist Patricia Morrison with him to Fur Bible. That aggregation released just one single in 1985, 'Plunder The Tombs'. He joined Nick Cave And The Bad Seeds the following year, just in time for the *Kicking Against The Pricks* tour. He remained with the band until 1992.

Although Powers would release a handful of material as a solo artist, it was clear he worked best within the framework of a band, and two years after leaving the Bad Seeds, Powers was back with a brand new group, Congo Norvell. Formed by Powers and Sally Norvell, the duo relied on a rotating roster of guest musicians to fill up the space. Indeed, their eponymous debut featured future Bad Seed Jim Sclavunos and grabbed Mick Harvey to produce four tracks. Congo Norvell would ultimately release three albums.

By the tail end of 1998 Powers was involved with yet another group, alongside Bob Bert (Sonic Youth), Jerry Teel, Jack Martin (both Little Porkchop) and Barry London (Stab City) as Knoxville Girls. With a sound that had been started by the founding members of New York's Little Porkchop, Knoxville Girls was flavoured with Blues and Country, with a little Rockabilly twang thrown in for good measure.

As one century ended and another began, Powers could be found in a myriad of guises, most notably working with electronic guru Khan.

SELECTED LISTENING

CRAMPS:
1981 *Psychedelic Jungle*

GUN CLUB:
1984 *Las Vegas Story*

CONGO NORVELL:
1994 *Music To Remember Him By*
1996 *The Dope, The Lies, The Vaseline* (withdrawn promo only)
1998 *Abnormals Anonymous*

KNOXVILLE GIRLS:
1999 *Knoxville Girls*
2000 *In The Woodshed* (live)

HUGO RACE

Hugo Race burst onto the Melbourne music scene in 1980 with his first band, Plays With Marionettes. Aggro and no-wave, the noise Plays With Marionettes unleashed was well received on the local circuit, already primed by bands like The Birthday Party and The Saints. Marionettes released two notable singles, 'Kitchen Kopf' and 'Hellbelly', before disbanding in 1984 when Race left to join Nick Cave on his legendary Man Or Myth? tour, then stayed to record Cave's solo debut.

The band was joined on this 1984 outing by another Melbourne music veteran, Edward Clayton-Jones, whose own band, The Fabulous Marquises, had crossed paths with Race's Marionettes during the early 1980s. While on tour in Europe, where Clayton-Jones was filling in for Blixa Bargeld, the pair hatched the seeds of an all new band, The Wreckery, which was formed in 1985, adding Wild Dog Rodeo's organist Charles Todd, bassist Tadeusz O'Biegly and ex-Marionette-er Robin Casinader.

By the beginning of 1985, The Wreckery were in the studio cutting their debut, a mini-album titled *I Think This Town Is Nervous*, released by Hot in December. Another, *Yeh My People,* followed in 1987, as Race was working with Cave and John Hillcoat on the score for *Ghosts...Of The Civil Dead.*

August, meanwhile, saw the release of the Wreckery's first full-length album, *Here At Pain's Insistence.* The band would soldier on through 1988's *Laying Down Law,* the last album to feature Clayton-Jones before he quit. Race would keep the band together with a re-jigged line-up through the middle of the following year before he, too, quit.

After the wreck of The Wreckery, Race relocated to Berlin where he revived, in name anyway, Hugo Race & The True Spirit, an aggregation he'd formed in 1987 with Robin Casinader and Nick Barker. The True Spirit released two albums, *Earl's World* in 1990 and *Second Revelator* at the beginning of 1992.

The True Spirit would remain active through the late 1990s, across several more albums and a host of successful tours which brought in a number of guest musicians, among them Mick Harvey and members of Die Haut and Einstürzende Neubauten.

SELECTED LISTENING

THE WRECKERY:
1986 *I Think This Town Is Nervous*
1986 *Yeh My People*
1987 *Here At Pain's Insistence*
1988 *Laying Down Law*

THE TRUE SPIRIT:
1988 *Rue Morgue Blues*
1990 *Earl's World*
1992 *Second Revelator*
1994 *Stations Of The Cross*
1996 *Valley Of Light*
1997 *Wet Dream*
1998 *Chemical Wedding*
1999 *Last Frontier*
2001 *Long Time Ago*

CONWAY SAVAGE

Pianist Conway Savage bucked the system when he entered Melbourne's music scene in the early 1980s. Plying a ferocious country *à la* Hank Williams and Merle Haggard, Savage, Jim White (People With Chairs Up Their Noses, later Dirty Three), Nick Danyi, Jim Shugg and Dave Last formed Feral Dinosaurs in 1982.

The Dinosaurs hit hard with their first single, a cover of Don Gibson's 'Blue Day', included on 1984's *Asleep At The Wheel* compilation. While ensconced in this group, Savage struck out solo as well, joining Scrap Museum for 1984's 'Say Die' single, and then again after the band (now featuring Phill Calvert) had become Blue Ruin, for 1990's *I'm Gonna Smile* LP.

Two further Feral Dinosaur singles, 'Ramblin' Man' and '50 Miles From Home' followed in 1985 and 1986 before the band released their debut, the *You've All Got A Home To Go To* EP. After the Feral Dinosaurs disbanded, Savage lent his skills to the session circuit, most notably working with Dave Graney And The White Buffaloes during 1989 on his *My Life On The Plain* LP.

Savage joined the Bad Seeds in 1990, but still found time not only to work on his own, burgeoning solo career which put three albums on the racks between 1993 and 2004, but on several other exciting projects as well, appearing on Robert Forster's *I Had A Girl In New York* in 1995. Savage also partnered briefly with Falling Joys' singer Suzie Higgie during 1996, turning back to his country and blues roots to record an album with her. Described as a cross between Mazzy Star and Nick Drake, *Soon Will Be Tomorrow* was released in 1998.

Savage also stepped behind the boards, producing albums for Acuff's Rose and The Stream during the mid-1990s and again added his piano to another band, Maurice Frawley And The Second Hand Ringos in 1998.

FERAL DINOSAURS:
1985 *You've All Got A Home To Go To*

WITH DAVE GRANEY:
1989 *My Life On The Plain*

WITH SUSIE HIGGIE:
1998 *Soon Will Be Tomorrow*

CONWAY SAVAGE:
1993 *Conway Savage*
2000 *Nothing Broken*
2004 *Wrong Man's Hands*

JIM SCLAVUNOS

Although he'd steeped himself in the CBGB's Punk scene for years, drummer Jim Sclavunos first cut his teeth in brief stints with two of America's most influential bands, Sonic Youth for 1983's seminal *Confusion Is Sex,* and The Cramps, where he replaced the departing Nick Knox shortly after the release of 1991's *Look Mom, No Head!* LP. That led him to Rowland S Howard and Lydia Lunch that same year when he stepped behind the kit for their *Shotgun Wedding* project.

Other gigs followed, with Congo Norvell, Carmaig Deforest, Tav Falco's Panther Blues, Alex Chilton, Anna Domino, Alan Vega and 8 Eyed Spy (with Lunch), but Sclavunos really let rip when he joined the New York rock band Alice Texas in the late 1990s, appearing on their 2000 *Gold* debut. With so many fingers in so many fires, Sclavunos also found time for his own solo project, the Vanity Set.

Sclavunos joined the Bad Seeds in 1996.

SONIC YOUTH:
1983 *Confusion Is Sex*

THE CRAMPS:
1991 *Look Mom, No Head!*

ALICE TEXAS:
2000 *Gold*

VANITY SET:
2000 *Vanity Set*
2003 *Little Stabs Of Happiness*

THOMAS WYDLER

Swiss-born drummer Wydler joined the Bad Seeds in 1985, following his tenure with sometime Cave collaborators Die Haut. Content since then to remain within the framework of the Bad Seeds, Wydler finally stepped out on his own when he combined with former Swans/Iggy Pop (etc) drummer Toby Dammit, for the album *Morphosa Harmonia* – a record that defied every expectation of how two drummers should sound, as Wydler contributed synthesizers, and Dammit took lead vocals, albeit masquerading as a childrens' choir. Guests on this remarkable disc included Jochen Arbeit (Einstürzende Neubauten), Beate Bartel (Liaisons Dangereuses), Christoph Hahn (Angels Of Light) and Martin Peter (Die Haut).

SELECTED LISTENING

DIE HAUT:
1983 *Burnin' The Ice*

WITH TOBY DAMMIT:
2005 *Morphosa Harmonia*

BIBLIOGRAPHY

Aside from sources cited within the text, the following publications were consulted.

MAGAZINES AND PERIODICALS
Alternative Press; *Goldmine*; *Live! Music Review*; *Melody Maker*; *New Musical Express*; *Q*; *Vox*; *Select*; *Mojo*; *Record Collector*; *Rolling Stone*; *Spin*; *Uncut*; *Classic Rock*; *Loose Lips Sink Ships*, *Stereotype*.

WEBSITES
www.Nick-Cave.com *Nick Cave online*
http://home.iae.nl/users/maes/cave/ *Nick Cave Collector's Hell*
www.angelindevilsboots.com *excellent unofficial site*
www.sempel.com/ *Peter Sempel official website*

REFERENCE BOOKS & BIOGRAPHIES
Guinness Book of Hit Singles, Hit Albums
Martin C Strong: *The Great Alternative & Indie Discography*
Joel Whitburn: *Top Pop Albums, Top Pop Singles*
The Complete Book Of the British Charts
Ian McFarlane: *The Encyclopedia Of Australian Rock And Pop*
Ian Johnston: *Bad Seed: The Biography Of Nick Cave*
Robert Brokenmouth: *Nick Cave: The Birthday Party And Other Epic Adventures*
Ian Shirley: *Dark Entries: Bauhaus And Beyond*
Dave Thompson: *The Dark Reign Of Gothic Rock*
Dave Thompson: *Better To Burn Out: The Cult Of Death In Rock And Roll*

Other Titles available from Helter Skelter

Coming Soon

Save What You Can: The Day of The Triffids and the Long Night of David McComb   DUE: AUTUMN 2006
By Bleddyn Butcher

Finely crafted biography of cult Australian group and their ill-fated front man who was simply the greatest lyricist of his generation.

Charismatic front man McComb's finely crafted tales of misfits and troubled outsiders and lost souls, merged Dylan with Carver and a Perth sensibility to brilliant effect, while his sprawling melodies set against 'Evil' Graham Lee's slide guitar created an achingly beautiful sound best exemplified by critics' favourites, *Born Sandy Devotional* and *Calenture*. In spite of rave critical plaudits, the Triffids' sales were mediocre and in 1990 the band split and returned to Australia. McComb put out one excellent solo album in 1994 before the sense of ominous foreboding that lurked throughout his music was proved prescient when he collapsed and was rushed to hospital to undergo a full heart transplant. Months later he was back in hospital with even more agonising intestinal surgery. McComb made a partial recovery, but the medication he was taking kept him in a permanent state of drowsiness. On Saturday, January 30th, 1999, he fell asleep at the wheel of his car. Though McComb survived the crash and discharged himself from hospital, he died suddenly three days later.

Paperback   ISBN 1-900924-21-8   234 X 156mm   16pp b/w photos
UK £14.99   US $19.95

Belle and Sebastian: Just A Modern Rock Story DUE: SEPTEMBER 2005
By Paul Whitelaw

Formed in 1996, this enigmatic Glasgow band have risen to become one of Britain's most respected bands.

For years, Belle and Sebastian were shrouded in mystery – the 23-piece ensemble led by singer-songwriter Stuart Murdoch refused interviews and the band scarcely ever toured. Their early singles though built them a strong and committed cult following. Their debut mail-order only album *Tigermilk* sold out within a month of its release. The follow-up, *If You're Feeling Sinister*, with its Nick Drake-influenced melodies and dark, quirky lyrics, found favour in alternative circles as far a field as San Francisco, Japan, South America, and especially France where a 1996 poll by influential magazine Les Inrockuptiles placed them above Oasis. The 1998 album, *The Boy With the Arab Strap* entered the UK LP charts at 12. Their latest Trevor Horn-produced album *Dear Catastrophe Waitress* is their highest profile release to date.

This is not only the first biography ever written on the band, but the most official that might ever hit the market. The band have agreed to participate in the project and to give the author extended interviews, paraphernalia and both personal and publicity still photos. Stuart Murdoch himself has agreed to design artwork for the cover.

Paul Whitelaw is an arts writer from Glasgow who has met and interviewed Belle and Sebastian on several occasions and he was the first journalist to champion the band in print.

Paperback   ISBN 1-900924-98-6   234 X 156mm   16pp b/w photos
UK £14.99

David Bowie: The Shirts He Wears DUE: SUMMER 2005
By Jonathan Richards

A Bowie book with a difference, this is a study of Bowie as a cultural icon that draws together his music, artworks and fashion to paint a fascinating portrait of one of rock's most important figures.

Paperback   ISBN 1-900924-25-0   234 X 156mm   16pp b/w photos
UK £14.99   US $19.95

John Martyn DUE: SUMMER 2006
By Chris Nickson
First ever biography of the pioneering guitarist best-known for his still-revered 70s album *Solid Air*. Draws on interviews with many friends and associates.

Paperback   ISBN 1-900924-86-2   234 X 156mm   16pp b/w photos
UK £14.99   US $19.95

Rush: The Definitive Biography DUE: AUTUMN 2005
By Jon Collins
Acclaimed Marillion biographer Collins draws on hundreds of hours of new interviews to tell the full in-depth story of the enduring Canadian trio who are one of the most successful cult groups in the world. From early days in Canada to platinum albums, stadium shows and the world's stage, taking in tragedy, triumphs and a wealth of great music, this is the definitive study of one of rock's great enigmas.

Paperback   ISBN 1-900924-85-4   234 X 156mm   16pp b/w photos
UK £14.99   US $19.95

Action Time Vision: The Story of Sniffin' Glue, Alternative TV and Punk Rock DUE: 2006
By Mark Perry
The legendary founder-editor of *Sniffin' Glue* – the definitive Punk fanzine – gives his own account of the Punk years. An eyewitness account of the key gigs; an insider's history of the bands and personalities; the full story of the hugely influential fanzine and the ups and downs of Perry's own recording career with Alternative TV.

Paperback   ISBN 1-900924-89-7   234 X 156mm   16pp b/w photos
UK £14.99   US $21.95

The Who By Numbers   DUE: AUTUMN 2006
By Alan Parker and Steve Grantley
Detailed album-by-album, song-by-song commentary on the songs of one of rock's most important and enduring acts, by Sid Vicious biographer and Lennon expert Parker, teamed with Stiff Little Fingers' drummer, Grantley.

Paperback   ISBN 1-900924-91-9   234 X 156mm   16pp b/w photos
UK £14.99   US $19.95

John Lydon's Metal Box: The Story of Public Image Ltd
DUE: 2006
By Phil Strongman
In between fronting rock's most iconoclastic group, the Sex Pistols, and re-emerging in the 21st century as a reality TV hero on *I'm A Celebrity*, Lydon led the post-Punk pioneers Public Image Ltd who tore up the rulebook and merged disco funk and industrial Punk to create coruscating soundscapes with catchy tunes – from *Death Disco* and *Flowers of Romance* to *Rise* and *This Is Not A Love Song* – and caused riots at their gigs. An essential chapter in the growth of post-Punk music and one that reveals Lydon as always forward-thinking and always compelling.

Paperback   ISBN 1-900924-66-8   234 X 156mm   16pp b/w photos
UK £14.99   US $19.95

Music in Dreamland: The Story of Be Bop Deluxe and Bill Nelson DUE: 2005
By Paul Sutton-Reeves
Draws on hours of new interviews with Bill Nelson and other members of the band, as well as admirers such as David Sylvian, Stone Roses' producer John Leckie, Steve Harley and Reeves Gabrel. Cover artwork especially designed by Bill Nelson himself.

Paperback   ISBN 1-900924-08-8   234 X 156mm   16pp b/w photos
UK £14.99   US $19.95

'77 – The Year of Punk and New Wave
By Henry Bech Poulsen
As 1967 was to the Haight-Ashbury scene, so 1977 was to Punk: a year in which classic singles and albums by all the key bands made it the only musical movement that counted, and before its energy and potential was diluted and dampened by the forces of conservatism and commercialism. '77 tells the story of what every Punk and new wave band achieved in that heady year – from The Pistols, Clash and Damned to The Lurkers, The Adverts and The Rezillos, and everyone in between.
Paperback   ISBN 1-900924-92-7   245 X 174mm   512 pp Illustrated throughout
UK £16.99   US $25.00

Linda Ronstadt: A Musical Life
By Peter Lewry
Ronstadt's early backing band became The Eagles and she has had success with songs by Neil Young, Jackson Browne and Hank Williams. After a US number 1 single and Grammy winning country rock albums in the 1970s, she has continued to challenge preconceptions with albums of Nelson Riddle-produced standards, a record of mariachi songs and a collaboration with Dolly Parton and Emmylou Harris. This is her first ever biography.
Paperback   ISBN 1-900924-50-1   234 X 156mm   256pp, 16pp b/w photos
UK £16.99   US $25.00

Suede: An Armchair Guide
By Dave Thompson
The first biography of one of the most important British Rock Groups of the 90s who paved the way for Blur, Oasis et al. Mixing glam and post-Punk influences, fronted by androgynous Bret Anderson, Suede thrust indie-rock into the charts with a string of classic singles, in the process catalysing the Brit-pop revolution. Suede's first album was the then fastest selling debut of all time and they remain one of THE live draws on the UK rock circuit, retaining a fiercely loyal cult following.
Paperback   ISBN 1-900924-60-9   234mm X 156mm   256pp 8pp b/w photos
UK £14.00   US $19.95

Currently Available from Helter Skelter Publishing

True Faith: An Armchair Guide to New Order
By Dave Thompson
Formed from the ashes of Joy Division after their ill fated singer Ian Curtis hung himself, few could have predicted that New Order would become one of the seminal groups of the 80s, making a series of albums that would compare well with anything Joy Division had produced, and embracing club culture a good ten years before most of their contemporaries.

From the bestselling 12 inch single 'Blue Monday' to later hits like 'Bizarre Love Triangle' [featured in the movie *Trainspotting*] and their spectacular world cup song 'World In Motion' the band have continued making innovative, critically revered records that have also enjoyed massive commercial success.

This book is the first to treat New Order's musical career as a separate achievement, rather than a postscript to Joy Division's and the first to analyse in depth what makes their music so great.
Paperback   ISBN 1-900924-94-3 8   234mm X 156mm   256pp 8pp b/w photos
UK £12.99   US $19.95

Wheels Out of Gear: Two Tone, The Specials and a World on Fire
By Dave Thompson
When the Punks embraced reggae it led to a late 1970s Ska revival that began in Coventry with Jerry Dammers' Two Tone record label and his band, The Specials. Original 60s rude boy fashions – mohair suits, dark glasses and the ubiquitous pork pie hats – along with Dammer's black & white themed logo were the emblems for a hugely popular scene that also comprised hit-making groups

such as Madness, The Beat and The Selecter.
Paperback   ISBN 1-900924-84-6   234 X 156mm   256pp, 16pp b/w photos
UK £12.99   US $19.95

Electric Pioneer: An Armchair Guide to Gary Numan
By Paul Goodwin
From selling 10 million records in 2 years, both with Tubeway Army and solo, to more low key and idiosyncratic releases through subsequent decades, Gary Numan has built up an impressive body of work and retained a hugely devoted cult following. Electric Pioneer is the first ever guide to his recorded output, documenting every single and album and featuring sections on his live shows, memorabilia and DVD releases.
Paperback   ISBN 1-900924-95-1   234 X 156mm   256pp, 16pp b/w photos
UK £14.99   US $19.95

Al Stewart: Lights, Camera, Action – A Life in Pictures
By Neville Judd
Best known for his 70s classic 'The Year of The Cat', Al Stewart continues to record and tour and retains a large and loyal international fan base. This is a unique collection of rare and unpublished photographs, documenting Al's public and private life from early days in 1950s Scotland, through to his success in Hollywood and beyond.
Luxury Paperback   ISBN 1-900924-90-0   310 X 227mm   192pp All pages photos,
16pp of colour
UK £25.00   US $35.00

Sex Pistols: Only Anarchists are Pretty
By Mick O'Shea
Drawing both on years of research and on creative conjecture, this book, written as a novel, portrays the early years of the Sex Pistols. Giving a fictionalised fly-on-the-wall account of the arguments, in-jokes, gigs, pub sessions and creative tension, it documents the day-to-day life of the ultimate Punk band before the Bill Grundy incident and Malcolm Mclaren-orchestrated tabloid outrage turned their lives into a media circus.
Paperback   ISBN 1-900924-93-5   234mm X 156mm   256pp 8pp b/w photos
UK £12.99   US $19.95

Bob Dylan: Like The Night (Revisited)
By CP Lee
Fully revised and updated edition of the hugely acclaimed document of Dylan's pivotal 1966 show at the Manchester Free Trade Hall where fans called him Judas for turning his back on folk music in favour of rock 'n' roll. The album of the concert was released in the same year as the book's first outing and has since become a definitive source.
  'A terrific tome that gets up close to its subject and breathes new life into it... For any fan of Dylan this is quite simply essential.' *Time Out*
  'Putting it all vividly in the context of the time, he writes expertly about that one electrifying, widely-bootlegged night.' *Mojo*
  'CP Lee's book flushed 'Judas' out into the open.' *The Independent*
  'An atmospheric and enjoyable account.' *Uncut* (Top 10 of the year)
Paperback   ISBN 1-900924-33-1   198mm X 129mm   224pp 16pp b/w photos
UK £9.99   US $17.95

Everybody Dance
Chic and the Politics of Disco
By Daryl Easlea
Everybody Dance puts the rise and fall of Bernard Edwards and Nile Rodgers, the emblematic disco duo behind era-defining records 'Le Freak', 'Good Times' and 'Lost In Music', at the heart of a

changing landscape, taking in socio-political and cultural events such as the Civil Rights struggle, the Black Panthers and the US oil crisis. There are drugs, bankruptcy, up-tight artists, fights, and Muppets but, most importantly an in-depth appraisal of a group whose legacy remains hugely underrated.

Paperback   ISBN 1-900924-56-0   234mm X 156mm   256pp 8pp b/w photos
UK £14.00   US $19.95

This Is a Modern Life
Compiled by Enamel Verguren

Lavishly illustrated guide to the mod revival that was sparked by the 1979 release of *Quadrophenia*. *This Is a Modern Life* concentrates on the 1980s, but takes in 20 years of a mod life in London and throughout the world, from 1979 to 1999, with interviews of people directly involved, loads of flyers and posters and a considerable amount of great photos.

'Good stuff … A nice nostalgic book full of flyers, pics and colourful stories.' Loaded

Paperback   ISBN 1-900924-77-3   264mm X 180mm   224pp, photos throughout
UK £14.99   US $19.95

Smashing Pumpkins: Tales of A Scorched Earth
By Amy Hanson

Initially contemporaries of Nirvana, Billy Corgan's Smashing Pumpkins outgrew and outlived the grunge scene with hugely acclaimed commercial triumphs like *Siamese Dream* and *Mellon Collie and The Infinite Sadness*. Though drugs and other problems led to the band's final demise, Corgan's recent return with Zwan is a reminder of how awesome the Pumpkins were in their prime. Seattle-based Hanson has followed the band for years and this is the first in-depth biography of their rise and fall.

'Extremely well-written … A thrilling and captivating read.' *Classic Rock*

'Sex, bust-ups, heavy metal, heroin death and a quadruple-platinum dream-pop double album… The first ever 'serious' Pumpkins biography.' *NME*

'A fascinating story … Hanson has done her research.' *Q*

Paperback   ISBN 1-900924-68-4   234mm X 156mm   256pp, 8pp b/w photos
UK £12.99   US $18.95

Be Glad: An Incredible String Band Compendium
Edited by Adrian Whittaker

The ISB pioneered 'world music' on '60s albums like *The Hangman's Beautiful Daughter* – Paul McCartney's favourite album of 1967! – experimented with theatre, film and lifestyle and inspired Led Zeppelin. *Be Glad* features interviews with all the ISB key players, as well as a wealth of background information, reminiscence, critical evaluations and arcane trivia, this is a book that will delight any reader with more than a passing interest in the ISB.

Paperback   ISBN 1-900924-64-1   234mm X 156mm   288pp, b/w photos throughout
UK £14.99   US $22.95

ISIS: A Bob Dylan Anthology
Edited by Derek Barker

ISIS is the best-selling, longest lasting, most highly acclaimed Dylan fanzine. This ultimate Dylan anthology draws on unpublished interviews and research by the *ISIS* team together with the best articles culled from the pages of the definitive Bob magazine. From Bob's earliest days in New York City to the more recent legs of the Never Ending Tour, the *ISIS* archive has exclusive interview material – often rare or previously unpublished – with many of the key players in Dylan's career: friends, musicians and other collaborators, such as playwright Jacques Levy and folk hero Martin Carthy.

Fully revised and expanded edition features additional previously unpublished articles and further rare photos;

'Astounding … Fascinating… If you're more than mildly interested in Bob Dylan then this is an essential purchase.' *Record Collector*

'This book is worth any Dylan specialist's money.' Ian MacDonald – **** *Uncut*

Paperback   ISBN 1-900924-82-X   198mm X 129mm   352pp, 16pp b/w photos
UK £9.99   US $17.95

Waiting for the Man: The Story of Drugs and Popular Music
By Harry Shapiro

From marijuana and jazz, through acid-rock and speed-fuelled Punk, to crack-driven rap and ecstasy and the dance generation, this is the definitive history of drugs and pop. It also features in-depth portraits of music's most famous drug addicts: from Charlie Parker to Sid Vicious and from Jim Morrison to Kurt Cobain.

Chosen by the BBC as one of the Top Twenty Music Books of All Time.

'Wise and witty.' *The Guardian*

Paperback   ISBN 1-900924-58-7   198mm X 129mm   320pp
UK £10.99   US $17.95

Jefferson Airplane: Got a Revolution
By Jeff Tamarkin

With smash hits 'Somebody to Love' and 'White Rabbit' and albums like *Surrealistic Pillow*, Jefferson Airplane, the most successful and influential rock band to emerge from San Francisco during the 60s, created the sound of a generation. To the public they were free-loving, good-time hippies, but to their inner circle, Airplane were a paradoxical bunch – constantly at odds with each other. Jefferson Airplane members were each brilliant, individualistic artists who became the living embodiment of the ups and downs of the sex, drugs and rock 'n' roll lifestyle.

Tamarkin has interviewed the former band members, friends, lovers, crew members and fellow musicians to come up with the definitive full-length history of the group.

"A compelling account of a remarkable band." *Record Collector*

"A superb chunk of writing that documents every twist and turn in the ever-evolving life of a great American band." *Record Collector*

Paperback   ISBN 1-900924-78-1   234mm X 156mm   408pp, 16pp b/w photos
UK £14.99   US No rights

Surf's Up: The Beach Boys on Record 1961-1981
By Brad Elliott

The ultimate reference work on the recording sessions of one of the most influential and collectable groups.

'factually unimpeachable ... an exhausting, exhilarating 500 pages of discographical and session information about everything anybody connected with the group ever put down or attempted to put down on vinyl.' *Goldmine*

Paperback   ISBN 1-900924-79-X   234mm X 156mm   512pp, 16pp b/w photos
UK £25.00   US No rights

Get Back: The Beatles' Let It Be Disaster
By Doug Suply and Ray Shweighardt

Reissued to coincide with the release of *Let It Be ... Naked*, this is a singularly candid look at the greatest band in history at their ultimate moment of crisis. It puts the reader in the studio as John cedes power to Yoko; Paul struggles to keep things afloat, Ringo shrugs and George quits the band.

'One of the most poignant Beatles' books ever.' *Mojo*

Paperback   ISBN 1-900924-83-8   198mm X 129mm   352pp
UK £9.99   No US rights

The Clash: Return of the Last Gang in Town
By Marcus Gray

Exhaustively researched definitive biography of the last great rock band that traces their progress from pubs and Punk clubs to US stadiums and the Top Ten. This edition is further updated to cover the band's induction into the Rock 'n' Roll Hall of Fame and the tragic death of iconic front man Joe Strummer.

'A must-have for Clash fans [and] a valuable document for anyone interested in the Punk era.' *Billboard*

'It's important you read this book.' *Record Collector*

Paperback   ISBN 1-900924-62-5   234mm X 156mm   512pp, 8pp b/w photos
UK £14.99   US No rights

Steve Marriott: All Too Beautiful
by Paolo Hewitt and John Hellier

Marriott was the prime mover behind 60s chart-toppers The Small Faces. Longing to be treated as a serious musician he formed Humble Pie with Peter Frampton, where his blistering rock 'n' blues guitar playing soon saw him take centre stage in the US live favourites. After years in seclusion, Marriott's plans for a comeback in 1991 were tragically cut short when he died in a house fire. He continues to be a key influence for generations of musicians from Paul Weller to Oasis and Blur.

'One of the best books I've read about the backwaters of rock music.' *Daily Mail*

'A riveting account of the singer's life, crammed with entertaining stories of rebellion and debauchery and insightful historical background... Compulsive reading.' *The Express*

'Revealing... sympathetic, long overdue.' ****Uncut*

'We won't see the like of him again and *All Too Beautiful* captures him perfectly. A right riveting read as they say.' Gary Crowley, BBC London.

'Hewitt's portrayal makes compelling reading.'**** *Mojo*

Hardback   ISBN 1-900924-44-7   234mm X 156mm   352pp 32pp b/w photos
UK £20   US $29.95

Love: Behind The Scenes
By Michael Stuart-Ware

LOVE were one of the legendary bands of the late 60s US West Coast scene. Their masterpiece *Forever Changes* still regularly appears in critics' polls of top albums, while a new-line up of the band has recently toured to mass acclaim. Michael Stuart-Ware was LOVE's drummer during their heyday and shares his inside perspective on the band's recording and performing career and tells how drugs and egos thwarted the potential of one of the great groups of the burgeoning psychedelic era.

Paperback   ISBN 1-900924-59-5   234mm X 156mm   256pp
UK £14.00   US $19.95

A Secret Liverpool: In Search of the La's
By MW Macefield

With timeless single 'There She Goes', Lee Mavers' La's overtook The Stone Roses and paved the way for Britpop. However, since 1991, The La's have been silent, while rumours of studio-perfectionism, madness and drug addiction have abounded. The author sets out to discover the truth behind Mavers' lost decade and eventually gains a revelatory audience with Mavers himself.

Paperback   ISBN 1-900924-63-3   234mm X 156mm   192pp
UK £11.00   US $17.95

The Fall: A User's Guide
By Dave Thompson

A melodic, cacophonic and magnificent, The Fall remain the most enduring and prolific of the late-70s Punk and post-Punk iconoclasts. *A User's Guide* chronicles the historical and musical background to more than 70 different LPs (plus reissues) and as many singles. The band's history is also documented year-by-year, filling in the gaps between the record releases.

Paperback   ISBN 1-900924-57-9   234mm X 156mm   256pp, 8pp b/w photos
UK £12.99   US $19.95

Pink Floyd: A Saucerful of Secrets
By Nicholas Schaffner

Long overdue reissue of the authoritative and detailed account of one of the most important and popular bands in rock history. From the psychedelic explorations of the Syd Barrett-era to 70s superstardom with *Dark Side of the Moon*, and on to triumph of *The Wall*, before internecine strife tore the group apart. Schaffner's definitive history also covers the improbable return of Pink Floyd without Roger Waters, and the hugely successful *Momentary Lapse of Reason* album and tour.

Paperback   ISBN 1-900924-52-8   234mm X 156mm   256pp, 8pp b/w photos
UK £14.99   No rights

The Big Wheel
By Bruce Thomas

Thomas was bassist with Elvis Costello at the height of his success. Though names are never named, *The Big Wheel* paints a vivid and hilarious picture of life touring with Costello and co, sharing your life 24-7 with a moody egotistical singer, a crazed drummer and a host of hangers-on. Costello sacked Thomas on its initial publication.

'A top notch anecdotalist who can time a twist to make you laugh out loud.' *Q*

Paperback   ISBN 1-900924-53-6   234mm X 156mm   192pp
UK £10.99 $17.95

Hit Men: Powerbrokers and Fast Money Inside The Music Business
By Fredric Dannen £14.99

Hit Men exposes the seamy and sleazy dealings of America's glitziest record companies: payola, corruption, drugs, Mafia involvement, and excess.

'This is quite possibly the best book ever written about the business side of the music industry.' *Music Week*

'This is simply the greatest book about the business end of the music industry.' *Q*****

'So heavily awash with cocaine, corruption and unethical behaviour that it makes the occasional examples of chart-rigging and play list tampering in Britain during the same period seem charmingly inept.' *The Guardian*.

Paperback   ISBN 1-900924-54-4   234mm X 156mm   512pp, 8pp b/w photos
UK £14.99   No rights

I'm With The Band: Confessions of A Groupie
By Pamela Des Barres

Frank and engaging memoir of affairs with Keith Moon, Noel Redding and Jim Morrison, travels with Led Zeppelin as Jimmy Page's girlfriend, and friendships with Robert Plant, Gram Parsons, and Frank Zappa.

'Long overdue reprint of a classic 60s memoir – one of the few music books to talk openly about sex.' *Mojo*

'One of the most likeable and sparky first hand accounts.' *Q*****

'Miss Pamela, the most beautiful and famous of the groupies. Her memoir of her life with rock stars is funny, bittersweet, and tender-hearted.' Stephen Davis, author of *Hammer of the Gods*

Paperback   ISBN 1-900924-55-2   234mm X 156mm   256pp, 16pp b/w photos
UK £14.99 $19.95

Psychedelic Furs: Beautiful Chaos
By Dave Thompson

Psychedelic Furs were the ultimate post-Punk band – combining the chaos and vocal rasp of the Sex Pistols with a Bowie-esque glamour. The Furs hit the big time when John Hughes wrote a movie based on their early single 'Pretty in Pink'. Poised to join U2 and Simple Minds in the premier league, they withdrew behind their shades, remaining a cult act, but one with a hugely devoted following.

Paperback   ISBN 1-900924-47-1   234mm X 156mm   256pp, 16pp b/w photos
UK £14.99 $19.95

Marillion: Separated Out
By Jon Collins
From the chart hit days of Fish and 'Kayleigh' to the Steve Hogarth incarnation, Marillion have continued to make groundbreaking rock music. Collins tells the full story, drawing on interviews with band members, associates, and the experiences of some of the band's most dedicated fans.

Paperback   ISBN 1-900924-49-8   234mm X 156mm   288pp, illustrated throughout
UK £14.99 $19.95

Rainbow Rising
By Roy Davies
The full story of guitar legend Ritchie Blackmore's post-Purple progress with one of the great 70s rock bands. After quitting Deep Purple at the height of their success, Blackmore combined with Ronnie James Dio to make epic rock albums like *Rising* and *Long Live Rock 'n' Roll* before streamlining the sound and enjoying hit singles like 'Since You've Been Gone' and 'All Night Long'. Rainbow were less celebrated than Deep Purple, but they feature much of Blackmore's finest writing and playing, and were one of the best live acts of the era. They are much missed.

Paperback   ISBN 1-900924-31-5   234mm X 156mm   256pp, illustrated throughout
UK £14.99 $19.95

Back to the Beach: A Brian Wilson and the Beach Boys Reader REVISED EDITION
Edited by Kingsley Abbott
Revised and expanded edition of the Beach Boys compendium *Mojo* magazine deemed an "essential purchase." This collection includes all of the best articles, interviews and reviews from the Beach Boys' four decades of music, including definitive pieces by Timothy White, Nick Kent and David Leaf. New material reflects on the tragic death of Carl Wilson and documents the rejuvenated Brian's return to the boards. 'Rivetting!' **** Q

'An essential purchase.' *Mojo*

Paperback   ISBN 1-900924-46-3   234mm X 156mm   288pp
UK £14.99 $19.95

Harmony in My Head
The Original Buzzcock Steve Diggle's Rock 'n' Roll Odyssey
By Steve Diggle and Terry Rawlings
First-hand account of the Punk wars from guitarist and one half of the songwriting duo that gave the world three chord Punk-pop classics like 'Ever Fallen In Love' and 'Promises'. Diggle dishes the dirt on punk contemporaries like The Sex Pistols, The Clash and The Jam, as well as sharing poignant memories of his friendship with Kurt Cobain, on whose last ever tour, The Buzzcocks were support act.

'Written with spark and verve, this rattling account of Diggle's time in the Buzzcocks will appeal to those with an interest in Punk or just late-1970s Manchester.' *Music Week*

'This warts 'n' all monologue is a hoot...Diggle's account of the rise, fall and birth of the greatest Manchester band of the past 50 years is relayed with passion and candour...but it works best as a straightforward sex, drugs and rock 'n' roll memoir.' – *Uncut* ****

Paperback   ISBN 1-900924-37-4   234mm X 156mm   224pp, 8pp b/w photos
UK £14.99 $19.95

Serge Gainsbourg: A Fistful of Gitanes
By Sylvie Simmons
Rock press legend Simmons' hugely acclaimed biography of the French genius.

'I would recommend *A Fistful of Gitanes* [as summer reading] which is a highly entertaining biography of the French singer-songwriter and all-round scallywag' – JG Ballard

'A wonderful introduction to one of the most overlooked songwriters of the 20th century' (Number 3, Top music books of 2001) *The Times*

'The most intriguing music-biz biography of the year' *The Independent*

'Wonderful. Serge would have been so happy' – Jane Birkin
Paperback   ISBN 1-900924-   198mm X 129mm   288pp, 16pp b/w photos
UK £14.99 $19.95

Blues: The British Connection
By Bob Brunning
Former Fleetwood Mac member Bob Brunning's classic account of the impact of Blues in Britain, from its beginnings as the underground music of 50s teenagers like Mick Jagger, Keith Richards and Eric Clapton, to the explosion in the 60s, right through to the vibrant scene of the present day.
'An invaluable reference book and an engaging personal memoir' – Charles Shaar Murray
Paperback   ISBN 1-900924-41-2   234mm X 156mm   352pp, 24pp b/w photos
UK £14.99 $19.95

On The Road With Bob Dylan
By Larry Sloman
In 1975, as Bob Dylan emerged from 8 years of seclusion, he dreamed of putting together a travelling music show that would trek across the country like a psychedelic carnival. The dream became a reality, and On The Road With Bob Dylan is the ultimate behind-the-scenes look at what happened. When Dylan and the Rolling Thunder Revue took to the streets of America, Larry 'Ratso' Sloman was with them every step of the way.
'The War and Peace of Rock and Roll.' – Bob Dylan
Paperback   ISBN 1-900924-51-X   234mm X 156mm   448pp
UK £14.99 $19.95

Gram Parsons: God's Own Singer
By Jason Walker £12.99
Brand new biography of the man who pushed The Byrds into country-rock territory on Sweethearts of The Rodeo, and quit to form the Flying Burrito Brothers. Gram lived hard, drank hard, took every drug going and somehow invented country rock, paving the way for Crosby, Stills & Nash, The Eagles and Neil Young. Parsons' second solo LP, Grievous Angel, is a haunting masterpiece of country soul. By the time it was released, he had been dead for 4 months. He was 26 years old.
'Walker has done an admirable job in taking us as close to the heart and soul of Gram Parsons as any author could.' **** Uncut book of the month
Paperback   ISBN 1-900924-27-7   234mm X 156mm   256pp, 8pp b/w photos
UK £12.99 $18.95

Ashley Hutchings: The Guvnor and the Rise of Folk Rock – Fairport Convention, Steeleye Span and the Albion Band
By Geoff Wall and Brian Hinton £14.99
As founder of Fairport Convention and Steeleye Span, Ashley Hutchings is the pivotal figure in the history of folk rock. This book draws on hundreds of hours of interviews with Hutchings and other folk-rock artists and paints a vivid picture of the scene that also produced Sandy Denny, Richard Thompson, Nick Drake, John Martyn and Al Stewart.
Paperback   ISBN 1-900924-32-3   234mm X 156mm   288pp, photos throughout
UK £14.99 $19.95

The Beach Boys' Pet Sounds: The Greatest Album of the Twentieth Century
By Kingsley Abbott £11.95
Pet Sounds is the 1966 album that saw The Beach Boys graduate from lightweight pop like 'Surfin' USA', et al, into a vehicle for the mature compositional genius of Brian Wilson. The album was hugely influential, not least on The Beatles. This is the full story of the album's background, its composition and recording, its contemporary reception and its enduring legacy.
Paperback   ISBN 1-900924-30-7   234mm X 156mm   192pp
UK £11.95 $18.95

King Crimson: In The Court of King Crimson
By Sid Smith £14.99

King Crimson's 1969 masterpiece *In The Court Of The Crimson King*, was a huge US chart hit. The band followed it with 40 further albums of consistently challenging, distinctive and innovative music. Drawing on hours of new interviews, and encouraged by Crimson supremo Robert Fripp, the author traces the band's turbulent history year by year, track by track.

Paperback   ISBN 1-900924-26-9   234mm X 156mm   288pp, photos throughout
UK £14.99 $19.95

A Journey Through America with the Rolling Stones
By Robert Greenfield
Featuring a new foreword by Ian Rankin

This is the definitive account of The Stones' legendary '72 tour.

'Filled with finely-rendered detail ... a fascinating tale of times we shall never see again' *Mojo*

'The Stones on tour in '72 twist and burn through their own myth: from debauched outsiders to the first hints of the corporate business – the lip-smacking chaos between the Stones' fan being stabbed by a Hell's Angel at Altamont and the fan owning a Stones' credit card.' – Paul Morley #2 essential holiday rock reading list, *The Observer*, July 04.

Paperback   ISBN 1-900924-24-2   198mm X 129mm   256pp
UK £9.99 $19.95

The Sharper Word: A Mod Reader
Edited by Paolo Hewitt

Hewitt's hugely readable collection documents the clothes, the music, the clubs, the drugs and the faces behind one of the most misunderstood and enduring cultural movements and includes hard to find pieces by Tom Wolfe, bestselling novelist Tony Parsons, poet laureate Andrew Motion, disgraced Tory grandee Jonathan Aitken, Nik Cohn, Colin MacInnes, Mary Quant, and Irish Jack.

'An unparalleled view of the world-conquering British youth cult.' *The Guardian*

'An excellent account of the sharpest-dressed subculture.' *Loaded*, Book of the Month

Paperback   ISBN 1-900924-34-X   198mm X 129mm   192pp
UK £14.99 $19.95

BACKLIST

The Nice: Hang On To A Dream By Martyn Hanson
1900924439   256pp   £13.99
Al Stewart: Adventures of a Folk Troubadour By Neville Judd
1900924366   320pp   £25.00
Marc Bolan and T Rex: A Chronology By Cliff McLenahan
1900924420   256pp   £13.99
Razor Edge: Bob Dylan and The Never-ending Tour By Andrew Muir
1900924137   256pp   £12.99
Calling Out Around the World: A Motown Reader Edited by Kingsley Abbott
1900924145   256pp   £13.99
I've Been Everywhere: A Johnny Cash Chronicle By Peter Lewry
1900924226   256pp   £14.99
Sandy Denny: No More Sad Refrains By Clinton Heylin
1900924358   288pp   £13.99
Animal Tracks: The Story of The Animals By Sean Egan
1900924188   256pp   £12.99
Like a Bullet of Light: The Films of Bob Dylan By CP Lee
1900924064   224pp   £12.99
Rock's Wild Things: The Troggs Files By Alan Clayson and J Ryan
1900924196   224pp   £12.99
Dylan's Daemon Lover By Clinton Heylin
1900924153   192pp   £12.00
XTC: Song Stories By XTC and Neville Farmer
190092403X   352pp   £12.99
Born in the USA: Bruce Springsteen By Jim Cullen
1900924056   320pp   £9.99
Bob Dylan By Anthony Scaduto
1900924234   320pp   £10.99

Firefly Publishing: An Association between Helter Skelter and SAF

The Nirvana Recording Sessions
By Rob Jovanovic £20.00

Drawing on years of research, and interviews with many who worked with the band, the author has documented details of every Nirvana recording, from early rehearsals, to the *In Utero* sessions. A fascinating account of the creative process of one of the great bands.

The Music of George Harrison: While My Guitar Gently Weeps
By Simon Leng £20.00

Often in Lennon and McCartney's shadow, Harrison's music can stand on its own merits. Santana biographer Leng takes a studied, track by track, look at both Harrison's contribution to The Beatles, and the solo work that started with the release in 1970 of his epic masterpiece *All Things Must Pass*. 'Here Comes The Sun', 'Something' – which Sinatra covered and saw as the perfect love song – 'All Things Must Pass' and 'While My Guitar Gently Weeps' are just a few of Harrison's classic songs.

Originally planned as a celebration of Harrison's music, this is now sadly a commemoration.

The Pretty Things: Growing Old Disgracefully
By Alan Lakey £20

First biography of one of rock's most influential and enduring combos. Trashed hotel rooms, infighting, rip-offs, sex, drugs and some of the most remarkable rock 'n' roll, including landmark albums like the first rock opera, *SF Sorrow*, and *Rolling Stone*'s album of the year, 1970's *Parachute*.

'They invented everything, and were credited with nothing.' Arthur Brown, 'God of Hellfire'

The Sensational Alex Harvey
By John Neil Murno £20

Part rock band, part vaudeville, 100% commitment, the SAHB were one of the greatest live bands of the era. But behind his showman exterior, Harvey was increasingly beset by alcoholism and tragedy. He succumbed to a heart attack on the way home from a gig in 1982, but he is fondly remembered as a unique entertainer by friends, musicians and legions of fans.

U2: The Complete Encyclopedia By Mark Chatterton £14.99

Poison Heart: Surviving The Ramones By Dee Dee Ramone and Veronica Kofman £9.99

Minstrels In The Gallery: A History Of Jethro Tull By David Rees £12.99

DANCEMUSICSEXROMANCE: Prince – The First Decade By Per Nilsen £12.99

To Hell and Back with Catatonia By Brian Wright £12.99

Soul Sacrifice: The Santana Story By Simon Leng £12.99

Opening The Musical Box: A Genesis Chronicle By Alan Hewitt £12.99

Blowin' Free: Thirty Years Of Wishbone Ash By Gary Carter and Mark Chatterton £12.99

www.helterskelterbooks.com

All Helter Skelter, Firefly and SAF titles are available by mail order from
www.helterskelterbooks.com

Or from our office:
Helter Skelter Publishing Limited
Southbank House
Black Prince Road
London SE1 7SJ

Telephone: +44 (0) 20 7463 2204 or Fax: +44 (0)20 7463 2295

Mail order office hours: Mon-Fri 10:00am – 1:30pm,

By post, enclose a cheque [must be drawn on a British bank], International Money Order,
or credit card number and expiry date.

Postage prices per book worldwide are as follows:

UK & Channel Islands	£1.50
Europe & Eire (air)	£2.95
USA, Canada (air)	£7.50
Australasia, Far East (air)	£9.00

Email: info@helterskelterbooks.com